The BOOK of LIFE

BIBLE TREASURES

Jesus in the Midst of the Doctors

By Heinrich Hofmann (1824–1911)
In the Dresden Galleries, Dresden

THE Bible has been the inspiration of the world's greatest artists. They in turn, under this high inspiration, have by their masterpieces of painting and sculpture, made characters and events of the Bible more clearly and vividly alive to young and old.

This famous painting of Jesus at the age of twelve in the Temple at Jerusalem is one of the most popular pictures in homes and schools all over the world. The interesting Bible story which this picture so beautifully portrays is told only in the Gospel of Luke and is given under the heading, "The First Visit to Jerusalem," in THE BOOK OF LIFE, Volume 7, pages 51 and 54.

As you read this swift Bible narrative, which is all that the Gospels say about Jesus between the ages of twelve and thirty, it is easy to understand why this dramatic incident in the boyhood of Jesus has ever kindled the enthusiasm of artists. Painters of many periods and nations have portrayed this important event of Jesus astounding the Doctors of Law by His questions and wisdom.

"Jesus in the Midst of the Doctors" is the most famous of all Hofmann's works and one of the most widely known and loved pictures of Jesus. Note the earnestness and the spirituality in the face of the boy-Christ. It is beautiful yet perfectly natural as he stands in the midst of a scholarly group of men varying in ages from alert, keen middle age to the very old and serene—the idly curious, the open-minded, the unbelieving, the almost convinced.

In these faces around Him is seen widely differing attitudes and understanding. These characters represent the world and its different attitudes towards Jesus and His teachings. As you study this picture, what do you see in each of these faces?

VOLUME 2

BIBLE TREASURES

THE

BOOK of LIFE

ARRANGED AND EDITED BY

NEWTON M. HALL, A.M., D.D., *Pastor and Christian Educator,*
Author of Civic Righteousness and Civic Pride

IRVING F. WOOD, Ph.D., D.D. *Professor of Religion and Bible,*
Author of The Spirit of God in Biblical Literature

Joint Authors of The Bible Story; Early Days of Israel; Days of the Kings
of Israel; Adult Bible Classes and How to Teach Them

JOHN RUDIN &
COMPANY, INC.
Chicago

ACKNOWLEDGMENTS

We gratefully acknowledge our indebtedness to the following for valued editorial counsel and assistance: V. Raymond Edman, Ph.D., L.L.D., President, Wheaton College; Paul E. Kretzmann, Ph.D., D.D.; the late George L. Robinson, Ph.D., D.D.; Merrill C. Tenney, Ph.D.; the late Professor Robert L. Cooke, Ed.D.; John Luchies, Th.D.; Professor Kenneth S. Kantzer, Ph.D.; all distinguished and devout Biblical scholars, teachers and authors; Louise Rock, Children's Religious Book Editor; Moody Press for *Stories of Hymns We Love;* Dr. Wm. S. McBirnie; Lewis Bayles Paton, D.D., Hartford Theological Seminary; Edgar J. Goodspeed, Ph.D.; Elihu Grant, Ph.D., Professor of Biblical Literature, Haverford College; Henry Thatcher Fowler, D.D., Professor of Biblical Literature, Brown University; Mr. and Mrs. W. A. Pottenger; Mr. Charles F. H. Crathern, Jr.; the American Passion Play of Blooming-ton, Illinois, and Bess Hibarger for helping to assemble Passion Play pictures; The Pilgrim Press; Edwin Markham; Houghton, Mifflin and Company; Fleming H. Revell & Company; The Abingdon Press; British Broadcasting Corporation, Copyright, London, W. 1.

We make grateful acknowledgment to the following Art Galleries for permission to use their pictures: Metropolitan Art Museum of New York; British Museum of London; Boston Museum of Fine Art; National Gallery, London; National Tate Gallery, London; The Louvre, Paris, France; National Museum, Naples, Italy; National Gallery, Dresden, Germany; Galleria Ambrosiana, Milan, Italy; The Art Institute of Chicago; Curtis & Cameron, Incorporated.

For special contributions by Professor Robert Seneca Smith; Clara Bodman Hawks; Mrs. Louise Hall Tharp; Cecilia Rudin; Helen Rudin; and Frances Olcott; and many others for their help, the publishers here wish to extend grateful and sincere appreciation.

The pictures by James J. Tissot are reproductions of original paintings of the "New Testament" at the Brooklyn Museum, New York, and of the "Old Testament" at the Jewish Museum, New York. Permission for use by John H. Eggers Publications, New York, who have exclusive publication rights. These photos, and others, were taken by Three Lions, Inc., New York. Other photos in color are used by permission of International Publishing Co., Ltd., Jerusalem, and Wide World Photos.

PREFACE

VOLUME Two is planned for boys and girls who have advanced beyond the beginner-reader stage. They now need stories with fairly simple vocabulary and, at the same time, more comprehensive themes and more difficult subjects.

The pictures are especially chosen with children and youth in mind. Manners and customs of daily living, child life, and objects of interest are shown. Not only is background material presented on the country of Palestine, but also on the great nations so closely related to Hebrew history. By studying the pictures in this volume, boys and girls will gain a greater knowledge of life in Bible times.

The Bible stories in this volume are those which would be of special interest to active youth of today. Here boys and girls will read exciting stories which will inspire them to live their lives today for Christ. These Bible stories are based on actual Bible passages, but are worded so that today's children will find them clear and meaningful. These same stories may also be read, in Bible language, in later volumes.

The Story of the Hebrew People is a "thumbnail sketch" of early Hebrew history. It presents a "bird's-eye" view of the Bible and places Bible stories in their proper historical order. Once the purpose and direction of Bible history is understood, the entire Bible becomes more meaningful.

These stories, which bring the Bible to life, will lead the children on to more serious study of their Bible as they grow older.

CONTENTS

VOLUME TWO
PART I

ADORATION OF THE SHEPHERDS
A molding by D. Mastroianni

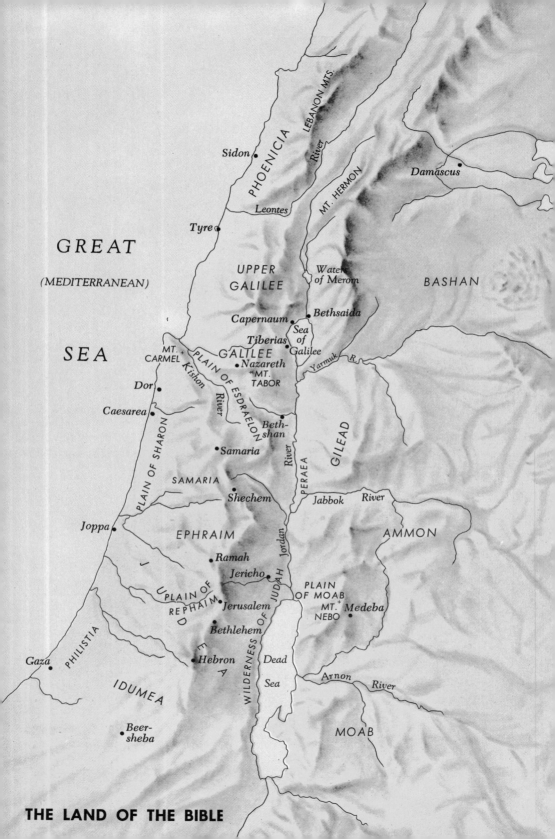

THE LAND OF THE BIBLE

In the Land of the Bible

A LITTLE CHAPTER ABOUT NAMES

NAMES OF THE PEOPLE

THE people who wrote the Bible were called Hebrews in the very ancient time. That meant, "those who had come from another land," "the people from over there."

The nation was also called Israel, because that was the name of one of the old heroes from whom the nation came.

A very prominent part of the nation, a tribe as they called it, was named Judah. From Judah came the greatest kings of the nation. Its greatest city, Jerusalem, was in the land of the tribe of Judah. At last, after many wars and great defeats, Judah was all of the nation which was left.

Then the name "Judean" began to be used for all the Hebrews. From "Judean" came the shorter word "Jew." The Hebrews are usually called Jews in the New Testament. Ever since the New Testament time, "Jew" has been the common name for all the Hebrew race.

NAMES OF THE LAND

The land where the Hebrews lived had two names. Curiously enough, neither is from the names of the Hebrews, but of other peoples.

The old name in the Bible books is Canaan. That is from a people who were living in the land when the Hebrews came there, the Canaanites. The Hebrews first began to call the country "The Land of Canaan,"

13

and "Canaan" it continued to be long after all the people first called Canaanites had disappeared.

The other name only came in use later. It did not begin with the Hebrews, but with the people who came to the country by sea, to trade and to do business.

Near the sea, in the southern part of Canaan, is a plain. This plain was not held by the Hebrews, but by a people called Philistines. For a long time the Philistines and the Hebrews were not friendly neighbors, but later they learned to live together without quarreling.

When people from the sea landed on the coast and came to the towns to buy and sell, they did not meet the Hebrews, but the Philistines. They called the name of the land Philistia. That was also the name which the Hebrews used for the plain by the coast, where the Philistines lived.

The people who traded changed the name "Philistia," in their language, to "Palestine." They began to call all the country by this name. In the New Testament time that was the name by which the country was usually known among the peoples of the world. And Palestine has been the most usual name for it ever since; but in the Bible itself the name is used very rarely.

Remember, then, that there are three names for the people:

Hebrews
Israelites
Jews,

and two names for the land:

Canaan
Palestine.

THE MOUNTAINS

The land of the Bible is a land of hills. On the western side is a level plain which, toward the south, is twenty miles wide, but becomes narrower as one goes north. Except this plain, almost all the land is hills and narrow valleys.

"I will lift up mine eyes to the hills," said a Psalm writer.

There is almost no place in the land where you cannot lift up your eyes to the hills. In the west, near the plain, there are rounded hills. They become higher to the east, till the center of the land is a high range of hills, with rounded tops and steep sides.

Then, a little farther east, the hills suddenly break down into steep valleys, with great rocks on the sides. There are precipices and strangely carved cliffs.

The hills end at the bottom of the deep valley of the Jordan. But the valley is nowhere more than a few miles wide, and on the other side the hills rise once more, towering up and up till they are as high on the eastern side of the Jordan as they are on the western side.

Is it any wonder that the words "mountain" and "hill" are found hundreds of times in the Bible?

When an old Hebrew poet wished to picture the power of God, he said,

"Which by his strength setteth fast the mountains."

—Psalms 65:6.

When a poet wanted to say that the most stable things would be changed, he said,

"Every mountain and hill shall be made low."

—Isaiah 40:4.

When another poet wished to say that God's power was eternal, he said,

MOUNT GERIZIM—THE MOUNT OF BLESSING

This mountain, the Mount of Blessing, is 2,848 feet high; and its neighbor, the Mount of Cursing, is 3,077 feet high. These noble mountains are near Shechem.

"Before the mountains were brought forth,
Or ever thou hadst formed the earth and the world
Even from everlasting to everlasting,
Thou art God." — Psalms 90:2.

Palestine has a number of very famous mountains. The Mount of Olives is close to Jerusalem, on the eastern side. Jesus had friends in a village on it, Bethany. Once he looked over at Jerusalem from the side of the mount and wept over the city, because he loved it so much and saw the troubles which would come to it. As he came down the road toward Jerusalem one day, the people met him with palm branches and shouts of praise, as was befitting a great king. So Palm Sunday began on the slope of the Mount of Olives.

Mount Tabor is in the middle of the country, looking out on the southern side over the fields on a plain below. It stands out beyond the hills behind it,

MOUNT OF TRANSFIGURATION
AS SEEN FROM AN EXCAVATION

a great dome, round with a flat top. The mountain
has looked down on peaceful harvests and on bloody
battlefields, for many armies have camped on its sides
and fought on the plain below.

One of the battles was fought in the early days
of Israel, when a woman, Deborah, urged a chief, Barak,
to gather the people against their enemies. All night
long they came to the camp on the mountain side.
When it was day they went down to fight in the plain,
and a great storm of wind and driving rain broke in
the faces of the enemy and gave the Hebrews the victory over a stronger force. They kept the memory of
it in a splendid poem, The Song of Deborah, which
you will find in another volume of this set.

Not far from Tabor, rising out of the plain, its
high, round top looking straight out to sea, is Mount
Carmel. It is the only mountain in the land where
the Hebrews lived which stands right on the seashore.
It can be seen by travelers from far away inland and
by sailors far out on the sea; so it was always a famous
mountain. Before the Hebrews came into the land
the people had climbed up its steep sides and built an
altar to God on its top, because it seemed to them
that they were nearer to God here than in the plain
below. When the Hebrews came into the land, they
also built an altar to God there.

Once upon a time, the people had forgotten to worship God. His altar on Carmel was broken down,
and nobody came up there any more to worship him.
They thought that other gods were better than their
God. Then a great prophet, Elijah, sent word all
about among the people, "Come up to the old altar
on Carmel"; and they all came, wondering what was
going to happen. They found Elijah and the priests

Beautiful Mount Hermon

From International Publishing Co., Ltd.

MOUNT Hermon is a beautiful mountain that marked the frontier between Palestine and Lebanon. From its snowy summit flow streams of clear water used to irrigate semi-arid areas nearby. It is the traditional "Mount of Transfiguration" where Jesus went with three of His disciples, Peter, James, and John; and from which He descended to help those who were sick and needy, especially a father and his little boy.

of the other god, Baal. Then Elijah made them choose between their own God and Baal. "If our Lord is God, follow him; if Baal, follow him," he cried. All day the prophets of Baal called upon their god to send down fire upon their altars; but nothing happened. Then Elijah prayed to God, and God sent a great fire down to the old altar Elijah had rebuilt to worship him. Then the people cried, "Baal is not god; we will follow the true God!"

Away off to the north is a range of mountains, the Lebanons. Most of the range lies outside the land in which the Hebrews lived, but it was very familiar to them. Hebrew villages reached high up on the southern slopes.

In the high Lebanons the snow lies late in the spring. Trees and plants grow there which are not found in the lower country. The most famous kind of tree is the cedar of Lebanon, great trees with dense tops and huge trunks. The Hebrews always spoke of these trees as the greatest and most splendid they knew. Once a great king, Solomon, built a house in which

MOUNT TABOR

This is one of the beautiful mountains of Palestine. Early tradition fixes the scene of the Transfiguration on this mountain but this cannot have been, because it is known that the top of the mountain was covered by houses at the time of Jesus.

to worship God. He wanted to make it the finest and most stately building in all the land, and he sent to Lebanon for cedars as its timber.

When a poet wished to picture the future of his nation as splendid with the gifts of prosperity from God he said,

"The glory of Lebanon shall be given unto it."

Isaiah 35:2.

The highest mountain of all in the land is Mount Hermon. It stands in the north, on the very edge of the country of the Hebrews, but it is so high and so separate from other mountains that it can be seen from far. From the hilltops in almost all the land a part of the view is the great, bare top of Hermon. Most of the year it is white with snow. Even when most of the country lies hot under the sun, and the children are picking flowers on the grassy hillsides and the wheatfields are green in the valleys, Hermon wears his white snow-cap. The most important river of the land, the Jordan, begins under the snow banks of Hermon.

The people in old time liked to worship God on the top of mountains, as they did on Carmel; but Hermon was too high, its top too cold and bleak, to think of such a thing in connection with it. It stood apart from all the rest of the land, like the great white throne of God.

"I will lift up mine eyes unto the hills"; and highest and grandest of all was lofty Hermon.

THE JORDAN

The land where the Hebrews lived had not many rivers, but there was one river which every child knew about. It was the Jordan.

Most of the Hebrews lived on a long line of hills

The Jordan River

(Photographed by Three Lions, Inc.)

THE Jordan is one of the best-known rivers in all of the world, not because of its length or width, but because so much of Bible history is associated with it.

This lovely view shows us this famous river near its beginning. It rises on the slopes of Mt. Hermon, which is snow-capped all the year round; and flows southward into the Sea of Galilee. Then it flows out of that Sea ever southward and downward until it pours into the Dead Sea.

In Galilee the Jordan flows swift and cold from its unfailing source in the snows of Mt. Hermon through a lovely countryside of hills and plains. The hillsides are pasture lands for flocks of sheep, and the fertile plains are irrigated with waters from the rivers. When Jesus lived in Galilee, the area was more densely populated then than now, with lovely villages in the valleys and populous cities surrounding the Sea of Galilee. The upper Jordan, shown in this picture, is a clear and cheery stream, but in the rainy season it can become a raging torrent.

And Elisha sent a messenger unto him, saying, Go and wash in Jordan seven times, and thy flesh shall come again to thee, and thou shalt be clean . . . Then went he down, and dipped himself seven times in Jordan, according to the saying of the man of God: and his flesh came again like unto the flesh of a little child, and he was clean. (2 Kings 5:10-14.)

running from north to south through their narrow land. On the east of this line of hills lies the valley of the Jordan. It runs the whole length of the land. From most of the hilltops one can look down into the valley. From many of them can be seen the green line of trees and bushes on the banks of the Jordan. So when the boys led the sheep up to the pastures on the high hills they could very often look down at the Jordan, in the deep valley below.

The Jordan begins high up on the slopes of Mount Hermon. It tumbles over the rocks, a little stream gathering other streams on the way, till it flows slowly and quietly between grassy banks into a little lake called Huleh. After passing through this it roars down a rocky channel to another and larger lake, the Lake of Gennesareth, or Sea of Galilee. At the southern end of this lake the Jordan begins its course as the largest river of the land.

In one respect this is the strangest river in all the world. From the Sea of Galilee all the way down it lies lower than the water in the ocean itself. It is below the level of the sea. Most rivers run down to the sea. If the Jordan reached the sea, it would have to run up hill.

The valley of the Jordan is a great hollow with hills on each side. Usually it is only a few miles across, and the river winds continually about from one side to the other; and always it is getting down, down, further, till it is far below the level of the sea.

The Jordan is not a large river. In the early summer it overflows its banks and is so deep that it cannot be forded. The rest of the year, even where it is largest, there are places where men can wade across and donkeys can bring goods safely over on their backs.

THE JORDAN RIVER

This is the famous river which flows through the eastern part of Palestine. It can be forded, especially at high water, only in certain places. It was a defensive barrier against the frequent raids of the eastern tribes. Many bloody encounters took place at the "ford of the Jordan" in Old Testament times.

The wheat grown on the hills to the east was thus brought to Jerusalem.

But if it is lower than the sea, how can it ever run into the ocean? It does not run into the ocean. It goes into the Dead Sea, and stops. It goes no farther.

But if it keeps running in and never out, why does not the Dead Sea become filled up and run over? Because the valley is hot. The sun beats down into it so that it evaporates the water from the Dead Sea as fast as the River Jordan brings it down, and so the sea does not become more full. If you put a dish of water on the stove where it is warm it will all go off in steam unless you keep putting more water in. So the water of the River Jordan all goes off in steam from the Dead Sea, and never runs into the ocean at all.

Truly, that is a very curious river.

THE DEAD SEA

The Dead Sea is the strangest lake in the world.

It is the deepest valley in the world. It lies over a thousand feet below the level of the sea. If the ocean

could flow in, the water would fill up the whole valley
of the Jordan to the Sea of Galilee.

It is the saltest lake in the world. It is much salter
than the ocean itself.

It lies shining and rippling in the sun, but no fish
live in it. No reeds or rushes grow along the edge of the
water.

There is no town on the lake. Only sand and rock
border it. The whole country about looks desolate and
dead. That is why it is called the Dead Sea.

THE SPRINGS

The Hebrews had a pretty name for the springs
of water. They called them "the eyes of the land."

They were very fond of their springs. Most of
the lands about theirs were very dry. In the winter,
when there was rain, grass grew, but in the long summer the sun shone hot every day and the grass dried
up and the ground became parched and dry.

There were very few springs in those lands, and
each one was very precious. The shepherds guarded
the water very carefully that none should be wasted.
If there was not enough water for their flocks the lambs
would die, and the shepherds must buy the right to
water their sheep at some other well.

Now in the land of the Hebrews every spring was
precious, too, but not as much so as in the lands about
them, where the shepherds lived. Water is so common
in the lands where most of us live that we would think
Canaan very dry, but it was so much more plentiful
than in lands about them that it seemed to the Hebrews very well watered. They were very proud of the
springs of water and of the brooks which flowed from
them.

One of the writers of the Bible describes Canaan as "a good land; a land of brooks of water, of fountains and springs, flowing forth in valleys and hills." And so it was, compared with some of the dry and thirsty lands about it.

The people cared so much for the springs that they settled near them. In time towns grew up, and sometimes, where there was a large spring flowing all the year, these became cities. The greatest city of all, the city that was long the capital of the land and is to this day the center of all the country, Jerusalem, stands where it does because long ago, long before the time of the Hebrews, somebody settled near a fine spring. That spring furnished water to the city all through the long ages. David drank from its water. Because even so fine a spring would not supply all the water needed, Solomon brought water in pipes from another place, but still the spring kept giving its water to those who came for it. It was flowing when Jesus came to the city. Thousands and thousands of women and girls have come down to the spring with water pots on their shoulders to get water for their homes. Cities have been destroyed and kingdoms overthrown and people of different races have come to drink its waters, but the spring kept right on flowing. It is flowing to-day, as it was long, long ago, when a village first gathered there because the spring gave them good water.

What happened at Jerusalem happened at many other places. The spring made the town; and then it kept on flowing age after age, no matter what happened to the town. And always people who lived near came to get its water.

Sometimes the spring had a name. If a town arose near by, the town was called by the name of the spring.

MARY'S WELL AT NAZARETH

WATER SKINS OF PALESTINE

These strange-looking objects are skins so often used in the East as receptacles for water or wine. Ropes are attached so that the skin may be carried over the shoulder.

There were towns called En-shemish, The Spring of the Sun, and En-gedi, The Spring of the Little Goats, and En-gannim, The Spring of the Gardens, and En-hakkore, The Spring of the Partridge.

The springs were one of God's best gifts to the people. One of the writers of the Psalms, giving a picture of the loving care of God, says,

"He sendeth the springs into the valleys,
Which run among the hills.
They give drink to every beast of the field."
—Psalms 104:10,11

Another Bible writer, who wishes to show how God blesses those who trust him, says,

"Thou shalt be like a watered garden,
And like a spring of water, whose waters fail not."
—Isaiah 58:11.

SHEEP AND SHEPHERDS

In the land of the Bible there were a great many sheep. They were not kept in fields with fences about. They roamed over the hills and found pasture where they could.

How could they be kept out of the fields of grain? Would they not wander away so far they could not get back home? In the mountains there were sometimes wild animals; how could the sheep be safe from them? A shepherd went out with the flocks of sheep. Sometimes the shepherd was the owner of the sheep. Sometimes he was hired to care for the sheep. Sometimes he was a boy, often the son of the owner.

The stories of Jacob tell how his sons went with the flocks of their father.

King David was a shepherd boy in his youth, and cared for his father's sheep.

It was the work of the shepherd to take care of the sheep. He must lead them to good pasture. He must take them each day to a spring for water. In countries where there were no springs, he took them to a well and drew water for them.

Sometimes the daughters of the owner went with the sheep as shepherds.

Once upon a time Moses made a long journey, and at evening came to a well where the daughters of a shepherd chief were waiting with their flocks. He helped them draw water, and was so kind to them that their father took him into his home, and for a long time Moses was a shepherd.

The shepherds did not drive their flocks. They went before them and the sheep followed after. The sheep soon got to know the shepherd and would follow wherever he went. The shepherd knew the sheep,

THE PET SHEEP

The mother and the pretty girl seem very fond of this great black sheep.
Do you think that it is sick or are they just giving it dinner from the basket?
The Eastern peoples are very much attached to their sheep.

"If a man have an hundred sheep, and one of them be gone astray, doth he
not leave the ninety and nine, and goeth into the mountains, and seeketh that
which is gone astray?"—*Matthew 18:12.*

too. Being with them day by day, he often gave names
to them. One would be "Spotty," and another "Blacky."
A little lamb so active he could hardly keep his feet
on the ground was "Frisky," and a slow and heavy
sheep, "Lazy-bones." And so each one had some
name that fitted him. The sheep knew their names
and would come when they were called.

The shepherd carried a long stick that he sometimes used as a staff. At the end was a bend, making
a great hook. With this he could reach down and
help a little lamb up a steep rock. This was called
the shepherd's crook. David carried also a sling and
perhaps a hunter's knife.

Shearing Sheep in Palestine

From International Publishing Co., Ltd.

FROM time immemorial sheep and goats have been the principal possessions of the inhabitants of Palestine. A man's wealth was measured by the size of his flock. From them he had milk and meat for food and also wool for clothing. Sheep-shearing time was an occasion for feasting and rejoicing. It was a harvest festival, a harvest of wool and not of wheat. While being sheared of the wool that had grown heavy throughout the year, the sheep were silent and submissive. The Bible tells of the silence of Jesus before His accusers: "As a sheep before her shearers is dumb, so He openeth not His mouth" (Isaiah 53:7).

The shepherd was always ready to help the sheep when they could not help themselves. Sometimes a sheep was weak and not able to go as far as the others could. Sometimes a sheep fell among the rocks and hurt himself. Then the shepherd took it up on his shoulder. The sheep lay quietly, for he knew and trusted his shepherd. If a little lamb was too tired to keep up with the sheep, the good shepherd picked him up and made a great fold in his robe, put the little lamb in it, and carried him in his bosom.

Then if the shepherd found that a lamb was missing when he got back to the fold at night, what did he do? Why, of course, the shepherd started straight back to find him. The poor lamb might have fallen and been hurt, or he might have wandered out of sight of the rest and then not known how to find them.

A SHEPHERD WITH A KID

A shepherd of Palestine with a little new-born kid in his arms. The shepherds of the East are very faithful and very gentle with their flocks. The sheep know the good shepherd's voice, and follow him but they will not follow a stranger.

If it were left out all night the dogs or wild beasts might kill it. So out the shepherd would go, taking a few dates to eat on the way. He would call the lamb by name, and peer into all the hollows in the hills, looking for the white coat of the sheep in the gathering darkness of the night. When at last he found it he put it on his shoulder and came back to the fold. As he drew near he called to the other shepherds, "I've found the lamb. I've found the lamb that was lost."

Is it any wonder that the shepherd came to love the sheep, and the sheep loved the shepherd?

SHEEP ON THE SLOPES OF MOUNT CARMEL

This flock of sheep is feeding on the slopes of Mount Carmel.

When the writers of the Bible want to say that God loves the people and cares for them, they sometimes call the people sheep and God their shepherd. Everybody in the Bible country knew what that meant. It was the best way possible of saying, "God knows everyone of you. God loves you. God will take good care of you. God wants you to love and trust him as the sheep do the shepherd."

Sometimes the rulers were called "shepherds of Israel," because they ought to care for the people.

Once the Hebrews were driven out of their country. They felt that the rulers, who ought to have protected them like shepherds, had been selfish and greedy, and had not done their duty.

In Babylon, where they had been sent, one of their number spoke to them in God's name, and said that God condemned the shepherds who had fed themselves, but had not fed the flocks. Now God said he himself would be their shepherd. They were like sheep which had been lost. They were out in the forest, scattered, away from the fold.

He would bring them to their fold, and even in the forest he would make it safe for them to lie down and sleep. For thus saith the Lord God:

"Behold, I, even I, will both search for my sheep, and will seek them out. As a shepherd seeketh out his flock in the day that he is among his sheep that are scattered, so will I seek out my sheep; and I will deliver them out of all places where they have been scattered in the cloudy and dark day. I will feed them in good pasture. I will feed my flock, and I will cause them to lie down," saith the Lord God. "I will seek that which was lost, and bring again that which was driven away, and will bind up that which was broken, and will strengthen that which was sick. And they shall dwell safely in the wilderness and sleep in the woods. And ye my flock, the flock of my pasture, are men, and I am your God," saith the Lord Jehovah.

The whole of Ezekiel 34 is about how God will be the shepherd of his people.

Do you know the Shepherd Psalm? It is the twenty-third Psalm, and begins:

"The Lord is my shepherd, I shall not want."

THE HOUSES

"What a queer-looking building!" said Harold. "It does not look like a house at all."

Harold was looking at the picture of a house in the Bible lands of the olden time. It did look queer to him; but think how very, very queer our houses would have looked to a Hebrew child of the old time, if he could have seen them.

The house looked like a square block of stone. On one side it had a low door. There were no windows. "What did they do for light?" asked Harold.

MOHAMMEDAN SCHOOL IN PALESTINE

This strange square structure is used as a Moslem school. The pupils sit around their teacher on the floor chanting monotonously the words of the Koran.

THE HOUSETOPS OF JERUSALEM

The flat housetops of the East are a favorite place in the evening and they are used as a sleeping place at night. The roofs are commonly, but not always, flat and are usually formed of a plaster of mud and straw, laid upon boughs or rafters, but, upon the flat roofs, tents or booths of boughs are often raised to be used as sleeping places in summer.

NAZARETH
Looking over the housetops of modern Nazareth.

Light could come in the door: If they had windows they would have had no glass to put in them. In that climate they lived out of doors more than we do, and did not need to have so much light in the house.

"There is no chimney. Did they never build a fire? Where was the stove?"

There was no stove. Most of the cooking was done out of doors, over an open fire. In the long summer they needed no fire to keep them warm. In the short winter it was wet and sometimes cold. In the hill country there was sometimes even a little snow, but it soon melted away. When it was cold the people put some live coals in a dish of iron or clay and set it in the middle of the room. This did not make the room very warm, but it was the best they could do.

If the house was large, it was built about a court, which was a small open yard. From a corner of the court a stone stair went up to the flat roof. If there was no court, the stairs went up on the outside of the house.

The roof was a very important part of the house. In the better houses it was made very thick and solid and surrounded by a little wall, so that people would not fall off. In the hot weather the people lived on the roof much of the time. They sat there, where they could catch any wind there might be; at night they slept there.

Sometimes they built a room on the roof.

There was once a prophet named Elisha. He was often a welcome guest at a certain house. The owners of the house wished to make a room where he could stay when he pleased, and they built it on the roof.

AN ADOBE VILLAGE IN PALESTINE

While some of the modern houses in Palestine are well built of stone, others are built of sun-dried clay bricks, or simply plastered up with mud like the adobe huts of New Mexico. Notice the ladder by which one goes to the roof.

The woman said to her husband, "Let us make a little chamber, I pray thee, on the wall; and let us set for him there a bed, and a table, and a stool, and a candlestick: and it shall be, when he cometh to us, that he shall turn in thither."

In a story about Peter, it is said that at one time he went up on the housetop to pray.

Houses of stone with roofs so solid were of the better class. The houses of the people in the villages were often built of mud, or, where they could be made, of clay bricks. They were of one story only, often with only one or two rooms. The roof was made of a layer of poles and brush, covered over with mud. In the rainy season grass often grew on the roof, but when the rain ceased and the sun shone hot, the grass soon withered.

Holy Family

By Simone da Pesaro (Simone Cantarini, 1612-1648)
In the Borghese Gallery, Rome, Italy
Color Photograph by Alinari Brothers, Florence

THIS charming painting represents Mary holding the infant Jesus whose hand John the Baptist is kissing, while Joseph thoughtfully looks on. About Mary's head is a white turban. Joseph, an elderly, bearded man in peasant's dress, is leaning on a staff. John is dressed in a camel's hair garment, symbolic reference to his later life in the desert prior to his ministry. We notice that the painter has taken the artistic privilege of making John far more than six months older than Jesus. Do you like this picture? The atmosphere of quiet devotion and human tenderness is quite appealing.

The life of the painter, Simone Cantarini, called Simone da Pesaro, was not as happy as the life he was able to give the people he painted. His disposition was naturally morose and irritable, we are told, and wherever he went he created trouble for himself and others. He was born in 1612 at Oropezza near Pesaro, whence comes the name Simone da Pesaro; ("da" means of). He studied with various Bolognese masters, especially Guido Reni (1575-1642), but grew so vain and arrogant that he was forced to leave Bologna. He went next to Rome, where he studied the works of the great masters, and from there to Mantua. Humiliated by his want of success in painting a portrait of the Duke of Mantua, he moved on to Verona where he died in 1648, some say of poison.

In his painting he copied the popular style of Guido Reni with great success. His works as an engraver are held in high esteem.

It is interesting to compare Pesaro's work with that of contemporary artists such as Sassoferrato, page 194, and dalle Notti, Volume 1.

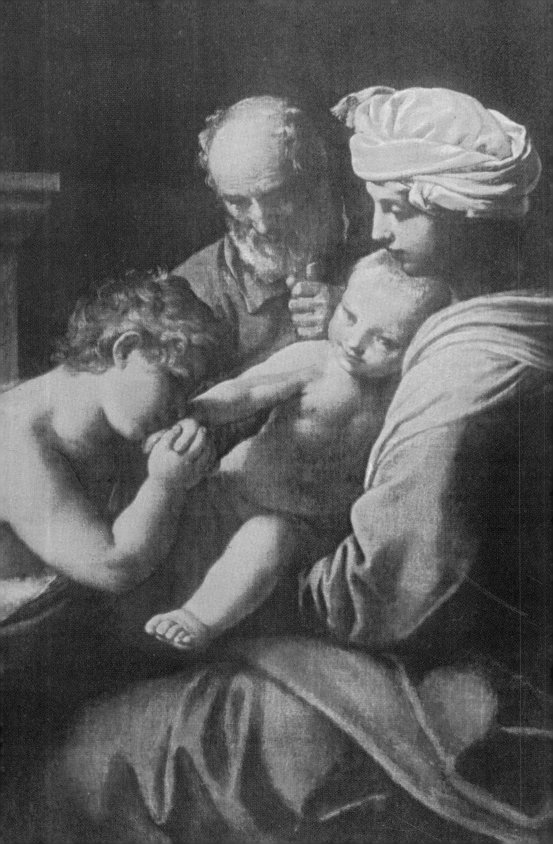

The prophet Isaiah compared a weak nation to the grass on the housetop.

"Therefore their inhabitants were of small power, they were dismayed and confounded: they were as the grass of the field, and as the green herb, as the grass on the housetops, and as corn blasted before it be grown up."   —Isaiah 37:27.

A Psalm writer says of wicked people,

"Let them be as the grass upon the housetops,
Which withereth before it groweth up."   —Psalms 129:6.

Such mud houses must be constantly cared for or the rain would get into the roof and begin to wash away the walls, and in a little while the house would fall down. Then only a heap of earth marked the place where the home had been.

Earlier than the house, in the history of Israel, was the tent. Away back in the early days of the Hebrews, in the times which the oldest stories of the nation told of, the people had been shepherds, wandering about

BETHANY

a wide country to feed their sheep. Then they had no houses; but every family had its tent of black camel's hair cloth. They set up their tents near a spring, and if the pasture became poor, or if a stronger tribe drove them away, they folded up their tents and went away.

They never forgot that once their homes had been in tents. Long after they had settled down in cities and villages, and lived for generations in houses, they spoke of their homes as tents. Once they refused to obey a king, and the people all cried, "To your tents, O Israel"; that is, "We will go home and leave the king."

When the writer of a Psalm wanted to say that he chose God rather than riches, he said,

"I had rather be a door-keeper in the house of
    my God
Than to dwell in the tents of wickedness." —Psalms 84:10.

So all the people you read about in the Bible lived in either a house of stone, a house of earth, or a tent. Most of the houses would seem very bare and very poor to you.

It makes much less difference what kind of a house a person lives in, than what kind of a person lives in the house.

THE CITIES

A city in our land has rows and rows of business blocks, some of them very high. It has great factories, with tall chimneys pouring out smoke. Then it has long streets of houses, standing back from the streets, often with yards about them. Outside of the city itself, sometimes miles away from the center of the city, are suburbs full of houses of people who do business in the city. By and by the houses grow less

WEAVER IN PALESTINE

This picture shows a weaver at work in his shop at Ramallah. Weaving is, as it has always been, one of the principal industries of Palestine.

numerous and at last, gradually, the real country appears, with only an occasional farmhouse.

In the land of the Bible the cities were different in many ways. Imagine yourself going toward one of them. You are not on a railroad train or an automobile or a trolley car, but perched up high on a camel. In front of you are other camels, and behind you still others. You have been riding so long that you are tired, and in a hurry to get to the city. But you see no signs of it anywhere. Instead of a plain, with a great city by some river in it, you are climbing a hill.

You come in sight of a hilltop. It has a town on it. Another hilltop in the distance has another town on it. Where is the city to which we are going? Oh! That is on a hilltop, too.

Why are all cities on hilltops? Because, in the old days when they were first built, the country was full of fighting tribes, and the hills could be defended from attack more easily than the valleys.

Still we are climbing up the narrow track. The leader of our caravan says that we are almost at the city. But where are the suburbs? Not a single house do we pass. We might be a thousand miles from any city, so far as appearances go. In the Bible land nobody lived outside a village or city, except the wandering tent-dwellers. Even the farmers lived in villages and went out to their work.

We make a turn in the road, and there, ahead of us on the top of the steep hill, is a high, gray stone wall. That is the wall of the city. Every city had walls higher than the houses and so thick that they could not be broken through. This was to protect the people in time of war, or from the raids of bands of robbers. In one side of the wall is a gate which is shut at night. The people who live in the city do not mean to have anybody come in without their knowledge.

The city seems small to us. It seemed quite large enough to the men who had to build that wall all about it.

Inside the gate is an open place, which the Bible often speaks of as "the broad place." Here the people gather if there is news to be heard or a proclamation from the king to be read. Out of that go the streets. They are often very crooked and usually very narrow. Sometimes if a man reaches out his arms he can touch the houses on each side. When a loaded donkey or camel comes along, it takes up the whole street.

There are no pretty yards, with houses standing amid great trees. In the walled city they could not afford to waste space that way. The houses are a solid row on each side of the streets. There are no windows in the front, only a door without any ornaments. The houses are built of stone, and a street is a narrow alley between two gray stone walls. Some of the houses have little gardens with a few flowers and perhaps a small tree, but that is behind the house, shut off from the street.

There are no great factories with roaring machinery and tall chimneys. Only a few things are made, and they are made in the homes. A blacksmith makes knives and ox-goads at the back of his house. A carpenter makes benches and tables and ox-yokes in a room of his house. The women spin thread and weave cloth in their own houses.

You ask, "Shall we go into the stores?" No, we

BARBER AT MICHMASH

This barber of Palestine is shaving the head of his customer (or shall we say his victim?), at his out-of-door shop in the neighborhood of the place made famous by the exploits of Jonathan, the son of Saul.

shall go to the stores, but we shall not go into them. In one of the narrow streets the fronts of the houses are open in a series of little booths. The merchant sits in the middle of the booth and can reach nearly everything without getting up, it is so small. A few large boxes would contain all his goods. The customers stand in the street outside.

One merchant sells cloth; another, sandals; another, pottery; another, barley or wheat; another, jewels and silver; another, the rare spices and precious oils

A STREET MARKET
Great heaps of fine-looking cauliflower are piled up on the curb for sale.

from Arabia or Egypt. In the morning the merchant takes down his shutters, and the store is open. At night he puts them up, and the store is closed.

In most cities there was one house larger and stronger than the others. Outside it looked quite as bare as the rest. It was the castle. In it the governor of the city lived, with the soldiers who guarded the walls and gates. It was made very strong so that it might stand an attack. Sometimes it was able to stand if all the rest of the city was taken. Usually it had a great tower from which watch was kept over the city. To it the people often fled when there was danger.

You see that the city in the old Bible lands was built for war, not for peace. That accounts for its place on a hill, for its walls and narrow streets, for its

Excavated Ruins at Hazor

From International Publishing Co., Ltd.

PALESTINE is an old land where many civilizations have arisen, flourished, and then fallen into decay. It has been invaded many times by foreign armies who have destroyed its cities and villages. In time the desolate areas would be re-populated and the new inhabitants often built their homes on the ruins of a previous settlement. Present-day students of archaeology and ancient history uncover the ruins of these old civilizations and make important and informative discoveries that corroborate the Bible account.

afford to waste space that way. The houses are a solid row on each side of the streets. There are no windows in the front, only a door without any ornaments. The houses are built of stone, and a street is a narrow alley between two gray stone walls. Some of the houses have little gardens with a few flowers and perhaps a small tree, but that is behind the house, shut off from the street.

There are no great factories with roaring machinery and tall chimneys. Only a few things are made, and they are made in the homes. A blacksmith makes knives and ox-goads at the back of his house. A carpenter makes benches and tables and ox-yokes in a room of his house. The women spin thread and weave cloth in their own houses.

BARBER AT MICHMASH

This barber of Palestine is shaving the head of his customer (or shall we say his victim?), at his out-of-door shop in the neighborhood of the place made famous by the exploits of Jonathan, the son of Saul.

You ask, "Shall we go into the stores?" No, we shall go to the stores, but we shall not go into them. In one of the narrow streets the fronts of the houses are open in a series of little booths. The merchant sits in the middle of the booth and can reach nearly everything without getting up, it is so small. A few large boxes would contain all his goods. The customers stand in the street outside.

One merchant sells cloth; another, sandals; another, pottery; another, barley or wheat; another, jewels and silver; another, the rare spices and precious oils

A STREET MARKET

Great heaps of fine-looking cauliflower are piled up on the curb for sale.

from Arabia or Egypt. In the morning the merchant takes down his shutters, and the store is open. At night he puts them up, and the store is closed.

In most cities there was one house larger and stronger than the others. Outside it looked quite as bare as the rest. It was the castle. In it the governor of the city lived, with the soldiers who guarded the walls and gates. It was made very strong so that it might stand an attack. Sometimes it was able to stand if all the rest of the city was taken. Usually it had a great tower from which watch was kept over the city. To it the people often fled when there was danger.

You see that the city in the old Bible lands was built for war, not for peace. That accounts for its place on a hill, for its walls and narrow streets, for its strong gates, and for its castle with the tower. Now men build cities for peace and not for war. The Bible compares God to the castle-tower, which makes the city safe.

"The name of the Lord is a strong tower;
The righteous runneth into it, and is safe."
—Proverbs 18:10.

"Thou hast been a shelter for me;
And a strong tower from the enemy." —Psalms 61:3.

"The Lord is my rock, and my fortress, and my deliverer;
My God, my strength, in whom I will trust;
My buckler, and the horn of my salvation, and my high tower." —Psalms 18:2.

JERUSALEM

The most famous city in the land of the Bible was Jerusalem. It is a very old city. It is older than London or Rome. As for New York, or any of our American cities, they are mere babies in age compared with it.

When Jesus lived, it was very old. The Hebrews called it the city of their fathers.

But it was older than the Hebrew nation. When they came into the land it was already there. It was so strong that the shepherd Hebrews could not take it. For a long time the old inhabitants lived in it, and kept the Hebrews out.

At last a great king, David, was able to take it. He came there to live, and from that time it was the Hebrew capital, as Washington is the capital of the United States; and London, of the British Empire.

It is still the chief city of the land, and the people of Israel love it still.

BAZAAR AT DAMASCUS

"The bazaars of Damascus are a perpetual banquet of color. In the long tunnels of streets, shot by solid shafts of light, all is beautiful—the old walnut wood, the brown tobacco bales, the carpets, the spotted brown scones in the bakers' shops, the tawny sweetmeats, the golden Hauran wheat, the piles of green melons, the tables of snow from Hermon, the armor and rich saddle bags."

JERUSALEM ACROSS THE VALLEY OF HINNOM

"Up to Jerusalem," they said; and that was right. From any part of the country they had to climb hills to get to Jerusalem.

Some cities are on rivers or harbors, where the ships can unload goods from all the world. Not so Jerusalem. It was up in the hills. The only way to get there was by mule or camel, up the steep paths on the mountain sides. The city stood on a hill, with valleys on the east and the west. On the south the two valleys joined, and the hill stood up sharp and steep above the deep valley. Only on the north was the land as high as the city, and even there, in ancient times, a little valley cut part way across.

How did a city ever rise on a bare hilltop like that? Because in ancient times the hilltops were the safest places. Many of the people

JAFFA GATE OF JERUSALEM

about were wild and lawless, and war and raids of robbers were common.

But it did little good to live on a hill unless there were also walls about a city. So Jerusalem had its walls. They were great, high stone walls, with walks along the top protected by smaller outer walls, where soldiers could stand and protect the city from attack.

And was it ever attacked? Yes, often, in spite of its strong walls and the deep valleys about it.

Sometimes the walls were overthrown, but they were always built up again.

The last time it was taken was by the Allies in World War I. Their great cannon could have broken the wall down, thick as it is, but General Allenby, the head of the army of the Allies, said that not a shot must be fired at the sacred city. So the walls still stood just as they did before that war. In the Bible times the kings lived in Jerusalem, as long as the Hebrews had kings. King Solomon built palaces and a temple there. The temple was destroyed and then built up again. Later it was made larger and more splendid. It was built of white stone, and could be seen

A SHOP IN PALESTINE

STREET IN JERUSALEM

gleaming in the sunshine from far away. It was a very wonderful building for those days.

This larger and more splendid temple was the one Christ knew. He taught in the open grounds within its walls. He never stayed long in the city, but, like all his people, he loved it.

How much the people loved Jerusalem is shown by some of the poems about it. Sometimes the poems call it Jerusalem, and sometimes Zion. The name Zion belonged at first to a special part of the city, but came to be used for all of it.

Here is one of the prayers for Jerusalem:

"Do good in thy good pleasure unto Zion;
Build thou the walls of Jerusalem." —Psalms 51:18.

Here is part of a poem by a man who wished the good of the city:

"Pray for the peace of Jerusalem:
They shall prosper that love thee.

Peace be within thy walls,
And prosperity within thy palaces." —Psalms 122:6,7.

The people rejoiced that God himself dwelt in the temple at Jerusalem. One poet ended a poem:

"Blessed be the Lord out of Zion,
Which dwelleth at Jerusalem
Praise ye the Lord." —Psalms 135:21.

As he stood on the walls of Jerusalem and looked out on the hills on all sides, a poet thought, "That is like God's care; it always surrounds his people," and he wrote,

"They that trust in the Lord shall be as Mount Zion,
Which cannot be removed, but abideth forever.
As the mountains are round about Jerusalem,
So the Lord is round about his people
From henceforth and forever." —Psalms 125:1, 2.

The first Christians were Jews, and loved Jerusalem as much as any one. One of them, expressing the assurance of a great future when all the world should be God's, called that glorious time the "New Jerusalem."

"I saw," he said, "the Holy City, New Jerusalem, coming down from God out of heaven." —Revelation 21:2.

And each good thought or action moves
The dark world nearer to the sun.
—*John Greenleaf Whittier.*

Children at Play in the Open Air

Photographed by Three Lions, Inc.

PEOPLE in Palestine like to live in the open—thanks to the mild climate. Here is a group of children playing in the street outside their homes. Note how plain and crude these dwellings are—yet these children had never known anything other, and they are quite happy.

How the People Worshiped God

DID they have churches, with seats for the people, and music and prayers and preaching? No; neither churches nor church services.

If you had seen the places where they worshiped, you would have wondered what they were for.

In the very early times they were only a bare rock, or a few stones piled up. They were very often on the top of a hill, for it seemed to these early people that they were nearer to God on the top of a hill than in the valley, and so they went up to the hilltops to build altars on which to worship God. They came to call any place where God was worshiped a "high place."

Later on God directed them to destroy all the other high places and to worship only at Jerusalem, God's chosen city.

There, in the city where the kings lived, a temple was built, finer than any other of the temples. This temple was very splendid, and the people were very proud of it.

Later the other temples and altars were all given up, and this temple became the only one the Hebrews had in all the land.

What was the worship, and what were the altars for?

The worship was sacrifice. The altars were places to give the sacrifice to God. Usually it was given to him by burning it; "burnt offering" it was called. Sometimes it was grain, or other things from the fields. More often an animal from the flocks was brought to the temple and

59

killed. Then a part of the animal was burned on a fire of wood on the altar. Part of it went to the priest who had charge of the temple. Often part of it was cooked and eaten by the family who had brought it. In eating it, they were coming into fellowship with God. It was as though they and God were eating together. They were showing God how they wanted him to be with them.

Sometimes the sacrifice was an offering to God. They wanted to give him a gift and so they brought him an animal from the flocks. They did it when they wanted to thank him. These offerings were an Old Testament picture of Christ, the blessed Lamb of God, who was to be sacrificed for us.

Sometimes they brought God a gift when they were sorry they had done wrong.

We do not offer burnt offerings on an altar now, but we still want to have God with us.

There is a verse in the New Testament which says, "Behold, I stand at the door, and knock: if any man hear my voice, and open the door, I will come in to him, and will sup with him, and he with me." — Revelation 3:20.

IN THE NEW TESTAMENT TIMES

When Jesus and his friends lived, there was a temple at Jerusalem, just as in the last part of the Old Testament times. Jesus went to the temple when he was in Jerusalem. The people called it the "House of God." It was the place where they brought their sacrifices. Every day offerings were made on the great altar before the temple, and at certain times in the year, called feasts, thousands of people came to the temple to worship, until the city was filled with the pilgrim hosts.

But in the days of Jesus this was not all. Every village and town had what was called a synagogue. That was much more like a church than was the temple. It was a room in which the people gathered on the Sabbath. There was a platform with a desk, somewhat like a pulpit, where the leader of the worship stood. He did not conduct the whole service himself. He might call on any one in the congregation to read the Scriptures or prayers, or to speak. Once Jesus went back to his early home at Nazareth, and on the Sabbath went to the service, just as he used to do when he was a boy and he read the Scripture and afterward spoke.

The service began with the recitation of a passage commencing, "Hear, O Israel, the LORD our God is one LORD; and thou shalt love the LORD thy God with all thy heart and with all thy soul and with all thy might."

Once when Jesus was asked what was the greatest commandment, he repeated this, which began the Sabbath service.

After this passage came some prayers, then the reading of the Scripture.

Then if any one was present whom the people wished to hear, there might come a sermon, and the service closed with a prayer and a benediction.

Does that seem to be very much like a church service? Yes, it was, because the Christian churches borrowed from the synagogues their way of worship. They loved the service there. When they gathered to worship God as Christians, they did it in the way they had always done. Changes came in as time went on, but the general Christian way of worship has always been something like the way in which Jesus worshiped when he was a boy.

A Little Journey in the Land of the Bible

DO YOU like to take journeys?
Will you come with me on a journey?
We will try to see what the land where the
Hebrews lived was like. We will make little
maps as we go on, so that we can understand it better.

THE GREAT SEA

West of the land, toward the place where the sun goes
down, was the great sea. The shore stretched almost
straight north and south. To the east lay the land, and to
the west the water, as it is in the map.

The people of the Land of the Bible were not sailors. King Solomon had a navy of merchant ships which voyaged to distant lands and brought back many interesting things, but the people were for the most part shepherds and farmers who lived on the hills and in the valleys away from the sea. They could see the ocean from their hilltops and often their poets wrote of the sea, but they did not often sail on the blue waters of the Mediterranean. The

LAND OF THE BIBLE

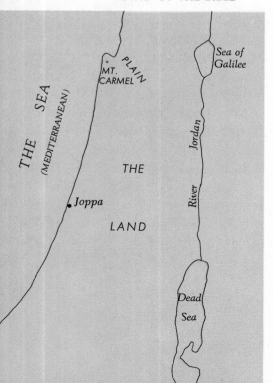

CAMELS READY FOR A JOURNEY

people of the coast were traders and colonists, the Hebrews were stay-at-home people.

As the Hebrew boys and girls looked out over the water, they could see no land to the west. The ships could sail and sail and sail, straight on, a long way before finding land.

JOPPA

The shore was mostly low and sandy. Now and then a little point of rocks put out, but most of the way the waves tumbled on the sand, with now and then a swamp where a stream cut through the sandbanks. At one place, where there were a little hill and some rocks, was a town, Joppa. It stands there still, and is called Jaffa. The harbor is not good, but ever since the Bible days ships have come to Joppa and loaded and unloaded.

MOUNT CARMEL

About fifty miles farther north is a great hill rising right up from the sea. It is Mount Carmel, and is the only hill along the whole coast. The sailors can see its round top from far off over the water, when they can see no land.

Now let us turn our backs to the sea and face the east, and begin our journey. But we shall not take a railroad. O dear no! Not in the times of the Bible! There is a railroad from Jaffa now, but we will travel as the people did when Jesus lived.

TRAVELERS ON FOOT IN PALESTINE

These sturdy peasants are trudging along on foot, driving their donkeys before them, bringing produce to Jerusalem.

A LONG JOURNEY ON FOOT

And how was that? For most strong men and boys, it was on foot. The king's messengers rode on horses, and galloped along as fast as they could. Rich men sometimes rode on donkeys. So sometimes did women and little girls, while the men walked by their side.

When men went on long journeys to other countries, across the great, wide desert places where there was no water for many miles, they sometimes went on camels, tall animals with long legs and long necks. Camels can go for days without water; and their broad, flat feet walk easily over the soft sand. We shall see camels walking on the great road which goes up the coast, bearing on their backs the goods of distant lands to sell in far-off cities. But we will travel afoot; only any who are lame or weak or not able to walk long distances, may ride on donkeys.

THE PLAIN

And so we start from Joppa. It will be more than one day's journey. For about twenty miles we go over a plain.

Large Rocks in the Sinai Desert

From International Publishing Co., Ltd.

THE desert of Sinai into which Moses led the twelve tribes of Israel was a "vast and howling wilderness," an area of very scant rainfall and therefore incapable of sustaining a population of any size. Moses had been a sheep herder in this area before he returned to Egypt to deliver his people from slavery. In these desolate surroundings God provided manna day by day for food, and water out of the flinty rock because there was no such provision by nature for the Israelites. The very desolation of their surroundings emphasized their complete dependence upon God.

It is dotted with mud-walled villages, and in the summer it is rich with waving wheat and barley. Near the villages are little groves of fig and olive and pomegranate trees. Off to the south, the plain stretches far and far, beyond the borders of the land. To the north, it goes on, growing a little narrower, till it

ARABS WITH CAMELS

ends in low hills, back of Mount Carmel.

UP INTO THE HILLS

When we have gone for a long time, we come to low, round hills. We follow up a winding valley between the hills. All this country was rich farming land, and many of the hills were crowned with little villages.

WATER CARRIER
IN JERUSALEM

This belt of low hills lasts ten or fifteen miles. Then the country changes again. The hills become much higher and steeper. They look like bare stone ridges. Often the dirt has been washed off and the gray rock appears. Deep gullies have been worn by the winter rains of centuries.

A CARAVAN CROSSING A FIELD

The four camels with their packs are crossing the plowed fields to reach the fine new military road.

The few roads wind up these gullies. Villages are not so numerous as they were on the lower hills. Here and there are little fields on the hill side, sometimes made by building a stone wall and piling earth behind it, till a long, winding, narrow strip of ground is formed, only a few feet across, and on this men raise a little grain.

TRAVELING IN PALESTINE

The white horse in this little caravan carries a palanquin, a sort of a little house, in which women make long journeys in the East. A woman is sitting in this one. Behind come two men. Do you notice how high they sit in their saddles? And a little dog is trotting with them.

Up the road winds, higher and higher to the hills. We begin to be tired. Shall we ever get to the top?

Yes, be patient. We shall be there at last.

ON THE TOP OF THE HILLS

Finally the valleys grow wider. We can see over the hills, instead of being shut up in narrow valleys. We are at last on the tops of the hills.

But do not think it is all level. Not at all. There are many hills, but they are all

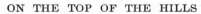

OLD ROMAN BRIDGE
IN HILL COUNTRY

about the same height, and the valleys between them are not very deep.

On the tops of some of the hills we see villages. Little fields of grain are in the wide hollows. There is a path running over a hill, and down here by the road is a spring of water. We see more people than in the steep valleys up which we have come. There in the distance is a shepherd leading his sheep. Here is a little boy running beside a donkey loaded with straw.

Here we come to a great, widespread tree. It is an olive tree, such as has grown in this country for many centuries. We will stop under it for a little while, and talk about these hills.

CAMEL

This is a "close up" view of one of the "locomotives" of the East. Sometimes the camels are called ships and sometimes locomotives.

Back from the coast, behind the plain, runs a long range of hills, like the backbone of the country. It begins far north of this land of Palestine, and goes farther south, till the hills flatten out into the desert lands. North of Palestine it is a range of mountains called Lebanon. Here in Palestine it is a range of hills running right down through the center of the land.

It is one hundred and fifty miles from the upper end of the land to the lower. Ask your father to tell you what place is one hundred and fifty miles from where you live. All that way the hills go, only broken at one place where they become low, just east of Mount Carmel. There a plain, called the Plain of Esdraelon, stretches right across the land.

A CARAVAN IN PALESTINE

The camels of the caravan are marching along in a row, carrying heavy burdens of merchandise.

Most of the stories the Bible tells took place on this long line of hills. Down to the south lived Abraham and Isaac and Jacob in their shepherd tents, and far off in the north, where the hills are called the Hills of Galilee, Jesus lived when he was a boy.

THE FAMOUS CITIES OF THE HILLS

Most of the famous cities of the Hebrews were on the hills. Hebron was south of us, and Jerusalem and Bethlehem near us, and north were Bethel and Shechem and Samaria and Nazareth and many others.

If you should write out the famous stories of the Bible on separate pieces of paper and scatter them over a great map at the places about which they tell, the places all up and down this ridge of hills would be white with them.

Before us is the most famous city of all, Jerusalem.

JERUSALEM

Now that we have rested we will go on. And here are the gray walls of Jerusalem, on a hill ahead of us. They are thick stone walls, with heavy gates that were shut at

The Jordan Valley

From International Publishing Co., Ltd.

THE Jordan River winds its way through a deep rift valley southward from the Sea of Galilee to the Dead Sea. To the east (on the left hand side) is the hill country of Ammon, Moab, and Edom; and to the west is the wilderness. It was from the wilderness of Judea on the right that John the Baptist came and preached to large crowds who assembled to hear him beside the Jordan. In the river he baptized those who were sorry for their sin.

night. Then all the little children thought, "We are safe now. No robbers can get into the city."

The story of Jerusalem is a long, long story, and we have not time for it now. It begins before the Hebrews came to Palestine, and is not finished yet. Jerusalem is still the greatest city in Palestine. Here David lived, and many other men and women about whom the Bible talks. Here Jesus came with his father and mother when he was twelve years old, and here at last he was crucified. O yes! It is the most interesting city in the whole world, and sometime you will want to learn all you can about it.

But now come to a hill just east of Jerusalem and look off. What do you see?

THE ROAD WHICH GOES UP TO JERUSALEM

"Away off in the east," you say, "I see a faint blue streak, and what looks like a line of rocks above it, with a long, straight, flat top."

Yes, that is a line of rock, and the faint blue streak is the water of the Dead Sea. It lies away down in a deep valley, far below where we stand on the top of the hills. Into the northern end of the Dead Sea flows the Jordan.

The Jordan River flows through the strangest valley in the whole world, and we are going to visit it.

DOWN TO THE JORDAN AND THE DEAD SEA

So we start down the road to the east. Almost immediately we begin to go down steep hills; and we keep on going down steep hills for almost twenty miles. We thought the hills on the west side were steep; those on the east are steeper. We thought the mountain sides there rugged and bare; these are still more rugged and bare. Great cliffs rise at times above the road, and on the other side are deep ravines, with jagged, rocky sides. And always we are going down, down, down. The sun beats down, and, if we are making the journey in the summer, it becomes very hot. No villages are on the way, for there is no land on which any crops can be raised; nothing but bare rocks. In the Bible times they called this region "The Wilderness of Judea"; and a very good name it is for the country.

GOING TO MARKET

The woman on the little donkey and the boy with the pleasant face are bringing their produce to market in a town of Palestine.

A FAMOUS RIVER

At last we turn about a cliff, and there below lies a flat valley eight or ten miles across. It looks like a sandy floor, as it stretches out below us. A line of willows and other little trees goes across it, winding about, and among the trees we now and then see a gleam of water. It is the Jordan River, with its fringe of trees on the bank.

The Jordan valley lies right along the east side of the long line of hills, with another line of hills on the further side of it. It is like a deep trough. It is as though a giant

plow had plowed a furrow straight down the ninety miles of Palestine. And what a deep furrow it is! At the Dead Sea, the glint of whose waters we saw from the hills, the valley is thirteen hundred feet lower than the sea. It is the deepest valley in all the world which is not filled with water.

Away off in the north, on the side of a high mountain called Hermon, there is a spring of clear, sparkling water. That is where the Jordan begins. It comes tumbling down till it finally comes into a lake about seven miles across and twenty miles wide, with hills all about it. This is the Sea of Galilee. When Jesus lived there were towns on the bank and fishing boats on the lake. Jesus had friends in the towns. Some of them were fishermen. He loved the blue waters of the lake and the beautiful green hills about it.

From this lake the Jordan River runs down the bottom of the valley, winding from side to side. The valley grows wider as it comes down, and the hills higher.

ON THE ROAD TO BETHLEHEM FROM JERUSALEM

At last the Jordan runs into the Dead Sea. This sea stretches about forty miles from north to south.

THE DEAD SEA

The Jordan River is usually muddy, but the Dead Sea is bright and clear. But you must not try to drink from it. The water is saltier than the Great Sea, and tastes like all the bad things you have ever tasted. Do the fish like it? Why, there are no fish in it. There are no fish that can live in that water. Do you see why it is called the Dead Sea?

And where does the water run from the Dead Sea? It does not run at all. It has reached the bottom here, and can go no farther.

But the Jordan River keeps running in and no water runs out? Yes. Then why does not the Sea get higher and higher till it runs over the edge of the valley, as a bath tub runs over when the faucet is left open?

Now this is what makes it such a strange lake. It would get higher and higher till it ran over if it were in a cool country; but away down in that deep valley the sun shines very hot, and the water dries up as fast as it runs in. The same thing happens to it as does to a kettle of water on the stove. The kettle will be all dry after a while

THE DEAD SEA

© MPS

"INN OF THE GOOD SAMARITAN"

Let us go down from Jerusalem to Jericho some twenty-three.miles away. Here by the roadside, before we reach Jericho, stands this quaint inn.

Here or near here, it is said, stood the inn the Saviour spoke of, to which the good Samaritan carried the wounded man who had fallen among thieves, and took such tender care of him.

Today this more modern building is called the Inn of the Good Samaritan. Read pages 272-278 and Luke 10:30-37, Volume 7:174-6.

if no new water is put in. So this lake would dry up if it were not for the fresh water which the Jordan pours in.

THE LAND OF MOAB

Now look at the hills across the valley to the east. The Hebrews never lived on those east of the Dead Sea. They were called Moab. But Hebrews lived in the hills farther north, east of the Jordan, which they called Gilead and Bashan. There were never as many people here as in the country west of the Jordan. Great herds of sheep and cattle roamed over the hills. In some parts there were forests, and, in other parts, wide fields of grain. A few of the Bible stories are about what happened east of the Jordan, but the greater number of them belonged to the western hills.

So we have seen the four regions of the Bible land: the plain along the coast; the hills in the center of the land; the deep Jordan valley; and the hills east of the Jordan. We have made the journey quickly on paper! But to take the long journey on foot would require several days.

Here are the four sections. Now our little journey from Joppa to the Jordan is done. The tents are up. The donkeys are tied, and we will say a prayer before we lie down to sleep under the bright stars, which keep watch over us.

REGIONS OF THE BIBLE LAND

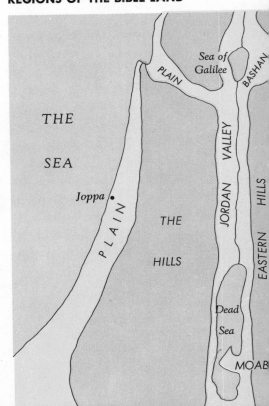

GLORIOUS SUNSET HOUR

The sunset to the west beyond the Sea of Galilee throws its glorious afterglow upon the eastern clouds.

Sunrise over the Sea of Galilee, where the Lord Jesus walked upon the waves, brings light and health and warmth to the world. But we thank the Lord for the sunset, for its blessing of rest, "For so he giveth his Beloved sleep." Read Psalm 127:2, Volume 6:290.

"LILIES OF THE FIELD"

Of every color are the flowers, white, yellow, pink, blue, purple; the most brilliant of all are the big tall Syrian anemones, royal scarlet, with a crown in each flowercup.

"Consider the lilies of the field," said the Saviour in his flower-sermon, showing the care of the Heavenly Father for his children. And these Syrian anemones are claimed to be the "Lilies of the Field." Matthew 6:28-34, Volume 7:103.

John the Baptist

By Andrea del Sarto (1486-1531)

In the Pitti Gallery, Florence, Italy

Color Photograph by Alinari Brothers, Florence

WE HAVE here an ideal representation of a youth, the Renaissance ideal, and ours, which makes visible for us those human qualities which we instinctively call "highest." This young athlete looks out upon the world with confidence, aware of his unique powers, ready to reveal his vision to men, his relaxed grace suggesting the composure which preludes action. He represents the embodiment of the heroic in man—man as he could be—should be.

Around him are the symbols of the Baptist. A goatskin is knotted about his shoulders. The bowl of purification is in his right hand, and the scroll of the prophets upon which his soul has fed is in his left. The slender reed cross appears in the corner. Over his arm falls a red mantle, symbolic of his zeal for things divine.

The story of John the Baptist as retold by the authors begins on page 210. From the Biblical account of his life, found in Volume 7, we learn that John "was in the deserts till the day of his showing unto Israel," that he was a hermit who lived on "locusts and wild honey" while brooding upon the people's sins, and that his audacious, vehement preaching startled the whole Jewish world into wakefulness. Thus we visualize the Baptist as a less placid, less socialized, but no less heroic person than del Sarto portrays here. Although Raphael's painting (Volume 7:284) conveys more of the smoldering energy of the Forerunner, we must add to these Renaissance ideal conceptions the uncontrolled fire in the eye and the frenzy of soul of the ascetic who cries, "Woe is me if I preach not repentance."

Andrea, son of Agnolo the tailor ("sarto"), was called "The Faultless Painter." The tragedy in the life of this gifted man is narrated in Robert Browning's noble poem "Andrea del Sarto." Another painting by del Sarto is in Volume 7, page 106.

Stories of
Old Testament
Days

Stories of Joseph

THE SHEPHERD BOY

DREAMED A DREAM.—Dreams were considered very important in Eastern countries.

SHEAVES:—Bundles of grain. Though Jacob was a shepherd, doubtless he raised a little grain.

ONCE, long ago, there was a shepherd named Jacob, who had twelve sons. Ten of them were great, stalwart men, but the two youngest were still growing up. The older of the two was named Joseph and the younger, Benjamin.

Of all the sons Joseph was the father's favorite. His father liked to keep him about the tent when the rest went far off over the hills with the flocks. Jacob made for the boy a coat such as rich men wore. It was far too fine to wear when working about the sheep. The fact is, Jacob thought his favorite was a little too good to do rough work, and wanted to make it easy for him. Perhaps if their mother had lived, it might have been different, but she was dead, and all the father's love for her had gone out to these boys.

It is no wonder that Joseph came to think well of himself. One day he had a dream which he told to his brothers.

"I dreamed," he said, "that we were binding sheaves in the field, and behold! my sheaf stood up, and all yours came around and bowed down to my sheaf."

His brothers sneered at him. "You think, do you, that we are going to bow down to you?" they said.

PLOWING WITH OXEN IN PALESTINE

BLACK TENTS OF THE ARABS

Another day, when they were all gathered with their father about the tent door after the sheep were taken care of at night, he told another dream.

"I have dreamed again," he said. "I dreamed that the sun and the moon and eleven stars bowed down to me."

Even his father, who loved him, could see how foolish the boy was.

"Do you think that all the family are to bow down to you?" he said.

His brothers hated him. It was bad enough to have his father save him from all the rough work. It was worse for him to put on airs, and think he was better than they. And, indeed, Joseph was on the way to becoming a selfish, spoiled boy, who thought, because he did not have to work as hard as others, he was somehow better than they.

—Now read this story in Bible language in Bible Heroes, Pioneers—Volume 3, page 133.

SOLD AS A SLAVE

BLACK TENTS:—The shepherds lived in tents woven of black goats' hair. In the New Testament, Paul was a maker of such tents.

TWENTY PIECES OF SILVER:—About twelve dollars.

COMPANY OF TRAVELING MERCHANTS:—A CARAVAN. The trade of the East was carried on by these caravans which had regular routes like our roads or railways.

The flocks of Jacob were so large that they sometimes had to go far away to find pasture. Sometimes the shepherds camped out on the hills, and did not come back to the black tents for days at a time.

One day, when the older brothers had been gone with the flocks for so long that Jacob wanted word of them, he called Joseph.

"Go up to Shechem," he said, "and find your brothers and the flocks, and see if all is well with them, and bring me word."

So off went Joseph, glad of the long walk up into the hills. He climbed the round limestone hills, and was soon out of sight of the familiar group of tents in the valley.

At last he came to Shechem. Here was the spring where he knew his brothers watered their flocks, but no one was there, nor could he see them anywhere on the hillsides. He followed up a valley, but they were not there. He went to the top of a hill but they were not on the other side.

Then he met a man, on a trail over the hills, who told him that his brothers had gone on to a place called Dothan, a dozen miles farther on. Joseph trudged on over more hills to find Dothan, where there was a spring and a wide, fertile field of pasture.

"I hope they will have a good dinner for me," he thought.

WATER BUFFALO IN EGYPT

These three Egyptian children are having fun with their strange steeds.

The water buffaloes are very valuable in Egypt as beasts of burden. They were used in Joseph's day. They were the fat and lean kine of Pharaoh's dream.

"And behold, there came up out of the river seven well favoured kine and fat fleshed; and they fed in a meadow."—*Genesis 41:2*.

WOODEN EGYPTIAN DOLLS

The little girls who played with these dolls lived in the 12th Egyptian Dynasty, about 4000 years ago.

MARBLES OF EGYPTIAN BOYS

These are stone marbles used by Egyptian boys. The children who played with these marbles lived more than 5000 years ago, but the marbles look very much like the stone "agates," with which boys play to-day.

JOSEPH SOLD BY HIS BROTHERS
A painting by Serehe Yemane Berhane

By and by he saw them in the distance, and went faster; for he was hungry and tired.

They had seen him, too.

"There comes that dreamer," one said.

"Let's kill him," another said, "and tell father that a bear ate him up. Then we shall see what becomes of his dreams."

How they hated him!

But the oldest, Reuben, said, "No, not kill him. Let's put him in this pit and leave him."

He hoped to come later and take him out.

So when Joseph came up, there was no rest and no good dinner waiting for him, but only hatred and black looks.

They stripped him of his fine coat and dropped him into an empty pit. Then they sat down to eat their own dinner.

A company of traveling merchants, with their goods on camels, came along. They were going far away to Egypt, with spices and rich goods. They stopped and talked with the shepherds at dinner. Then one of the brothers, Judah, said,

"Why kill Joseph? If we sell him to these merchants then we shall be innocent of the crime of killing him."

So they pulled the boy up out of the pit and sold him for twenty pieces of silver to the merchants. That was cheap for a slave, but perhaps they did not want the merchants to ask too many questions about how they came to have a slave boy to sell.

Then they sat down to finish their dinner and the merchants went on down the road toward distant Egypt with their newly bought slave. When Reuben, who had gone away, came back, he found Joseph gone. He

BOAT ON THE NILE

By courtesy of the Metropolitan Museum of Art,
New York

IN THIS picture, the slaves are working hard
at the oars. The helmsman stands in the
stern by the great rudder. The mast and
sail have been taken down. For full explana-
tion, see Volume 3.

soon learned what had happened, but could do nothing. The merchants would not give up their good bargain, even if he could overtake them. So Reuben, not to make enemies of his brothers, kept still in all that followed.

One bad deed leads to another. The brothers killed a kid, dipped the fine coat into its blood, and when they drove the sheep home again, threw it down before their father and said,

"This looks like Joseph's coat. You will know whether it is or not."

"Yes," said Jacob, "it is. Some wild beast has eaten him up."

For long years he mourned sorely for this son, and could not be comforted; so that the brothers, hard and heartless as they were, wished they had not done this wrong. But they dared not tell him the truth, not even when they had sons of their own, and knew how much fathers loved their children. —Read in Vol. 3, pp. 134-139.

JOSEPH IN EGYPT

CANAAN:—One of the names of Palestine, from which Joseph came.

YEARS OF FAMINE:—Years in which no food could be raised or so little that the people were in danger of starving.

Joseph had been brought up out of doors, and had never slept under any roof heavier than a tent. He was probably a fine, strong, bright-eyed boy, and sold well in the slave market in the great city in Egypt. One of the high officers of the land bought him. He had to learn new kinds of work, and a new language, for in Egypt they did not speak the language of the people of Canaan. He had hard work to do and no nice coat now to wear. But he was so cheerful and willing and honest that things went very well, considering he was a slave, until someone accused him falsely to his master. Then he was thrown into prison; and that was worse than being a slave. But his honesty and cheery way won him friends again, and by and by he was trusted to help the keeper of the prison.

In the same prison were two officers of the king. One morning Joseph found them troubled because they had each dreamed a dream, and could not tell what it meant. Joseph said that God had told him the dreams meant that one would be released, and the other not, and so it turned out.

For two years longer he stayed in prison, and the time must have dragged very slowly.

Then came a day when a messenger from the king, whom the Egyptians called the Pharaoh, appeared at the prison, and demanded Joseph. He hastened Joseph out of the prison, put on him finer clothes than he had ever seen before, and brought him before the great Pharaoh himself.

Now the reason was this: Pharaoh had dreamed a troublous dream, and none of the people whose business it was to tell what dreams meant could explain it. Finally the officer who had been in prison told of Joseph, and the Pharaoh hurriedly sent for him.

"I hear you can explain dreams," he said.

"No, but God can," Joseph replied.

Then Pharaoh told his dream. First he had dreamed that seven fat oxen were eaten up by seven lean oxen; then that seven full heads of grain were eaten up by seven shriveled heads.

"Both mean the same," said Joseph. "There will be seven fruitful years in Egypt, then seven years of famine. God has shown Pharaoh this beforehand, so that the famine can be prepared for in the years of plenty. Gather up food and build storehouses, and make ready for the years which will produce nothing."

Pharaoh was pleased with Joseph, and appointed him as the officer in charge of all the food supply for the country. He made Joseph the second man in the kingdom and gave him a fine chariot to ride in, and whenever Joseph went through the streets of the city men cried before him, "Bow the knee."

But life was not all parade and fine clothes. He had to see that in all Egypt grain was bought and storehouses were built, and that the farmers were not cheated and that the government got what it paid for. Joseph had never worked so hard before in his life.

All these years his poor father in the shepherd's tent mourned him as long dead.

JOSEPH AND HIS BRETHREN

COURT OF JOSEPH:—The place where he received people who had business with him.

INTERPRETER:—An officer who could speak both the Egyptian language and the language of other countries.

After the years of plenty came the years of famine. No grain grew in the fields, and the people would have died of starvation had they not been able to go to Joseph and buy food. Soon they came saying,

"Our money is gone, and our children are crying with hunger. Buy our cattle and give us grain."

So he did; and every day the great court of Joseph was filled with Egyptians, who bowed down before him and begged him to sell them food for their hungry children. Joseph was very glad to be able to do it. So much food had been collected in the plentiful years that now there was enough and to spare.

The Pyramids and the Sphinx

THE Pyramids are said by authorities to have been built as royal tombs, and also to have been used for astronomical observations. According to Herodotus 100,000 men were employed twenty years in building the great Pyramid, the Pyramid of Cheops. This Pyramid was originally 480 feet high with a base 764 feet square. It is believed that the Pyramid was once covered by a solid granite casing which has been removed. There are three "great" Pyramids and about forty others of lesser size.

The Sphinx is a huge rock image near the Pyramids and is older than some of them. Although it is badly defaced, still it has a certain high dignity and power. "Viewed now at a little distance, it has the calmness, the simple majesty that belong to high art. Old writers say that the face was once sweet and beautiful."

JOSEPH AND BENJAMIN
A painting by James J. Tissot

SLAVES BRINGING SUPPLIES OF FOOD

These slaves are bringing supplies of food: poultry, bread, and other supplies, to the steward of the king.

MODEL OF EGYPTIAN BUTCHER SHOP

MODEL OF EGYPTIAN GRANARY

In this model, the slaves are making bread: one is bringing water, others are kneading the meal, and one has a loaf of freshly made bread. For full description of these pictures see Volume 3.

One day, as Joseph sat in his court, he glanced down and saw a group of foreign-looking men in travel-stained clothing, standing timidly at the back of the court. He knew them. They were his brothers. All were there except Benjamin, the youngest. They did not know him. They may have wondered if one of the slave donkey-drivers they saw in the streets might be their brother, but they would never dream of looking for him under the fine robes of an Egyptian officer.

The famine had reached their land, and they had come to Egypt to buy grain, but they felt very strange in this fine court.

When their turn came, they bowed very low before the great officer and began to tell how their children were hungry, but he, talking Egyptian, broke in on them. The interpreter told them what he said, but they needed no one to interpret his black looks and harsh tone.

"You are spies," he said. "You have come to see how weak the land is."

"No, no," they replied, "we came to buy food. We are all one man's sons, we are not spies."

"Spies you are," he growled.

"No, we are twelve brothers; and one is dead and one is with our father, and we are come to buy food. We are not spies," said the frightened shepherds.

"I believe you are spies," he said, "but you may prove you are not. One may go back for your brother and the rest stay in prison."

And off to the prison he sent them.

Three days later he brought them in again.

"You may all go back except one," he said, "and take food for your children; but you must not come again unless you bring your youngest brother," for Joseph longed above all to see Benjamin.

Game of Draughts Played on a Low Table with Two Sets of Seven Men, One Set for Each Player.

From a Wall-Relief from the Tomb of Nykauhor at Sakkara. Now in the Metropolitan Museum of Art.

Dynasty V, about 2700 B.C.

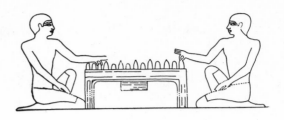

Girls Playing Ball, Two of Them Mounted on the Backs of Their Companions.

From a Wall-Painting in the Tomb of Basket at Beni Hasan.

Dynasty XII, about 2000 B.C.

Game Called "The Vase," represented as Played on a Circular Board with Round Men or Marbles. The Method Followed in Playing the Game is Not Known.

From a Wall-Relief in the Tomb of Shepsesre at Sakkara.

Dynasty V, about 2700 B.C.

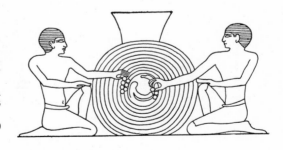

EGYPTIAN GAMES

So he put one, Simeon, in prison, and the rest went home with bags of grain on their donkeys' backs; and Joseph had ordered their money to be put into the bags with the grain, where they found it when they opened the bags.

They did not know what to make of it all, but they knew that they could neither free Simeon nor buy more food unless Benjamin went with them.

Benjamin had taken the place of Joseph in Jacob's love, and it was not easy to persuade the anxious father to let him go on the long journey, but at last Jacob consented.

One day, as Joseph sat in his court again, he espied the frightened faces of his brethren, and with them one whom he knew to be Benjamin.

He paid no attention to them, but turned and spoke to an officer, who went out. Soon they were called out of the court, taken to a fine house, and told that they were to dine with the great Egyptian officer.

Simeon joined them, they laid out the little presents they had brought, and wondered what was coming next.

Joseph came in and asked, "The old man, your father, is he yet alive? Is this your youngest brother?"

But even yet he did not tell who he was.

When they sat down at the table, they found they were seated in order of age. How should the Egyptian or his servants know that? It was all very strange.

The next day, as soon as it was light, they started for home with the grain they had bought, glad enough to be gone. But before long a messenger came riding after them.

"Why have you done evil for good?" he said sternly. "You have stolen my lord's silver cup from his house."

Bedouin Tent near Beersheba

From International Publishing Co., Ltd.

A BEDOUIN tent of today is very similar to that of Jacob in the days of the patriarchs. The tent was the home for all the family, including the families of the married children. It was a place of hospitality for friend and stranger alike. In such a tent and environment Jacob reared his large family. The father was revered by the members of his household, and led them in the worship of Almighty God. He gave the responsibility for daily duties to the sons who were sheep herders, much as is still true among the desert dwellers in the Middle East.

Here was further strange misfortune. That they should be taken for thieves!

They protested with many words that they were honest men and had stolen nothing.

"Search us," they said. "Whoever has stolen your lord's cup shall die and the rest of us will be your slaves."

"Very good," said the messenger, just as Joseph had told him to say, "but I will not be so hard on you as that. Whoever has stolen the cup shall be my lord's slave and the rest can go free."

CAMELS IN THE DESERT

For centuries the camel has been the "Ship of the Desert." Modern travelers use these faithful beasts just as the people did in the days of Abraham. The French Government is, however, experimenting with tractors which may take the place of the camels and the long caravans. What would the Patriarchs think of such a substitute!

Then he opened Benjamin's bag, and there in the top was Joseph's silver cup, for Joseph had given orders that it should be put there.

Joseph was trying to see whether they were still selfish, and would give up Benjamin to save themselves, or not.

The brothers were astounded, but they had no thought of riding away free and leaving Benjamin to his fate. They all went back to the harsh Egyptian officer to plead for their brother.

Then one of them, Judah, told the whole story: how Joseph was dead, how their old father loved Benjamin, how it would kill him if Benjamin did not come back! "Keep me as a slave," he begged; "only let Benjamin go to our father."

By that, Joseph knew that his cruel brothers had
learned love and loyalty. The need of harshness was
over. They had stood his test! He was ready to let
them know who he was.

"Let every one go out of the court," he cried; and
all the officers and interpreters and soldiers and clerks
went out, leaving the great officer alone with the group
of wondering shepherds.

Then Joseph stepped down from his great throne,
laid aside his rich robes, laid aside his harsh manner
and his Egyptian speech, and in the language of his
boyhood said, "I am Joseph. Does my father yet
live?"

And the strong men wept together.

Joseph sent his brethren back, with wagons and
camels, to bring his father and all their families and
their tents and their flocks to Egypt. The Pharaoh
gave them permission to settle in a part of the land of
Egypt. So Jacob saw his son Joseph again, and spent
his last years with him.

His brethren asked Joseph to forgive them for the
old wrong they did him.

"Forgive?" he said. "I forgave you long ago. You
meant it for evil, but God
meant it for good."

This is the wonderful
story of the shepherd boy
who became second to the
king in the great empire of
Egypt. —See Vol. 3, pp. 155-199.

BRONZE EGYPTIAN CAT
The cat was a sacred animal in
Egypt in the early days.

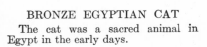

MOSES SAVED
FROM THE NILE
A painting by Orazio Gentileschi

The Story of Moses

THE BABY IN A FLOATING CRADLE

REEDS:—Tall river plants, growing close to the shore, partly in the water.

HEBREWS:—The descendants of the family of Jacob, who had come into Egypt when Joseph was second to Pharaoh. Joseph was dead and the Pharaohs had forgotten all about him and his service to the nation.

ONCE, in Egypt, there was a little girl named Miriam. She lived with her parents and her brother Aaron not far from the banks of a wide river. In some places along the side of the river were reeds. Miriam could reach in among the reeds and hide little baskets, and they would stay quietly, held by the stout stalks about them.

Out on the river, boats were often passing. They were not steamers, as on the large rivers to-day. They were boats with sails. If the wind was right the sail was up. If not, men rowed the boats with long oars.

Not far away was the palace of the king of the country. Little Miriam used sometimes to watch the soldiers go tramp, tramp, on the road to the palace.

Sometimes she saw the daughters of the king walking by the river, with their servants. But she never spoke to them. Oh no! She was only a poor girl, who was not even of the same race as they were. Her people were called Hebrews, and they had to work for the king, making bricks with which he built his great storehouses. The king and his people were Egyptians and the Egyptians always looked down on the Hebrews.

When mother stood in the door of their little house and called, "Miriam, Miriam, come now and help me," then Miriam would run home and tell her mother all about the beautiful princess, with her servants and her rich dress, who walked so often on the path by the river.

Now the Egyptians were afraid that if the Hebrews became too strong they would fight for their freedom. To keep them from becoming too strong, the king did a very cruel thing. He sent out word that all the little boy babies should be killed. If that were done for a time, then, later, there would not be so many men among the Hebrews to fight for their freedom.

ONE OF THE GREAT PYRAMIDS

By and by, a little baby was born in Miriam's home. Miriam loved her little brother. He looked up and smiled so cunningly, and she was soon very sure he knew her and reached out his little hands to her. At first she did not understand why her mother so often wept when she looked at the baby, and why she kept him hid in a room in the house, and was so anxious if he began to cry when any Egyptian was passing in the street. Then she learned about the new law, and she was afraid day and night that the soldiers would come and take the little baby away.

For three months the mother kept the baby hidden. But that could not go on. Sometime the baby would surely be found.

One day Miriam's mother said to her,

"Go down to the river and get me some reeds and grasses."

Miriam wondered what her mother would do, but she brought the reeds with tall, strong grasses. Her mother wove them into a little basket. She set the basket in the water, but the water came through the cracks, and the basket sank.

Then her mother took the basket and covered it with something that dried into a hard, smooth coating. Then she put it in the water again, and it floated on the top like a little boat.

Miriam was very curious about what it all meant. She thought the little boat would make a nice plaything, but her mother did not give it to her. Instead, she covered it inside with the softest cloth she had, and made a little nest, all cosy and warm.

Into that nest she put the little baby! Miriam wondered still more what her mother meant. Then she picked up basket, baby and all, and went out toward the river, telling Miriam to come with her. What could her mother want?

When they got to the river, Miriam began to see what the little basket that swam like a boat was for. Her mother put the little basket in a safe place among the reeds on the river, just as she had hidden her little baskets when she had been playing by the river.

Then her mother told Miriam what to do, and went back to the house; and Miriam stayed by the river. She felt very much grown up, because her mother had left her to watch the baby. If something happened, then she must do just as her mother had told her, and perhaps she could save baby brother's life.

Then that very thing her mother had talked of

PLEASURE BOAT ON THE NILE

really happened. The young princess came along the
river bank with her servants. Just as she was opposite the baby, she saw the little basket and stopped.
Miriam saw her point it out to a servant girl, and heard
her say, "What is that basket? Go bring it."

The girl brought the basket, and Miriam saw the
princess' look of astonishment as she said, "It is a
Hebrew baby!"

Miriam's heart was in her mouth. What would
the princess do? But Miriam went up, just as her
mother had told her to, and asked,

"Shall I bring you a nurse for the baby?"

Now the baby had begun to cry, and the kind heart
of the princess went out to the lonely little thing.

"Yes," she said. "Bring a nurse for it."

Miriam ran home and brought her mother.

The princess said, "Take this child home and take
care of it for me, and I will pay you."

So the mother was nurse for the baby, and the
child was safe because the king's daughter, the young
princess, had adopted him.

That is how Miriam saved her little brother.

The baby was called Moses, and grew up to be the
man who led his people out of Egypt.

—The Bible text vivid and brief is in Volume 3, pp. 203-205.

The Infant Samuel

By Sir Joshua Reynolds (1723-1792)

In the National Gallery, London, England

THE touching story of Samuel is given on the opposite page and the Bible text, in Volume 3, beginning on page 523.

This famous painting presents an idealized portrait
of a child, kneeling and looking upward toward a shaft
of light from heaven, with chubby hands pressed
together in an attitude of prayer. Against a dimly-
lighted background, the little boy's white-garmented
figure and lustrous hair shine forth.

Sir Joshua Reynolds was born at Plympton Earl, in
Devonshire, England, and early showed strong artistic
inclinations. After two years' study with Thomas
Hudson, a London portrait-painter, and several years
of painting for a living, Reynolds journeyed to Italy
where he spent three years studying the works of the
Italian masters.

Returning to London in 1752, Reynolds painted a
portrait of his friend Commodore Keppel which was so
much admired that he became immediately the most
celebrated portrait-painter in England. From then on
until his sixty-seventh year, he painted continuously,
producing in all the amazing number of some three
thousand pictures. The roster of people who sat to
Reynolds for their portraits includes nearly all the
noteworthy individuals of his day from King George III
down. Among the painter's life-long friends were Samuel
Johnson, Oliver Goldsmith, David Garrick, and
Edmund Burke.

Through writings and paintings, Reynolds promoted
an English school of painting. In the history of painting, the latter half of the eighteenth century belongs
especially to portraiture, and Reynolds and his com-
patriots, Hogarth and Gainsborough, were the foremost
portrait-painters in Europe at that time.

Reynolds was particularly successful in portraying
children in all their various moods. This painting of
the infant Samuel has been a popular favorite ever
since it was painted in 1776.

The Story of Samuel

THE BOY WHO LIVED IN THE TEMPLE

ONCE there was an old priest named Eli who was in charge of the most sacred place of worship the Hebrews had at that time. The people came there to worship. They brought offerings to give to God. Often it was a lamb; sometimes, if the person was poor, it was only a dove.

One day a woman came to the priest and brought, not a lamb, nor a dove, but a little boy. She said she had promised God that if she should have a son he should belong to God always. The only way she could think of was to bring him to the priest and give him to be a helper in the temple.

So the mother kissed her little boy and left him with the good old priest. The mother's name was Hannah and the boy's, Samuel. Hannah missed little Samuel about the home very much, but she never called him back. Every year, when she came up to the temple, she brought a little coat which she had made for him.

His father and mother did not live very far from the temple, and perhaps they came up to see him more often than once a year.

Samuel was happy in helping Eli about the temple. The old priest had two grown sons of his own, but they were not good men, and he came to love little Samuel, who was so obedient and cheerful. When Eli called, "Samuel, Samuel," the boy came running up with his cheery, "Here am I," and was ready to do

115

whatever Eli wanted. And so the old priest and the little boy were very happy together.

Every night the old priest lit a lamp in the temple. Then Eli and Samuel lay down and went to sleep.

One night they lay sleeping. It was before daylight and the lamp was still burning when Samuel awoke.

He thought he heard some one calling, "Samuel, Samuel."

He jumped up and ran to Eli. "Here am I," he said. "You called me."

"I called not, my son," said Eli. "Go lie down again."

Samuel went back and lay down. After a little he thought he heard Eli again calling, "Samuel, Samuel."

Again he jumped up and ran to Eli and said, "Here am I, for you called me."

Again Eli said, "I called not, my son. Go, lie down." And Samuel went and lay down again.

After a little he thought he heard Eli again: "Samuel, Samuel."

Again he ran to Eli and said, "Here am I. You surely called me." Then Eli, who knew that he had not called the boy, said to himself, "It must be God who is calling him."

He said to Samuel, "If you are called again, say, 'Speak, Lord, for thy servant hears.'"

So Samuel went and lay down once more.

After a little the voice came again, "Samuel, Samuel."

Samuel did as Eli had told him. He said, "Speak, Lord, for thy servant hears."

Samuel lived many years after this and led his people in battle, and brought many messages to them from God. It all grew out of the fact that he was a boy who came when he was called. —Read Vol. 3, pp. 523-557.

Presented to Samuel

By James J. Tissot (1836–1902)
Photographed by Three Lions, Inc.

The people of Israel had asked for a king and God had let them have their way. He had told His prophet Samuel to anoint Saul.

Saul was at his best in the early years of his reign, when he accepted the advice of God through Samuel. Samuel grew to love him and, at one time, prayed for him all night. The people were pleased with him, too.

Years later, Saul became disobedient and God could no longer use him as king. He sent Samuel to Bethlehem to anoint a new ruler. A man named Jesse lived there. "I have provided me a king among his sons," God said.

When the prophet reached Bethlehem, he invited the people to a sacrifice to the Lord.

Jesse came with seven sons. As each fine son passed before Samuel, the prophet thought, "This must be the man. He looks like a king." But God said, "The Lord seeth not as man seeth, for man looketh on the outward appearance but the Lord looketh on the heart." Samuel was puzzled. He asked Jesse if he had no other children. "There is one other," Jesse replied. "My youngest son is tending the sheep." He sent for him.

The artist has painted the moment when David and Jesse stand before the prophet. The young man's face is serious, for he knows that the prophet's visit is important. "What could he want with me?" he wonders.

Samuel gestures toward him. "This is the one the Lord has chosen," he says, as he anoints David to be the future King of Israel.

And from that very day, David of Bethlehem felt God near him in a very special way. He did not become king for many years, but those years were a time of preparation.

Putting on Saul's Armour

By JAMES J. TISSOT (1836–1902)
Photographed by Three Lions, Inc.

KING SAUL watches anxiously as his servants put his armour on David.

Only a shepherd boy, David had come to Saul offering to fight a giant Philistine, Goliath, who challenged the armies of Israel. The contest was to decide the winner in the war between the two nations.

The king was amazed. David was only a boy and Goliath was an experienced warrior.

David answered Saul's doubts by recalling the times he had defended his sheep against wild animals with only a sling and stones. "This Philistine has defied the armies of the living God. The Lord who delivered me out of the paw of the lion . . . will deliver me out of the hand of this Philistine."

Saul stared at the boy. Once, he, too, had been a man of faith. When he was anointed king, the spirit of God had come upon him and he had been able to fight in the strength of the Lord. Now, his faith had been dimmed by his disobedience to God and his reliance on worldly values.

"Go," he said, "and the Lord be with you." Yet, he directed David to put on his armour. In all Israel, only the king and his son had armour, for Israel had no metal workers at that time. A servant brought Saul's armour and began to dress David in it.

But David put the armour aside. He knew that his trust lay not in metal plates, but in the Lord. He must fight Goliath in his own way.

Thus, David left Saul's presence. Armed only with his faith in God and his sling, he went forward to face the giant.

Slinging the Stone

By James J. Tissot (1836–1902)
Photographed by Three Lions, Inc.

In this painting, the artist emphasizes the difference in size between Goliath and David. Goliath was nearly ten feet tall. He was the champion of the Philistine army.

The formidable giant was protected by armour covering most of his body and by a large shield. He carried a huge spear and a sword hung at his side. In contrast, David had five smooth stones in a sack at his side and a sling in his right hand; and in his heart was confident faith in the Lord God.

The sling was a long strip of leather with a pouch at the center. To use it, David placed a stone in the pouch and brought the ends together, so that the stone hung down, limply. Then, he swung the sling around and around his head, releasing one end to let the stone fly to the target.

Insulted at the idea of fighting a boy, Goliath shouted, "I will give your flesh to the birds and the beasts!"

David knew where his strength came from. Though Goliath had sword, spear, and shield, David warned, "I come to you in the name of . . . the God of the armies of Israel, whom thou hast defied. This day will the Lord deliver you into mine hand."

David reached into his sack, chose a stone for his sling, and cast it toward Goliath's head. It struck him squarely in the unprotected forehead and he fell forward on his face, defeated.

"So David prevailed over the Philistine with a sling and with a stone . . . And when the Philistines saw their champion was dead, they fled."

Friendship with Jonathan

By James J. Tissot (1836–1902)
Photographed by Three Lions, Inc.

There was great excitement in the army camp of Israel. David had slain Goliath and the Philistine army had been defeated. Everyone was grateful to the courageous shepherd boy.

Jonathan, King Saul's son, showed his feeling for David by giving him his bow and sword and placing his own princely robe around David's shoulders.

The artist shows us the beginning of the famous friendship between Jonathan and David. The two make a solemn promise to always be friends, for each loved the other "as his own soul." The soldiers find it hard to understand— the king's son embracing a common shepherd boy. Only Jonathan and David realize that true friendship has no requirement but love.

Jonathan was to prove his love for David many times. He would seek to explain David's actions to his father, the king. He would plead for him; he would warn him of danger. His love may have helped David forgive the hostility of Saul.

Years later, when Saul and Jonathan were dead, David, as the new king, had an opportunity to show his love for Jonathan. When told that Jonathan's son was made lame as he and his nurse fled the battle in which Jonathan was killed, David asked that the man be brought to him. "I will surely show thee kindness for Jonathan thy father's sake," he told him. And he gave him servants and land and a place at his own table.

So it was that the friendship of David and Jonathan survived from shepherd to King; from Prince to son.

Saul's Attempt on His Life

By James J. Tissot (1836–1902)
Photographed by Three Lions, Inc.

David's victory over Goliath had marked a turning point in his manner of living. No longer did he shepherd his father's sheep, for King Saul made him one of his personal staff, and he "went out withersoever Saul sent him, and behaved himself wisely; . . . and he was accepted in the sight of all the people . . ."

The people praised David in public and in private, claiming that his victories were ten times greater than those won by the king. Saul heard their words, and they made him angry. As he thought of David, he asked, "What can he have more but the Kingdom?" And from that day on, he eyed David with jealousy.

Yet when Saul was troubled or depressed, young David was often called to play his harp and sometimes the king was soothed.

David was a good musician. As he tended his father's sheep, he had often made music that quieted the restless animals. He had made songs to go with the music. One song began: "The Lord is my shepherd; I shall not want."

The artist has pictured one of these occasions when David is playing for the king, but this time the music does not soothe Saul. Instead, his jealous rage bursts into violence and he hurls his javelin at David, who quickly avoids it.

Sometime later, Saul again tried to pierce David with his javelin. Then, David knew it was no longer safe for him to stay at the king's palace. With the help of his friend Jonathan, Saul's son, David escaped into hiding.

Meeting with Ahimelech

By James J. Tissot (1836–1902)
Photographed by Three Lions, Inc.

THIS PICTURE tells the story of two men and five loaves of bread. Looking in the window is young David who had come to the priest, Ahimelech, for help.

David had been anointed as the future king of Israel and became the hero of the people. In admiration, the women had sung: "Saul hath slain his thousands, but David his ten thousands." King Saul became jealous of David's popularity and tried to kill the young soldier.

Without preparation or food, David and his men were forced to run from the king's anger. After three days in hiding, David went to Ahimelech at Nob, a city near Jerusalem.

Coming alone to the window, David asked the priest for bread. Ahimelech replied that all he had was holy bread. The holy bread, or shewbread, had just been taken from the tabernacle where it was kept in worship of God. Every week, it was replaced by fresh bread. The old bread could be eaten by the priests, but not by outsiders. Therefore, Ahimelech was reluctant to give it to David.

Questioning David, Ahimelech decided that he was clean according to God's law and gave him the bread. He also gave David the sword of Goliath, which was kept at the tabernacle.

Many years later, Jesus recalled this event when the Pharisees criticized His disciples for picking and eating grain as they walked through the fields on a sabbath day. After speaking of David's need, Jesus said, "The sabbath was made for man, and not man for the sabbath."

Do you think he meant that His way of loving and helping people is good on any day and more important than just keeping rules?

With Saul at the Cave

By James J. Tissot (1836–1902)
Photographed by Three Lions, Inc.

Once david and King Saul had been good friends. David had played music for the king; he had fought in the king's wars; he had even married the king's daughter.

Then King Saul had become jealous of him. He had plotted against him and, with many soldiers, followed David and his men into wild country, where they sought refuge.

At Engedi, near the Dead Sea, Saul paused to rest in a cave where David and his men were hiding. His men reminded David of the Lord's words, "Behold, I will deliver thine enemy into thine hand, that thou mayest do to him as it shall seem good unto thee." But David cut only a piece of cloth from the king's robe, to show how near he had been. A little later, he called out to Saul and tried to reason with him.

The artist shows David, outside the cave, kneeling before the king, as a loyal subject would. He raises his hand in a sign of peace.

David reminds Saul that he could have killed him but that he would never harm a man anointed by order of the Lord. He asks Saul to become a friend again.

The king looks down at the young man he has outlawed. He remembers David's courage and helpfulness and he weeps. He says: "Thou art more righteous than I . . . I know well that thou shalt surely be King." Then, he asks David to promise that he will be good to Saul's family when he becomes king.

David promised, but neither he nor the king, realized then that jealousy had so twisted Saul's mind that he would never be free of his hate and suspicion.

Taking Saul's Spear and Water Bottle

By James J. Tissot (1836–1902)
Photographed by Three Lions, Inc.

In the hill country west of the Dead Sea, David and his men were hiding from King Saul. Despite his promises, once again Saul's jealousy had overcome him and he sought to kill David. Two of David's scouts reported that Saul and his army were camped near Hebron.

"Who will go down with me to Saul's camp?" David asked, and Abishai, one of his thirty valiant men, volunteered. The two men made their way silently in the darkness of night. No sentry challenged them as they crept into Saul's camp, for everyone was asleep.

The artist shows them looking down at the sleeping king and his captain, Abner. Abishai grasps the king's spear as if to lift it from where Saul had stuck it in the ground. "God has delivered thine enemy into thine hand," he tells David. "Let me kill him."

David shakes his head. "Destroy him not," he cautions, "for who can stretch forth his hand against the Lord's anointed, and be guiltless?" And they departed, taking Saul's spear and water bottle. From a safe distance across the valley, David called loudly to Abner, rebuking him for not guarding the king.

Saul, too, awoke and recognized the voice. "Is this thy voice, my son David?" he asked.

"It is my voice, my lord, O King," David replied. He held up the king's spear and water bottle as proof that he would never harm God's anointed ruler.

Saul seemed to realize how foolish he had been. "Return, my son David," he begged. "I will no more do thee harm."

Yet, David knew he could never again trust Saul. Never again would they be friends.

DAVID IN THE WILDERNESS
A painting by James J. Tissot

Stories of David

GOD SEES THE HEART

ONCE a man went out to find a king. The man was named Samuel. It was the same Samuel who once lived with the old priest, Eli.

God said to him, "Go to Bethlehem. A man lives there named Jesse. One of his sons is to be king."

So Samuel went to Bethlehem. He made a feast, and asked some of the people to the feast.

When all had gathered he asked Jesse, and said, "Come to the feast, you and your sons."

All the people came, and Jesse and seven of his sons came.

They did not know that Samuel had come to find a king.

Samuel saw the oldest. He was fine and tall.

Samuel said to himself, "He must be the king, he looks so fine."

God said, "No, he is not the king, even if he is tall and fine. God sees the heart."

Then Samuel looked at the next.

He was tall and fine, too.

But God said, "No, he is not the king."

Then Samuel looked at the next. He was not so tall and not so fine.

God said, "No, he is not the king."

Then Samuel looked at the next. He was not so tall and not so fine.

God said, "No, he is not the king."

WOMEN OF BETHLEHEM

These women are carrying their heavy jars on the road near the old City of Bethlehem.

A FLOCK OF SHEEP ON THE HILLS OF PALESTINE

This is a large flock of sheep which the shepherd is leading along the road in the hill country of Palestine.

Then Samuel looked at the next. He was still less tall and fine.

God said, "No, he is not the king."

Then Samuel looked at the next. He was the youngest of the seven.

God said, "No, he is not the king."

And these were all the sons with Jesse.

Samuel said to Jesse, "Are all your sons here?"

Jesse said, "David, the youngest of all, is not here. He is only a boy, and is with the sheep while we are here."

"Send for him." said Samuel. "We will not sit down to eat till he comes."

Jesse sent for David. Samuel looked at him as he came. He was not so tall as the oldest, and not so fine as the next, and not so strong as any of them.

But God said, "He is the king, for his heart is right."

So, after he had learned many hard things, the boy who kept the sheep became king.

THE SHEPHERD BOY AND THE BEAR

BETHLEHEM:—A little town in the hills of Judea. It was not only the birthplace of the boy who was chosen king, but, many years later, Jesus was born there.

He was the youngest boy in the family. David was his name, and he lived in a village called Bethlehem. Not very far from Bethlehem begins wild, rocky land, which grows wilder and more rocky the farther one goes to the east. It is so rocky and barren and the hills are so steep that no one lived there. In the holes under the rocks bears lived, and even now and then a lion. In the spring the shepherds led their flocks a little way into this wild country, for after the winter rain the grass grew, and the sheep could find good pasture.

David used to lead his sheep there, too, though there was always a little danger from the wild beasts.

One day something happened which we should never know if he had not later mentioned it to show that he believed he could fight a great warrior, Goliath. The next story tells of David and Goliath. This is the story of what David did while he was still a shepherd. It must have been something like this:

One day he had led his flock far away from the others. He was following a little valley where the water ran in the early spring, and the sweet, green grass made fine pasture. The sheep moved slowly along, eating as they went, and the lambs jumped and played about in the bright spring sunshine. David kept close watch of the flock, for sometimes, the old shepherds said, wild beasts came up as far as this. If he should lose a lamb his older brothers would say that he was not fit to be trusted alone with the flock. He had his sling with him, and now and then tried it.

"Suppose that rock were a bear," he said. "His head would be the point sticking up. Could I hit him right in the eye?" Then he would sling a stone, and another, and another, and still another, till he could put a stone just where he wanted it. He almost wished a bear would come out and let him try it on his hard old head.

And while he was thinking that, what do you suppose happened? He saw a great bear rush out from behind a rock and catch a lamb in his jaws and start off.

Now nobody knows just what happened next, or how many stones David shot out of his sling before he hit the bear, or whether he lamed him first with a stone and then killed him with his long shepherd's knife. But when it was through, the bear was killed, and David took the poor, frightened lamb out of the bear's mouth. He must have bound up its wounds and taken it home that night very tenderly.

By being brave when he was all alone out in the pasture with the sheep, and watching over the flock his father put in his care, he became fit to be a king of his nation.

DAVID AND THE GIANT

PHILISTINES:—A warlike people, enemies of the people of Israel, with whom they were often at war.

COAT OF MAIL:—A coat made of metal, sometimes of chains woven together or of pieces of metal overlapping each other.

PRONE:—Flat.

David was the shepherd boy who afterwards became a great king in Israel.

One night when he came in with his sheep, he found all the village of Bethlehem astir. The streets were

full of men. Some of them had swords, and some were hastening home from the fields.

David put his sheep in the fold and ran home.

There he found that the land was at war. People called the Philistines, with whom they had fought many times before, had sent an army up into the hills where they lived. The king, Saul, had sent to all the towns and villages to call the men to his army. That was why men were hurrying home to get their swords.

Three of David's older brothers were going. It was the first time some of them had gone to the army, and it made them feel very important.

Perhaps David asked if he could go, but his father said, "No, you are too young. You must stay and help me with the sheep."

So that night the others went off, and David slept all night, and next morning led the sheep to pasture just as usual. What his father said, he must obey.

DAVID STREET IN JERUSALEM

This is a busy day in old David Street, Jerusalem. A little girl dressed in white and a little boy are going to school. There is a group of older children on the left, and many people are on the sidewalk. Perhaps a procession is to pass that way, or, perhaps, the people are only shopping. Jerusalem, after all these years, is still one of the important cities of the world.

Some days later his mother made some cakes and cheeses and wanted to send some of them to the boys in the army. So David's father said he might go, for he, too, wanted to hear from the boys.

Then they packed up some parched corn and other food for his brothers, and put up ten of the little, home-made cheeses for the captain of the boys' company, and David and a servant started early in the morning to go over the hills to the army.

When they came to it, David left the presents with the servant outside the camp and started to find his brothers.

Over on the other side of the valley he saw the Philistine army. They stood before their camp with swords and shields, as though they were ready to attack the Hebrews. Already Saul had sent out word for the Hebrew army to be ready, and the soldiers were gathered in front of the tents with drawn swords.

David found his brothers, and told them the news from home. While he was talking with them, a great voice boomed over the valley.

"Give me a man to fight with," the voice said. "Choose a man and let us fight together. If he kills me, we will be your slaves. If I kill him, you will be ours."

David looked across the valley, whence the voice came. In front of the Philistine army stood a man taller than any of the others; a very giant he looked. He had a helmet of brass, and a coat of mail with shining scales of metal, and his legs were covered with sheets of brass. He had in his hand a huge spear, and before him stood a man with a great shield. His name was Goliath and because he lived in the city of Gath, they called him "Goliath of Gath."

David had seen bears and lions while keeping his sheep, but he had never before seen so terrible an object as this huge warrior, with his armor gleaming in the sunshine.

"I defy the armies of Israel," Goliath shouted. "Give me a man that we may fight together."

But not a Hebrew dared accept his challenge. As they saw how huge he was, their hearts failed them, and they were sore afraid.

This was not the first time he had dared them to fight.

Day after day he had shouted his challenge across the valley, and nobody had accepted it. He grew more bitter every day, and scorned them for cowards who dared not fight.

"What shall be done to the man who kills this Philistine?" asked David.

His brother was angry at his question. "Have you run away to see the battle?" he asked. "What have you done with those few sheep in the wilderness?"

"What have I done now?" said David. "Is there not a reason?"

Reason enough, to be sure, when no one in all the army dared fight the giant!

Some one ran to the king and told him of David's questions, and the king said, "Bring him here." So the shepherd boy was taken to the king's tent.

But when the king saw how he was only a boy, he said, "You cannot fight this man. You are only a youth, and he a man of war from his youth."

David answered, "When I was keeping the sheep, a lion and a bear both came to take sheep from the flock, and I killed them. God will deliver this warrior into my hands as he did the lion and the bear."

Then Saul said, "You must wear armor, if you are going to fight him," and he put on David his own heavy armor.

But the shepherd boy was not used to armor, and he knew he could not fight in it; so he begged to be allowed to fight his own way, and the king consented.

David went down to the brook and carefully picked out five smooth, round stones. He had with him his shepherd's sling. He had spent many hours practising with it while the sheep were feeding, and he could sling a stone to hit any rock or tree at which he aimed. He chose stones just right to fit his sling.

He slipped these stones into his shepherd's bag, took his sling in his hand, and walked across the brook and straight up the slope toward the giant.

BLOCKING THE TRAFFIC IN
DAVID STREET, JERUSALEM

You will have to look rather closely to see the camel which is lying down with its burden right across David Street in Jerusalem. Perhaps his master is delivering goods to one of the shops or perhaps the camel is just tired and refuses to go any farther as they sometimes do. There seems to be no traffic officer to clear the way!

Goliath was still bellowing out his challenge, "send a man to fight," when he saw an unarmed shepherd boy, with no spear or sword, only a sling in his hand, coming towards him.

He was angry. This was an insult to his warlike power, to ask him to fight with a defenseless boy!

"Am I a dog?" Goliath shouted at him. "Come on and I will give your body for food to the birds."

"You come to me," said David, "with a sword and a spear. I come to you in the name of the God of the armies of Israel. He will give you into my hand."

Then he fitted a smooth stone into his sling, ran lightly toward the giant, and slung the stone straight at him.

Here came the value of all those hours of practice in the wilderness.

The stone sang through the air and buried itself right in the forehead of the great warrior, and his huge bulk came crashing down prone upon the ground.

The Philistine army behind gave a gasp. "Goliath of Gath is dead," they cried, and turned and fled. The soldier who bore Goliath's shield dropped it and ran with them.

The boy David ran up, drew the great sword of the giant and cut off his head with it. And all the army of Israel shouted with a great shout, "Goliath of Gath is dead, Goliath of Gath is dead."

If David had not learned to be brave when he was alone, fighting the beasts of the wilderness to protect his flocks, he never would have dared to fight with Goliath of Gath.

THE TWO FRIENDS

In Palestine there once were two friends, named David and Jonathan. Jonathan was the son of the king, Saul. He lived at the court, and had a place in the army. He was a brave young man. His father was fond of him, and all the people loved him. They had all looked to him to be king some day, in place of his father.

David had been a shepherd boy. He was a brave lad, too, but he had never been with the army till he had come to visit his brothers one day. Then he had killed the great giant Goliath, of whom all the army were so afraid they had not dared to fight with him. Then every one began to say how brave David was. When the army came back, and David came along with it, the people from the towns swarmed out to meet them. They had made a song, and sang it to the victorious army. Part of the song was this:

"Saul has slain his thousands, and David his ten thousands."

That was calling the youth David a greater warrior than Saul, who had led the army in many battles. Saul did not like that, and no wonder!

David was very sensible. He did not think he was a great warrior simply because he had killed one of the enemy, even if that man was a giant. Some young men might have strutted around and talked big and thought themselves better than the gray-headed old generals. Not he! He was the same modest, sensible youth he had been when he was a shepherd boy. The king gave him a place in the army, and all the people were talking about the brave deed he did, but he was not spoiled by it all.

ARAB AND HIS HUT

This hut which looks not unlike the wigwam of the Indian is made of slender withes.

It is pitched in the desert with high hills in the background.

As he was around the court week after week, kept there by the king's command, the king grew more and more jealous of him.

"What can the people give him more but the kingdom?" he muttered, as he noted how popular the young man was.

But his son, Jonathan, came to love David very warmly. He might, like his father, have been jealous of David. If the people should want David for king after Saul, where would he be? His father was asking that question, and at last became ready even to kill David, but Jonathan, with his big, unselfish heart, grew to love him more and more.

Now King Saul was at times more than half insane, and then the evil thoughts that were down in the bottom of his heart came up and governed his actions. David was skilful with the harp, and was sometimes called in to play before Saul when the dark moods were upon him. But one day Saul hurled his spear at him while he was playing. Another day he tried again to pin him to the wall with his spear; and Jonathan and all the court came to know how Saul had grown to hate David.

It became unsafe for David to be in Saul's presence, and he went home, away from the court. But still he was in danger.

Then came a time when he must decide whether he could stay even in his own home, or must go out and be a fugitive, living as best he could in the wilderness.

He and Jonathan had a long talk in the fields. They felt that it might be the last time they could talk together in safety. Jonathan was sure that the people's minds were turning more and more to David for the future king. It could not have been an easy thing for him to give up his hope of the kingdom; but he did it. He was sure the kingdom would go to David, and he asked David to promise kindness to his children in that day.

Jonathan was to sit at a feast with the king the next day. He would find out if the king was determined on the death of David and let him know. Three days later David was to be hiding near this field, and Jonathan would come here and let him know the result. So, after a long and loving talk together, the friends separated.

Jonathan went to the feast. The first day Saul said nothing about David. The second day, as they came to the table, he asked, "Where is David?"

Jonathan said that David had asked to be excused to go home. Then the king's anger broke. He stormed at Jonathan. He said that as long as David lived Jonathan would never be king. He ordered David's death. At last, in blind rage, he hurled his spear at Jonathan. In his mad fury he was willing to kill his own beloved son.

Jonathan left the table in sorrow and shame, but he still loved David.

The next day he took his bow and arrows and called a boy to go with him, and went out to the field.

When he met any one who asked him where he was going, he said, "Out to the field, to practise shooting at a mark."

So he was, but the trip had been arranged with David.

He came to the place where David had met him before.

"Now run and find the arrows I shoot," he said to the boy.

As the boy went, he shot an arrow beyond him, and called, "The arrow is beyond you."

That was the sign to David that there was danger in Saul's anger.

Jonathan called again to the boy, "Make haste, hurry up, don't stay."

That meant to David that he must flee as soon as possible.

The boy took up the arrow and came back. Then Jonathan said to him, "Here, take the bow and arrows back to the city. I will come later."

And the boy, who knew nothing of David's hiding near by, went away, while Jonathan walked on.

He and David were alone. David came out of his hiding place and the two friends met once more, for the last time, before David went out to live as he could, while Saul sought his life.

"God watch between us," they said.

It finally came out as Jonathan had seen it would. When Saul was dead, David became king. Jonathan had fallen in battle, and so did not see the throne, which might have been his, go to his friend; but David never forgot his love.

He wrote a poem about Saul and Jonathan, which ends thus:

"How are the mighty fallen in the midst of the battle!
Jonathan, thou wast slain in thine high places.
I am distressed for thee, my brother Jonathan:
Very pleasant hast thou been unto me:
Thy love to me was wonderful,
Passing the love of women.
How are the mighty fallen,
And the weapons of war perished!"

—See the Bible text of this beautiful story—Vol. 4, pp. 55-67.

DAVID AND THE THREE BRAVE MEN

CAVE IN THE WILDERNESS:—The country about Bethlehem, the pasture lands where David kept his flocks, has many of these great limestone caves.

On one occasion, David, who was then king of Israel, was at war with the Philistines.

They had come up from their home in the plain-country, and gone far into the hills where the Hebrews lived.

One day a man came running to the camp of the king.

"The Philistines have come to Bethlehem," he said.

Wilderness of Judea

From International Publishing Co., Ltd.

THE Wilderness of Judea lies on the eastern slopes of the Judean hills looking down toward the Jordan valley and the southern desert. It is rugged country with deep valleys and gorges on whose steep sides there are many caves. It was to this area that David fled from King Saul. Here David and his followers were able to hide from the royal army until the death of the king and the coronation of David at Hebron in the south of Judea. The wilderness is still a wild, desolate region where only a few nomads wander with their flocks of sheep and goats, for the pasture is very poor. The only roads are the paths made by gazelles, the mountain deer native to the region.

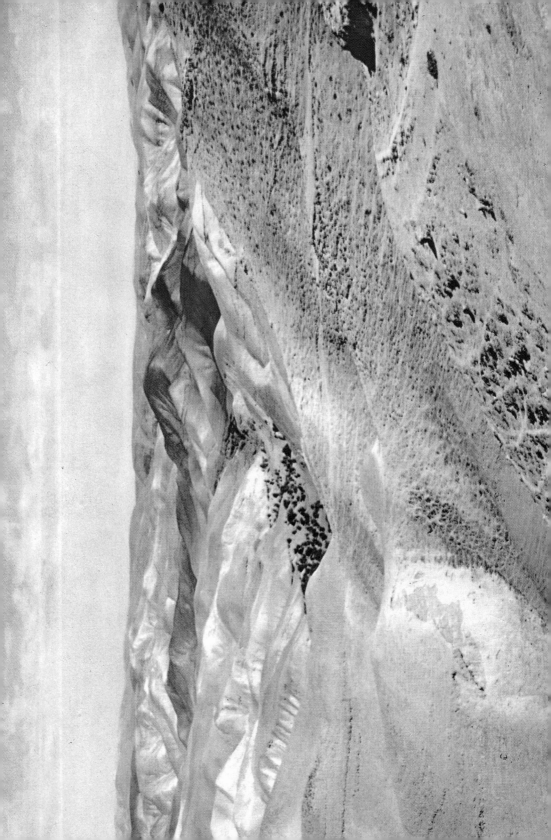

Bethlehem was the town where David had lived when a boy. He had played in its streets with his brothers. He had gone out to the pastures with his father's sheep and had brought them back to the fold at night, when the sun was setting over the houses of Bethlehem.

When he was tired with his work or play, and warm with the heat of the summer sun, he had gone to the well close by the town, and drunk of its cool water. All the village came to the well for water. They boasted that it had the best and coolest water of any well about. When men went away to distant places, they came back saying, "There is no water anywhere like the water of our well at Bethlehem."

And now the town and its well were in the hands of their enemies! That was hard for David to think of. He moved his army, which was not very large, into the country near Bethlehem, but the Philistines were so strong that he did not dare to attack them. He and his men camped about a great cave in the wilderness, and waited to see if a chance of attack would not come.

One day, when David was warm and tired, and weary with thinking how his old home was under the Philistine power, he exclaimed, "I wish some one would give me drink from the well at Bethlehem, which is by the gate."

It was only a wish, and he never dreamed that any one would really try to do it.

Three men of his soldiers heard the king's words.

They looked at each other and slipped out. "David shall have his wish," they said to each other as they met outside the camp.

A little later they were climbing up the hill toward Bethlehem.

The Philistines were camped about the town. Behind their tents lay the well. The three men watched them draw water from it as the sun went down, and saw how the tents stood in relation to it. They waited till the sun was set, and the stars were out, and the fires of the soldiers died down, and all the camp became quiet.

Then they crept down, moved quietly between the tents, and reached the well. Perhaps a camel lifted up his long neck to watch them draw water in the darkness, but the men all slept.

The next morning the three men were in David's camp again.

"Yesterday," they said, "you wished for water from the well of Bethlehem. We have brought it to you." Then they told him the story of their adventure, and how they had dared it for their love of him.

But David would not drink the water. "It is the blood of the men who risked their lives for me," he said. "It is too precious for me to drink. It is worthy to be a sacrifice to God"; and he poured out the water as his gift to God.

So here were noble men: the three soldiers who loved their leader, and the king who knew a brave deed when he saw it.

Let us be content to work,
To do the thing we can, and not presume
Because it's little.

—Elizabeth Barrett Browning.

The Young King and His Dream

UNDERSTANDING HEART:—Wisdom, knowledge.

ONCE there was a king of the Hebrews named Solomon.

When the people in the Land of the Bible talked of their kings, they called him the richest and wisest of them all.

His father David was king before him. Solomon had always lived in a king's palace, and had the finest things the kingdom could give. He had servants to wait on him, and horses to ride.

When he went out into the city street, very likely the people all made way for him. "Here comes the son of the king," they said, and stood aside for him to pass.

All that was very fine but it has spoiled a great many king's sons. It is not good for boys and girls to have too much done for them. It sometimes makes them lazy and selfish. But that was not the way with Solomon.

When David died and Solomon, still a young man, became king, he went to one of the great sacred places of the people to worship. And this is what the Bible says about what happened there:

When night came, Solomon lay down and slept. In his sleep he had a dream. He dreamed that God came to him and said, "Solomon, ask of me anything you want."

Now if Solomon had been as selfish as some he would have said, "I want riches. I want power. I want to be the greatest of all the kings. I want fine food to eat and fine clothes to wear, and a great army, and all the people bowing before me."

But he did not ask for riches or power or glory.

He said, "O God, all this kingdom has come to me from my father, and I am like a little child. I do not know how to rule it. Give me wisdom. Give me an understanding heart, so that I may rule this people."

So, because he was not proud or selfish, but was humble and childlike, God was pleased. He wanted to know how he could serve others, not how he could get good things for himself. And God gave him the wisdom for which he asked, and also he gave him that for which he had not asked, riches and honor.

"Happy is the man that findeth wisdom,
For the gaining of it is better than the gaining of
silver."
—Proverbs 3:13a, 14.
"Her ways are ways of pleasantness
And all her paths are peace."
—Proverbs 3:17.

—Read the Bible text—Vol. 4, pp. 193-195.

A FAMILY AT RAMALLAH

This is a family of the town of Ramallah near Jerusalem where, for a long time, a mission conducted by the Society of Friends has done a great deal of good for the people. Notice the mother with her strong patient face, the smiling little girl, the baby, the bright little boy looking up to his mother, and the older boy in the background.

The Little Slave Girl

SLAVE-MARKET:—In those days, slavery was everywhere common. Even young children captured by the enemy were sold to be slaves. So Joseph was sold and the little girl of the story, whose name we do not know.

ONCE there was a little slave girl in an ancient city called Damascus. This city was the capital of a country called Syria. The king of Syria lived there, and his generals and his officers. All the people of Damascus were very proud of the city, because it was so beautiful. Two rivers of clear water flowed through it, and by the side of the rivers were trees with green leaves and, in the fall, ripe fruit. The people thought their rivers were the most beautiful rivers in the world.

The land of Syria was neighbor to the land of the Hebrews, and there was war for many years between the Syrians and the Hebrews. That is why the little slave girl lived in Damascus. She was a Hebrew, and once when the Syrian armies made a raid into her land, she was captured and brought away. That was the way armies did in ancient war, and no one thought it was wrong.

The little girl was sold in the slave-market to Naaman, one of the great generals of the Syrians, who took her home to wait on his wife. They must have been kind to the poor little girl, for when her master became sick she was sorry and wished he could be made well.

Naaman had a fine house and many servants. He was a friend of the king, and when he went to court

139

A HOUSE ON THE WALL OF DAMASCUS

This house, built into the wall of the city, is like the one where Paul was entertained after his conversion.

"Then the disciples took him by night, and let him down by the wall in a basket."—*Acts 9:25*.

RIVER JORDAN NEAR JERICHO

all the people in the street bowed down to him. But none of this made him happy. He was a leper; and there was no cure known for the terrible disease of leprosy. So the great man in the great house was very unhappy. He could look forward only to suffering and pain.

Perhaps he had forgotten all about the little slave girl. She was so unimportant in the house that we do not even know her name. She kept thinking of her own home, and how the hills came close to the little village where she lived. She remembered hearing about a man who could make the sick well. Perhaps she still cried at night when she thought of the home she might never see again. But she was sorry for her good master and mistress. Perhaps she knew that her mistress cried at night, too, in spite of her fine house and beautiful clothes, when she thought how there was no help for Naaman.

One day the little girl said to her mistress, "Would God my master were with the prophet Elisha, in Israel! He would heal him of his leprosy."

Some one who heard it told Naaman what the little slave girl said, and Naaman told the king.

"There is a man in Israel," he said, "who can cure me of my leprosy."

The king was as eager as Naaman himself. He had been at war with the king of Israel, but if Naaman could be cured in Israel he would be a friend of the king's.

"I will write a letter to the king of Israel," he said, "and you shall take it and go to his city, Samaria."

Naaman set out from Damascus, with a company of guards and rich presents for the one who should cure him; and at home Naaman's wife had long talks with the little slave girl about the man in Israel who could cure her master.

But when the king of Israel read the letter from the king of Syria he was afraid; for it said, "I send with this Naaman, my servant, that you may cure him of his leprosy."

"Am I God, to kill and to make alive?" said the king of Israel. "How can I cure a man of leprosy? He seeks a quarrel with me!"

Through the land the story ran, and all Israel feared that Syria was planning to fight again.

Elisha the prophet heard of Naaman, and he sent word to the king, "Let Naaman come to me, and he shall know what Jehovah can do."

Now Elisha was the very man to whom the little slave girl meant her master to go, but between them the two kings had almost sent Naaman back without seeing the prophet.

LITTLE GIRLS OF PALESTINE

These little girls do not look as though they had very much time for play. It was a little girl much like one of these who was the captive maiden in the story of Naaman. The prophet Zechariah predicted that the time would come when

"There shall yet old men and old women dwell in the streets of Jerusalem, and every man with his staff in his hand for very age.

"And the streets of the city shall be full of boys and girls playing in the streets."—*Zechariah 8:4, 5.*

So Naaman came with his horses and chariots and all his band of soldiers and servants, and stood before the prophet's door.

But Elisha did not even come to the door to meet the great general. He only sent out a messenger who said, "Go and wash in the River Jordan seven times and you will be cured."

Then Naaman was angry that Elisha should have treated him with so little respect.

"I thought," he said, "that he would have come out, and stood, and called on his God, and raised his hand over me, and cured me. Go to the Jordan indeed! Are not Abana and Pharpar, the rivers of my own Damascus, better than the Jordan? May I not wash in them, and be cured?" He turned and went away in a great rage.

BREAD SELLER IN JERUSALEM

This boy is selling bread in the streets of Jerusalem. The round flat cakes do not look much like our loaves of bread. Do you see that he has a reserve supply on the stone near by? It cannot be as clean as the bread we use!

But some of his servants were cooler than their master. They came to him and said, "My father, if the prophet had told you to do some great thing, would you not have done it? Why not, then, this small thing?"

Then Naaman laid aside his anger, and went down the hills to the Jordan, and dipped himself seven times in the Jordan, as the prophet had told him, and he was cured.

And so, the Bible says, the great general, and the king, and the prophet, and God himself, all worked together for the cure of the leper, but it all started from the kind heart of the little Hebrew slave girl.

—Read this story in the words of the Bible—Vol. 4, pp. 437-441.

The Boy Who Was King

HIS name was Josiah. He was only eight years old when his father's death left him king.

Do you think it would be a fine thing to be king? I fear that this little king did not think so.

His father Amon had been king for only two years. Before that, he could remember that he was sometimes taken to see an old man with a gray beard. They told him it was his grandfather Manasseh, the man who had been king of the land for over fifty years. Then Manasseh had died and his father became king, and all the people shouted, "God save the king," when he took his seat on the throne in the great courtyard.

There were some things which the little boy did not know. He did not know that a great many of the people who shouted for the kings hated them in their hearts. They hated both Amon and the old king, Manasseh. The little Josiah did not know how cruel his father and grandfather were, and how they had killed innocent people. So he lived in the palace and played in its garden, and never dreamed that ill could come.

Then there was a night when he was wakened by the shouts of men rushing through the palace. He was frightened, but nothing happened to him. The next morning he was told that his father was killed in the night, and that now he must be king. His mother looked very frightened and very sad, but told him to be brave and good, because no one wanted to harm him.

Desert in North Palestine

From International Publishing Co., Ltd.

DURING the rainy season, which is our winter and spring, the landscape of Palestine abounds in beautiful flowers. During most of the year the land is dry and parched except where it is irrigated; and then suddenly the flowers burst forth, and the rose of sharon is among them. The prophet Isaiah foretold that "the desert shall rejoice and blossom as the rose; it shall blossom abundantly, and rejoice even with joy and singing" (Isaiah 35:1–2).

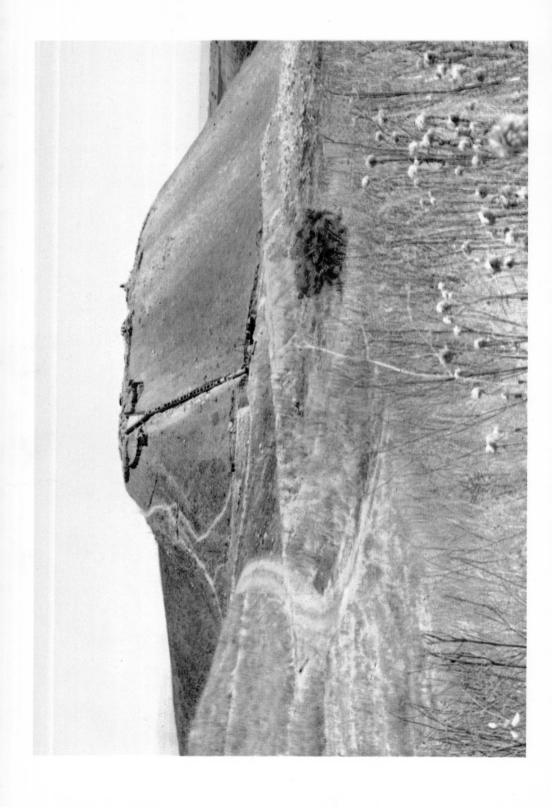

So that day the little boy was taken into the court-yard and again all the people shouted, "God save the king." Poor little fellow! He tried to be brave, but he was afraid of all the great whiskered men with drawn swords who stood on each side and behind him. He was glad to get away from it all to his mother, back in the quiet rooms where the women lived.

Now he had to spend part of every day with men who told him about the God who had given his nation their land; about King David, his own ancestor, who had founded the kingdom; about David's son, Solomon, who had built the great temple which stood close to the palace; about the laws of this kingdom he must rule; and about a great many other things he never before had heard of. As he grew older, he learned that his grandfather and father had hated the God of the nation and worshiped other gods. The people now in the court were devoted to God, and they taught the little king to love him for all he had done for the nation.

During all these years, the old temple, which had stood over three hundred years, since the days of Solomon, had been neglected. Josiah wanted to do what he could to undo the evil work of his father and grandfather. He determined that as soon as he could he would see that the temple was repaired. There were things which hindered, and he was a young man before he was able to do it.

At last, however, carpenters and masons were at work in the temple. They brought in timbers and hewn stone, and all the building and the courtyards about it were busy with men repairing the parts that were tumbling down.

Then Hilkiah, the high priest, said to the man in charge of the work, "I have found a book of the laws of our God."

Books in those days were not bound as they are now. They were written on long sheets of leather, and rolled up into rolls. One began reading at one side and unrolled as he read.

So the man in charge of the work, whose name was Shaphan, took the book home to read. As he read it he said, "These laws are not being kept. The king must know of this."

A FUNERAL PROCESSION
NEAR JAFFA GATE, JERUSALEM

Notice the cross carried in advance, the white umbrellas, the street venders with burdens on their heads in the rear.

The next time he went to the king to report on the work in the temple, he took the book along.

"Hilkiah the priest," he said, "has given me a book," and he unrolled it and read it.

The laws in this book were new to the king. He knew, as well as Shaphan, that they had never been kept. If they were really what Jehovah wanted, they ought to be observed.

Josiah sent to a wise and good woman, Huldah. She said that the laws in the book were really what Jehovah their God wished to have done. If they were not kept, evil would come on the nation, as it had in other days when the law was not kept.

It was not easy to put these laws in force. They said that no God except Jehovah must be worshiped; and in Jerusalem itself, close to the palace of the king, and in many of the towns about, there were altars raised to other gods. The priests of these altars were

THE WAILING PLACE OF THE JEWS

This ancient wall is the spot where the Jews gathered to bewail the fate of
Jerusalem. This custom is certainly as old as the Middle Ages. These people
would kiss the ancient stones and mourn the fate of their beloved city.

important people. Many were in favor of keeping the
worship of the other gods. The young king was not
sure but he would stir up a rebellion if he attacked
this old worship. He must have remembered that
night in his boyhood when armed men had rushed
into the palace and killed his father. Perhaps the
same thing might happen to him. Yet this law said
that these altars must be overthrown and he, the king,
must see that the law was obeyed. He would be dis-
loyal to his trust, not worthy to be a king, if he did not.

If he thought of danger, he said nothing of it. He
sent to all the leading men of the country.

"Come to the king's palace," the messengers said.

He was not content to get the great men. He sent
out word that all the people should gather.

When the young king came out of his palace, all
the great space was filled with people, wondering what
was coming. The king had the new-found book in
his hand. He unrolled it and read it, so that everybody
might understand what was to be done. Then he
said, "I have promised God that I would keep this

law,'' and he made them enter a covenant with him that the new-found law should be kept in the nation.

This was his way of bringing the people to his side.

Then he began by ordering all the images of the other gods which were still in the temple to be brought out and burned. Some of the people who were standing by may not have liked that, but they had promised to obey this law.

This king had a busy life, and not an easy one. He must sometimes have watched the little children playing in the streets, and wished he could, either as boy or man, have had some freedom from the labor and care of the kingdom. But he was a brave man, and never tried to shirk a task because it was hard. He had his reward. No king since the times of David and Solomon held so high a place in the memory of the nation as Josiah, the man who was king from his boyhood.

OLD WORLD RESTAURANT

Jerusalem Lies Waste

From International Publishing Co., Ltd.

THE valley of the Brook Kidron lies just east of the city of Jerusalem. The walls of the ancient city are on the crest of the narrow valley to the west, and the Mount of Olives is on the east. On the western slope there remain the gravestones and tombs from ancient times. It was considered to be a great honor to be buried in this place because it was believed that the resurrection and the judgment would begin here. On the east side of the valley and at the foot of the Mount of Olives is the Garden of Gethsemane. The Israelites had always great respect for the Kidron valley and for the sepulchres of their fathers, as mentioned by Nehemiah during the captivity in Babylon (Nehemiah 2:3).

The Story of a King's Officer

BABYLONIA:—A powerful country, the capital of which was Babylon. It was at this time in the hands of the Persians who had conquered it.

IN the court of the King of Persia was a Hebrew named Nehemiah. He was a high officer, and every day it was his business to come to the king. One day men came from Jerusalem to see him. "What is our city like?" he asked.

Then they told him how large parts of it had never been built since the days when Babylonia destroyed it, and how the walls still lay broken down, so that any strong band of raiders could capture and rob it.

It was a sorry story they had to tell, and it made Nehemiah very sad. Even the king noticed it, and enquired about it.

PLOWING WITH CAMEL
This farmer is using a camel to plow the rocky soil.

He made Nehemiah governor of Judah, and sent him back to Jerusalem to help his own people.

First Nehemiah walked around and looked at the walls. They still lay broken down.

Nehemiah talked to the people and said, "Come, let us build the walls again so that we will not be ashamed of our city. God has been good to me. The king sent me here to help build the walls."

"Let us start to build," said the people. At once they began getting ready to build.

Each family worked on that section of the wall nearest its own home. So all the way around the city, men were building the new walls.

Then someone told Nehemiah, "Our enemies plan to attack Jerusalem!"

Nehemiah told the workers, "While you are working or carrying stones, hold a sword in one hand. Be ready to fight at any minute."

So the men watched for the enemy and worked at the same time. And all around the city, the walls rose higher and higher as the people worked.

They worked two weeks, four weeks—five, six, seven weeks. They worked seven weeks and three days.

Then the walls were finished. All around the city were high walls. Nehemiah and all of the people had worked with a right good will. Once again the city was protected.

The Story of a Brave Queen

AT the time of this story, many Jews were living in the land of Persia, where they had been brought as captives many years before.

The king of Persia had as his queen a beautiful Jewish orphan named Esther, who had been brought up by her cousin Mordecai as his own daughter. This Mordecai was a good man and a leader of his people, but he had an enemy named Haman, a Persian prince highly placed in the king's court. Haman hated all Jews bitterly and plotted their destruction; but he hated Mordecai especially because when the king had honored Haman, Mordecai had refused to bow down to him, as the rest of the people did.

With clever cunning, Haman persuaded the king that the Jews were a danger to the kingdom, and an order went forth that on a set date all Jews should be slaughtered. Mordecai was much distressed, and asked Queen Esther to beg the king to spare the lives of her people. Esther feared greatly to do it, for any person, even the queen, who went before the king uninvited would be put to death unless the king held forth his golden sceptre. "Nevertheless," said she, "If you will pray with me, in three days I will do it; and if I perish, I perish."

On the third day Esther dressed herself in her queenly robes and presented herself before the king. As he saw her, God made her to find favor in his sight, and he held out his royal sceptre. "What is your wish?" said he; "You may have it, even to the half of my kingdom." "Only this for now," said Esther, "that the king and Haman

155

come to a banquet which I shall prepare." So the king
consented, and Haman was greatly flattered to be the
special guest. But as he was going home, Mordecai once
more refused to bow, which so enraged Haman that on
his wife's urging he built a gallows seventy feet high, with
the idea of asking the king's permission to hang Mordecai
on it because of his disrespect.

That night the king was sleepless, and he called for his
servants to read to him from the royal records. There it
was written that, months before, Mordecai had saved the
king's life by revealing a secret plot against the throne.
"And what reward," asked the king, "did Mordecai receive for his loyalty?" "Nothing," was the reply.

Just then Haman was admitted, and the king asked
him, "What shall be done for the man whom the king
desires to honor?" The delighted Haman, sure the king
was referring to him, proposed that he be dressed in royal
robes, given a crown, and allowed to ride through the
streets on the king's horse, led by a prince. "So be it,"
said the king, "Call Mordecai and give him this honor,
and you, Haman, shall be the man to lead his horse!" And
so it was done.

Then Haman was called to the queen's banquet, and
there Esther told the king of the evil plot against the
Jews. "Who dared to plan this wickedness?" cried the
king. "This Haman," replied Esther.

Immediately the king reversed the decree against the
Jews, and ordered that Haman should be hanged on the
gallows which he had built for Mordecai.

So the Jews were saved by the courage of the brave
Queen Esther, and every year since, the Jewish people
celebrate with joy and gladness the great day of their
deliverance from destruction.

—Read the whole story in Vol. 4, beginning on page 525.

ESTHER IS MADE QUEEN BY AHASUERUS
A painting by V. Bianchini

Adoration of the Shepherds

By Eanger Irving Couse (1866-1936)

In the Grace Methodist Church, Harrisburg, Pa.

Copyright by Curtis & Cameron, Inc., Boston, Mass.

OF THE many Bible stories about shepherds, our favorite is the one told in Luke. "And there were shepherds ... keeping watch over their flock by night, And, lo, the angel of the Lord came upon them and ... said, 'Fear not: for, behold, I bring you good tidings of great joy ... For unto you is born this day ... a Saviour, which is Christ the Lord.'" This beloved story is retold on pages 177-81 and in our best loved Christmas hymn, "Silent Night," in Volume 9.

In the picture we see the gentle mother seated by the tiny Christ Child, about whom a radiant light shines. Joseph stands quietly behind Mary in the manger shelter, while across a rock-strewn pasture three shepherds and a little boy come to worship. Do you not feel the mingled timidity and awe and faith of these simple folk who were the first worshipers of little Jesus? What do you think the boy's woolly lamb symbolizes?

The artist, Eanger Irving Couse, was born in Saginaw, Michigan, and died in Albuquerque, New Mexico. He studied at the Chicago Art Institute, the New York Academy of Design, the Paris Ecole des Beaux-Arts, and with Bouguereau (page 314) and Robert-Fleury.

He traveled throughout the West studying and painting Indians and southwestern scenes. During his long career, he won many prizes, helped establish the famous artist's colony at Taos, New Mexico and saw much of his work acquired by leading American museums.

The picture reproduced here was painted about 1900 for the Grace Church where it still adorns the space over the altar. You will want to compare Couse's painting with those by earlier artists from other countries—Correggio (page 183), Murillo (page 176), and LeBrun (volume 7:36).

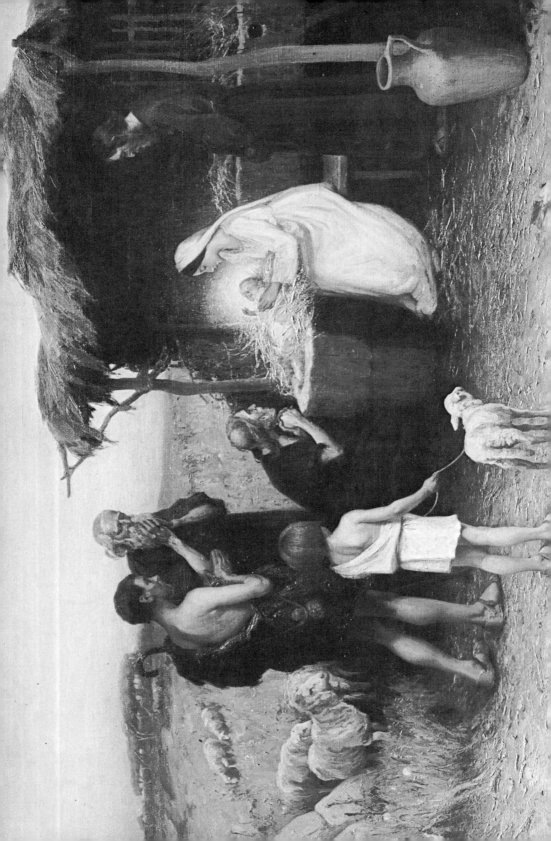

A Child's Life
of Jesus

A Child's Life
of Jesus

N another book of this set is the story of Jesus as the Gospels tell it.

Nothing can ever take the place of those stories. They are told very simply and very beautifully. In them we see Jesus as he lived and walked through the hills of his land and rested by the roadside and talked with the people who flocked to him, and at last died for them, for you and for me, because of his love for us all.

We hear his words of love and counsel. We listen to the wisest sayings ever uttered about God and what God wants us to do.

These little stories in this book are not to take the place of the Gospels. They are only meant to prepare you for them, so that a little later you can read them and understand them a little better.

Camel Caravan

(Photographed by Three Lions, Inc.)

TO the people of Palestine camels are "the ships of the desert." Caravans of camels are still seen entering the Holy Land from outlying regions, especially to the east and the south where the deserts prevail. These beasts of burden can travel where no horse can go, and sometimes even where twentieth century trucks cannot follow.

It was on camels that the Wise Men from the East came to Jerusalem because they understood that the King of the Jews had been born. From thence they were directed to the little village of Bethlehem, south of the capital city. There they found Joseph and Mary and the babe Jesus. At the command of the Magi, the camels kneeled down outside the house where they found the Lord Jesus, and from the backs of the camels were taken the gifts which were presented to little Lord Jesus.

A Child's Life of Jesus

THE PEOPLE OF JESUS' TIME

PRINCE OF PEACE:—This is perhaps the greatest of the titles of the Messiah. "My peace I leave with you," he said.

THE Hebrews in the time of Jesus were not a great nation. They were only a small part of the huge Roman Empire, and their country only a little province among the provinces which Rome governed. What seemed to many of the Hebrews worse, their God was despised by stronger nations because he was only the God of a little people; so, the others thought, he must be a little God.

The Hebrews knew he was the only true God. Did not the Scriptures tell that he made the world? Had he not guided the nation for hundreds of years?

The Bible through their teachers, the prophets, had promised them two things: (1) There should come a time when their nation would be great among the nations of the world; (2) When that time came, their God would be worshiped by all the world. And there was promised another thing: God would give them a great Prince, under whom all these happy things would come to pass. The Hebrew kings had, in the ancient days, been anointed when they were crowned; so they called this great king, who was to come in the future, "The Anointed"; in Hebrew that was "The Messiah."

The prophets gave the expected Messiah other great titles. Isaiah wrote: "For unto us a child is born, unto

165

us a son is given: and the government shall be upon his shoulder: and his name shall be called Wonderful, Counsellor, The Mighty God, The Everlasting Father, The Prince of Peace.

"Of the increase of his government and peace there shall be no end, upon the throne of David, and upon his kingdom, to order it, and to establish it with judgment and with justice from henceforth even for ever. The zeal of the Lord of hosts will perform this."

Some of the people were willing to forget these old promises and to live as though the nation had no hope. Some of them, however, remembered them, and longed for the glorious day to come. If the Roman officials were overbearing, they prayed God to send the Messiah. If other people scoffed at their weak God, they prayed that God would show his power.

They began to say to each other, "If Israel were only ready, God would send the Messiah"; "If we would only do our part, he would do his." One of them wrote, "If Israel would keep the law perfectly for a single day, the Messiah would come."

So a great many people were waiting quietly, with prayer in their hearts, to see what God would do.

In order to understand the beginning of the story of Jesus we must remember how so many praying people were waiting—waiting—waiting. If you had asked them for what they were waiting they would have said, "For the Kingdom of God."

QUESTIONS

Why did the Hebrews think their God was a great God?
What had the old prophets promised them?
What does "Messiah" mean?
What were the people of Jesus' time waiting for?
Is it always best for people to have everything they want at once?

THE MOTHER OF JESUS

MESSIAH:—The most common title for the one who was to "redeem Israel," for whom the people watched and waited.

Mary, the mother of Jesus, belonged to the people who were "waiting for the kingdom." Mary and Joseph wished that the Messiah would come; and they often prayed that they might be able to help the coming of the kingdom. But they were both humble people. Joseph was a carpenter. Mary's family were not people who had much influence in Israel because of wealth or position. They were good, honest, kind-hearted people; respected by their neighbors and earning their living by their work, just the kind of people who are, after all, the real strength of any nation.

One day, the Gospel of Luke says, Mary was visited by an angel, who greeted her as "highly favored of the Lord." Mary wondered what he meant. Why should she, a humble maiden, be "highly favored"?

Then the angel told her that the Holy Spirit should come upon her, and she should become the mother of the Messiah—the great King. Then the angel left.

But Mary's heart was filled with wonder and marvel.

In the Gospel of Luke there follows a most beautiful poem, in which Mary expressed her thought. It praised God because he lifts up the lowly and will bring the kingdom which so long ago he promised to his people. It is always a fitting song for those who, like the humble people in Israel, "wait for the kingdom."

Later this poem was called the "Magnificat," from the word with which it begins in Latin. It was often sung in the church services. Some churches use it still, and it is worthy of use by any Christian. It is a wonderful song of trust and hope.

The visit of the angel to Mary was called the "Annunciation," that is, the Announcement of the Christ that was to be. It was a favorite scene with the old church painters. They tried to express in the face of Mary all the wonder and worship and submission they could.

—Read the Bible text in Vol. 7, pp. 29-32.

THERE IS ROOM IN MY HEART FOR THEE

Thou didst leave Thy throne and Thy kingly crown
　　When Thou camest to earth for me:
But in Bethlehem's home there was found no room
　　For Thy holy nativity.
　　　　O come to my heart, Lord Jesus,
　　　　There is room in my heart for Thee.

Heaven's arches rang when the angels sang,
　　Proclaiming Thy royal degree;
But of lowly birth cam'st Thou, Lord, on earth,
　　And in great humility.

The foxes found rest, and the bird its nest
　　In the shade of the cedar tree;
But Thy couch was the sod, O Thou Son of God,
　　In the deserts of Galilee.

Thou camest, Lord, with the living word
　　That should set Thy children free;
But with mocking scorn, and with crown of thorn,
　　They bore Thee to Calvary:

When heaven's arch shall ring and her choirs shall sing
　　At Thy coming to victory,
Let Thy voice call me home, saying, "Yet there is room,
　　There is room at My side for thee":
　　　　And my heart shall rejoice, Lord Jesus,
　　　　When Thou comest and callest for me.
　　　　　　　　—*Emily E. S. Elliott.*

The Boy Jesus in the Temple

By William Holman Hunt (1827-1910)

In the Birmingham Gallery, Birmingham, England

ON PAGES 201-10 you will find the story of that important happening in the life of the boy Jesus which inspired this painting and the one on page 208. How different the two interpretations are! Which do you prefer?

Here the scene is placed in the Temple at Jerusalem, a magnificent temple built by Herod for the Jews in order to still their restlessness under his iron rule. "Forty and six years was this temple in building," we are told. Fabulous sums must have been spent on the spacious marble edifice, with its gold-plated, jewelled doors, intricately carved wall-screens, elaborately decorated pillars and hanging candelabra of silver. Untold sums poured into its treasury from the earnest, obedient believers, such as the young couple pictured in the background who are following a priest and his attendant, the mother carrying their first-born and the father the sacrificial lamb which he has just bought from the dealer.

What wealth and pomp are made visible, too, in the rich apparel of the seated "doctors," one of whom hugs possessively a great scroll of the sacred law. Pride mingles with scorn and cunning in their faces. No wonder the beggar at the door suffers unheeded; no wonder only one of these learned men has sensed the marvel of this young Prophet's insight!

Notice how these myriad details bring us to the center of interest, the simply clad boy Jesus. We see an anxious mother and a strong, virtuous father, both relieved to find their lost son and bent on taking him away at once. But the sturdy lad's attention is not so easily won. The clear, far-seeing eyes show that the soul within has been awakened by the discussions he has been having. Though as yet Jesus is but a boy, on his right is the great tradition which he is destined to fulfill and destroy, and on his left is the suffering world which he will serve and redeem.

Another of Hunt's carefully studied, highly symbolic pictures is in Volume 7, page 354.

The Church of the Nativity
at Bethlehem

(Photographed by Three Lions, Inc.)

WHEN Jesus was born in Bethlehem there were no churches like this one there, or anywhere in the world. Christian churches have been built because the Saviour came to Bethlehem. This church is built over the traditional place of the stable in whose manger the Christ-child was laid. The place is marked by a star with the inscription in Latin of John 1:14—"The Word was made flesh, and dwelt among us . . ."

Bethlehem is still a village located in the hill country of Judea south of Jerusalem. While not far from the capital city it has an atmosphere totally different from that of a large city. It seems so quiet, peaceful, and just the kind of village in which Jesus should be born.

> And Joseph also went up from Galilee, out of the city of Nazareth, into Judaea, unto the city of David, which is called Bethlehem . . . to be taxed with Mary his espoused wife . . . And she brought forth her first-born son, and wrapped him in swaddling clothes, and laid him in a manger; because there was no room for them in the inn. (Luke 2:4-7.)

ONCE IN ROYAL DAVID'S CITY

Once in royal David's city
    Stood a lowly cattle shed,
Where a mother laid her Baby,
    In a manger for His bed:
Mary was that mother mild,
Jesus Christ her little Child.

He came down to earth from heaven
    Who is God and Lord of all,
And His shelter was a stable,
    And His cradle was a stall;
With the poor, and mean, and lowly,
Lived on earth our Saviour holy.

And, through all His wondrous childhood,
    He would honor and obey,
Love, and watch the lowly maiden
    In whose gentle arms He lay;
Christian children all must be
Mild, obedient, good as He.

For He is our childhood's pattern;
    Day by day like us He grew;
He was little, weak and helpless,
    Tears and smiles like us He knew;
And He feeleth for our sadness,
And He shareth in our gladness.

And our eyes at last shall see Him,
    Through His own redeeming love;
For that Child so dear and gentle
    Is our Lord in heaven above;
And He leads His children on
To the place where He is gone.

Not in that poor lowly stable,
    With the oxen standing by,
We shall see Him; but in Heaven,
    Set at God's right hand on high;
When like stars His children crowned,
All in white shall wait around.

                —*Cecil Frances Alexander.*

JESUS IS BORN

WHAT DOES CHRISTMAS MEAN?

List:—A tax list. Under the Roman Government, taxes were very high and no one, not even the poorest, was allowed to escape.

Christmas is presents and shopping. It's turkey and candy and parties. It's trees and decorations and vacation. Christmas is all of these things—and none of these things.

The real Christmas is Jesus' birthday. God gave His own Son to the world as the first Christmas gift.

But Christmas is even more than Jesus' birthday. Jesus did not come so that He could be a Baby in a manger. He came so that He could die on the cross for the sins of the world. When we celebrate Christmas, we celebrate Good Friday and Easter, too. At Christmas time we do not worship the Baby Jesus. We worship Jesus, God's Son, who came to die on the cross for our sins, and rose again that we might have everlasting life.

THE LONG JOURNEY TO BETHLEHEM

Once upon a time, word went through all the towns and villages of Palestine that the Roman governor of the country wished to make a list of all the inhabitants. At Nazareth, in the northern part of the land, lived the carpenter Joseph and his young wife Mary. Their family belonged in Bethlehem, several days' journey to the south. The Jews took great pride in their families, and no one had a better right than the carpenter Joseph; for his family traced its descent back a long, long way to the most famous of all the ancient kings of the nation, King David. When they heard of the list, they wanted to be placed on it as of the town of Bethlehem, the home of the old King David.

Adoration of the Shepherds

By Murillo, Bartolomé Estéban (1617-1682)
In the Prado Gallery, Madrid, Spain

HERE a group of shepherds have come to pay homage to the Child still in the manger at Bethlehem. They are very humble people and their strong, rugged faces are lighted up with joy at seeing the Child.

These poor shepherds are giving the best gifts they have: a lamb, a basket of eggs, a hen.

The figures that first attract our eye are the lovely mother and Child. Their inner radiance makes these two stand out from the people around them.

Murillo, Spain's greatest religious painter, is especially noted for his delightful pictures of babies. Here, the charming, complete relaxation of the child's position, as well as the appealingly complacent, little face, are quaintly life-like.

Notice how well the artist has given the impression of softness and roundness in the baby's arms, contrasted with the firmness of the little round head, and the hardened, work-roughened hands of the kneeling shepherd.

The beautiful mother has a tenderly absorbed expression, such as we might see in real life, as she supports the baby so that the others may see him. Don't you think she has a lovely face? The white tones of her skin are set off by the velvety soft darkness of her hair.

We can only see part of the kneeling shepherd's face, but doesn't it have an interesting expression? Murillo's skill in realistic details is shown in the rough soles of the man's feet, and in the surprisingly natural lamb.

The tired, worn, resigned face of the old woman presents a marvelous contrast with the freshness and light of the Child.

"THERE WAS NO PLACE FOR THEM AT THE INN"

And so they went to Bethlehem. The young wife rode on a donkey, and the husband walked by her side. It was a long journey. They came into Bethlehem tired. It may have been almost night when they got there; for they found that all the places to stay were already filled. There was an inn, but the innkeeper said, "No place here. I am sorry, but the inn is full."

They tried to find a place to sleep, but everywhere they went, the people said, "No place here. Our house is full."

Now an inn was a large court-yard where the camels and donkeys were kept and where the luggage was piled up during the night, with rows of little rooms on one or two sides in which people slept, rolling out the blankets they carried with them. At best it would seem to us very poor; but Joseph and Mary did not have even that. The best they could get was a place among the oxen and camels and donkeys. So here they camped down for the night, in the stable with the animals, because there was no room for them in any house in Bethlehem.

And that is how it came about that Jesus was born in a stable.

THE SHEPHERDS IN THE WINTRY FIELDS

In the fields not far from the town that night there was a group of shepherds. They were staying out with their flocks, instead of bringing them into the fold. They lay looking up at the bright stars, and the only thing they heard was now and then the soft stirring of the sheep. Perhaps they had been talking of the great hope for the Messiah.

"Perhaps," said the oldest of them all, "our God will send him first to this town of ours, Bethlehem, where the great King David was born," and he turned to gaze where its walls cut the starry sky.

"If he only would!" said the youngest of them, scarcely more than a boy. "The Messiah would come down from heaven with splendor, and the angels of God would be about him, and I would say, 'Let me go with you. I am from Bethlehem, too.'" He stopped to dream how glorious it would be to follow the Great King.

Then spoke a gentle quiet man. "Remember, my boy, that David was only a shepherd lad like you at Bethlehem. Perhaps the Great King, too, will come first in humble station, not in power."

Perhaps they had been saying something like that; for they, too, were people "waiting for the kingdom."

While they lay on the ground, looking up into the starry skies, suddenly they saw an angel of God, and all the sky about him was bright with a glory such as they never had seen before.

THE SONG OF THE ANGELS

They were afraid. It was all very well to wish for the splendor of God, but when it came they were terrified. Then the angel spoke: "Do not be afraid. I bring you good news—good news for all the people. This day the Messiah is born here in Bethlehem. You may know him because he will be a little baby wrapped up, lying in a manger."

Then suddenly instead of one angel there was a great host, all praising God and saying,

"Glory to God in the highest,
And on earth peace, good will toward men."

Then it was all over. They were alone again, out in the rocky pasture, looking up at the great, empty, starry heavens.

The Madonna—Detail from the Holy Family

By Bernardino Luini (c.1475-c.1533)
In the Gallery Ambrosiana, Milan, Italy
From a Color Photograph by Anderson, Rome

THIS lovely head of the Madonna is a detail from a picture of the Holy Family which you will find in its entirety in Volume 9. Here we may study closely the beautiful features of the mother of Our Lord. Depth of religious feeling, serenity of mind and spirit, joy and sorrow are all expressed in this lovely face.

The artist, Bernardino Luini, worked in Milan and nearby towns and therefore belongs to the Milanese school. In his day Italy was divided into many independent city-states which rivaled each other in political, economic and cultural affairs. The inhabitants of these states were named from their native cities and localities. Thus a man from Milan was called a Milanese or a Lombard much as we speak of a man from Cleveland as a Clevelander or an Ohioan. Most of the large cities were centers of art where the knowledge of one generation of artists was passed on to the next in the botteghe (shops) of the master painters. Hence so-called schools of painting developed each with its own characteristics.

Bernardino Luini lived and worked in Milan at the time when the artistic teachings of the genius, Leonardo da Vinci, were guiding the local school of painters. Luini's work was naturally affected by this influence, especially in the types of faces he used. The painting by Luini shown here was based on a drawing by Leonardo and so great was the resemblance to Leonardo's work that it was long considered a work of the greater master. However, Luini was an original artist in his own right. Another of his illustrations, The Child John The Baptist, is shown in Volume 7, page 20. His paintings tell us that he was a man of sympathetic nature and deep religious faith.

But it was not all over for them.

"The Messiah has come!" whispered the old man.

"And we have seen his glory!" exclaimed the boy.

"He is a little baby in Bethlehem," said the quiet man.

And they arose that very hour and went straight to Bethlehem to find the little baby in the manger.

THE VISIT OF THE SHEPHERDS

He was not hard to find. There were lights in the court of the inn, as they looked through the gate, and there in the stable, among the animals, they found Mary and Joseph and the little baby lying in the manger, just as the angel had said.

Down they knelt before the manger; for they could not forget that the angel had said that the babe was the Great King; and they told Mary and Joseph and the others standing by what the angels had said.

Then the travelers who had been awakened wondered at the story; it seemed so impossible that this weak little baby could be the Great King. Probably most of them did not believe it. Why should the angels tell such good news only to poor shepherds, and not to the leaders of the people or the learned men?

It was a very natural question, but I think Jesus himself in later years gave the answer. He once said, "Blessed are the pure in heart, for they shall see God"; and I think these shepherds at Bethlehem must have been pure in heart.

As for Mary, she asked no questions at all, but laid these things away in her heart and thought of them often in later years.

And this is the wonderful story of the meaning of Christmas. —Bible text—Vol. 7, pp. 39-40.

QUESTIONS

What does Christmas mean?

Why did Joseph and Mary go to Bethlehem?

What happened when they arrived at Bethlehem?

What were shepherds doing in a field near by?

Why did they go to Bethlehem?

What did God give us at Christmas?

How can we thank him for his gift?

HOW THE WISE MEN FOUND JESUS

MAGI:—They were learned men and they made a special study of the stars, "astronomers" we should call them.

FRANKINCENSE AND MYRRH:—Rare gum and perfumes used as gifts to kings.

The Gospel of Luke tells how the shepherds found Jesus. The Gospel of Matthew has nothing about the shepherds, but it tells how wise men from far away came to the babe in Bethlehem.

This is the story:

THE VISIT OF THE WISE MEN

After Jesus was born in Bethlehem, some strangers appeared one day in Jerusalem, the capital city, which was not far from Bethlehem. Strangers often came to Jerusalem. Most of them were Hebrews, come from other countries to worship their God in the home of their fathers. These men were not Hebrews. They came from far off in the east, and were Magi, "wise men." They said that they had seen a star which meant that a great king had been born in Palestine and they started at once on the long journey across the desert to worship him.

Instead of going to see the great temple, or offering jewels from the east for sale in the market-place, they went about asking questions.

HOLY NIGHT
A painting by Antonio Correggio

"Where is the child born to be King of the Jews?" they asked.

All the people they asked shook their heads. "There is no such child," they said. "Why do you think there is?"

"We are students of the stars," they said. "We have seen a star in the east which is the star of the King of the Jews. Where is he?"

But the people could not answer.

Now the Jews were ruled in those days by Rome, a great city far off in Italy, but the Romans let some of the parts of their empire have kings and princes of their own, so long as Rome could rule through them. At this time the Jews had a king, Herod. He was an ambitious, blood-thirsty man whom the people feared. He heard about the visit of the wise men, and he wondered if it meant some plot of his enemies, or if a child had been born who would displace his family. He believed that the stars could tell what would happen, if people knew how to read their message. He knew, too, about the Messiah, for whom so many of the people hoped. Whatever lay behind this visit from the strangers, he thought was probably connected with that belief in a future great king, the Messiah.

"IN BETHLEHEM IS THE KING TO BE BORN"

He called the learned men of the Jews and said, "Tell me, where is this King Messiah to be born?"

They said, "In Bethlehem. There is an old prophecy which so says: 'And thou Bethlehem in the land of Judah art not the least among the princes of Judah for out of thee shall come a Governor who shall rule my people Israel.'"

Then King Herod sent secretly for the strangers.

"Tell me all about this. When did you first see the

The Madonna with the Rabbit

By Titian, Tiziano Vecellio (c. 1477-1576)

In the Louvre, Paris, France

IN THIS gracious, human scene, we have another variation of the "sacra converzatione," or communion of holy personages usually attending the Madonna and Child, which was such a popular devotional subject during the Renaissance. We have already seen pictures of this kind on page 183, and in Volume 7, page 60.

Here the lovely Madonna holds a white rabbit, which has attracted the Babe's attention, while the youthful St. Catherine, holding the Infant, leans graciously toward her. A basket of fruit lies open at Mary's feet, nearby a shepherd looks on, and sheep graze in the meadow beyond.

How beautiful are the serene young mother and her charming comrade, as they encourage the infant's joyous interest in the world about him. What a lovely pastoral symphony in the tranquil, shadowy countryside! It is not difficult to imagine the bright colors in the foreground—blending into the rich, modulated green of the landscape.

This interest in loveliness enhanced by splendor and color is typical of Venetian painting, which, simply as painting, is considered the most beautiful in the world. The glory of this school is to an unusual degree that of a single individual, Tiziano Vecellio of Cadore. Titian painted this picture in 1530 during middle age—a period of dramatic energy and color enriched by a spirituality readily apparent in The Entombment (Volume 7:262).

Carried off by the plague in 1576, Titian had lived nearly a century, and for over seventy years had been a famous painter. He began with the cool preciseness learned from Giovanni Bellini (see Volume Nine) and closed with a passionate mystery of expression which foretells Rembrandt (page 274). So far as Venice was concerned, Titian was its Renaissance.

star?" For he wanted to know how old this future king, if there was such a person, might be.

When the crafty old king had learned all they could tell him, he said,

"South of this city you will find a little town, Bethlehem. Go there and look. If you find him, bring me word, so that I may go and bow before him, too."

But what he really wanted was to put the innocent babe out of the way.

The wise men mounted their camels once again and started for Bethlehem. And when they looked up into the sky they saw the star of the king. It seemed straight ahead of them. All the way to Bethlehem it seemed straight ahead of them; and when at last they found Mary and Joseph and the little baby, it seemed to be shining down on them from directly above.

What a different group from the shepherds, with their rough sheepskin coats! These strangers may have had clothes that were worn and travel-stained, but when they took down the boxes from their camels and opened them, the gifts they took out were gifts of rich men. They laid by the little babe, born in a stable, gold and frankincense and myrrh—costly gifts from far-away lands.

That is the story of how God sent wise men from far away to find Jesus.

The end of this story is not so happy.

THE ANGER OF THE KING

The cruel old king was back in Jerusalem, waiting for the wise men to come back and tell him where the baby was. He hugged himself whenever he thought how cunning he had been to get them in their innocence to lay the foundation for his wicked plot. But perhaps the strangers were not so simple as the old king thought they were.

One of them had a dream in which God told him not to go back to Herod, and what they had seen of the king made them quite willing to take the dream as a warning and hurry out of the country on their tall camels by another way. Herod waited, but they did not come. The days passed, and still they did not come. He did not dare to send soldiers for them, because that would show the people his plan.

At last he found that they had gone away, but by that time they were over the borders of the little country, far off on the desert roads to the east, too far for his soldiers to follow even if he had wanted to send them.

THE ESCAPE TO EGYPT

While the baffled king was waiting and growing more angry every day, Joseph and Mary and the baby had gone off into Egypt; so while the wise men were going in one direction, the child Jesus was being taken in another; and the jealous king, Herod, was fuming and fretting back in his palace in Jerusalem.

Herod found out that the wise men had gone, and he was furiously angry. But no one thought to tell him that a carpenter named Joseph, with his wife and a baby on a donkey by his side, had been seen starting out on the ancient caravan road to Egypt. Nobody cared what humble people like that did, or where they went. So the king supposed that if the wise men had found any child, he must be still in Bethlehem. But he would not be there long! No one else, child or man, should be called King of Israel in his dominions while he lived!

THE SAD FATE OF THE LITTLE CHILDREN OF BETHLEHEM

One day the people of Bethlehem were amazed to see grim-looking soldiers filing through the gate of their town on the Jerusalem side. They grew pale, for Herod's soldiers were not welcome guests. The soldiers placed guards at all the gates, so that no one could escape. Then began scenes one does not like to think of. Cries and wailing went up from all the city, for the king had ordered that all the boy babies, under two years old, should be killed. If he did not know which baby he wanted to put out of the way, he would kill them all!

People mourned for the little babies, but when, not long after, the old king died, nobody was sorry.

Meantime the little Jesus was playing on the sands down in Egypt. When Herod was dead they came back and lived in a town called Nazareth

—Read the complete story in the Bible language, Vol. 7 pp. 44-51.

QUESTIONS

What strangers came to Jerusalem after the birth of Jesus?
Why did they come?
What did Herod want them to do?
What did they give Jesus?
What gifts can you give Jesus?

THE SPHINX

The Sphinx, with the Great Pyramid in the background. Tradition says the Holy Family rested here during their flight into Egypt.

BRIGHTEST AND BEST

Brightest and best of the sons of the morning,
  Dawn on our darkness and lend us Thine aid;
Star of the East, the horizon adorning,
  Guide where our infant Redeemer is laid.

Cold on His cradle the dewdrops are shining,
  Low lies His head with the beasts of the stall;
Angels adore Him in slumber reclining,
  Maker, and Monarch, and Saviour of all.

Say, shall we yield Him in costly devotion,
  Odors of Edom, and offerings divine,
Gems of the mountain, and pearls of the ocean,
  Myrrh from the forest, or gold from the mine?

Vainly we offer each ample oblation;
  Vainly with gifts would His favor secure:
Richer by far is the heart's adoration;
  Dearer to God are the prayers of the poor.

Brightest and best of the sons of the morning,
  Dawn on our darkness, and lend us Thine aid;
Star of the East, the horizon adorning,
  Guide where our infant Redeemer is laid.
                              —*Reginald Heber.*

AS JOSEPH WAS A-WALKING

A Christmas Carol

As Joseph was a-walking,
  He heard an angel sing:
"This night shall be the birth-night
  Of Christ our heavenly King.
His birth-bed shall be neither
  In housen nor in hall,
Nor in the place of paradise,
  But in the oxen's stall.

HOLY FAMILY IN EGYPT
A painting by Robert Leinweber

He neither shall be rockèd
  In silver nor in gold,
But in the wooden manger
  That lieth in the mould.
He neither shall be clothèd
  In purple nor in pall,
But in the fair, white linen
  That usen babies all."

As Joseph was a-walking,
  Thus did the angel sing,
And Mary's son at midnight
  Was born to be our King.
Then be you glad, good people,
  At this time of the year;
And light you up your candles,
  For his star it shineth clear.

The shepherds came a-walking,
     A-walking, a-walking,
The shepherds came a-walking
  With coats of hodden gray.
And when they slipped within the door
And stepped across the courtyard floor
Not a sleeper waked to see
Who these countrymen might be—
These men who tramp while others sleep—
These shepherds who have left their sheep

The wise men came a-riding,
     A-riding, a-riding,
The wise men came a-riding
  With robes of shining silk.
And when they opened wide the door
And marched upon the courtyard floor
All the people rose to see
Who these riders fine might be—
These men so richly clothed and grand
Like kings from some far distant land.

Madonna and Child

By Sassoferrato, Giovanni Battista Salvi (1605-1685)
In the Brera Gallery, Milan, Italy
Photograph by Anderson, Rome

THE Madonna and Child has ever been a favorite subject for painters. Here we see Mary holding the sleeping Child Jesus in her lap while an encircling cloud of cherubs' heads join her in sweet adoration. This charming motif of cherubs was especially popular with seventeenth century artists. Murillo, a Spanish artist of that period, used this background theme frequently. (See page 216, and Volume 7, page 293.)

If we compare this picture with earlier paintings by Fra Angelico da Fiesole or Raphael (page 248), we find the others more earnestly and nobly religious than this one. When we compare it with a modern painting by Couse (page 160), the modern is far more austere in feeling. These comparisons show us that Sassoferrato painted at a time when religious feeling differed greatly from that of preceding centuries and later times. This mildly cheerful, naïvely sentimental scene, showing no trace of grandeur or formality, is distinctly of the seventeenth century. If we compare it with other Italian pictures of the same time (p. 42, 1:146), or with the contemporary Spanish artist, Murillo (page 216), we can better understand the spirit of the century. Today many of these pictures seem more than a little affected, but that is merely because we no longer express our religious feelings in what was then an entirely sincere way.

Giovanni Battista Salvi, called Sassoferrato from his birthplace, was the son and pupil of Tarquino Salvi, a mediocre painter. Giovanni later studied and copied the works of the great masters in Rome, being particularly influenced by Raphael's Florentine manner. He settled in Rome, devoted himself principally to painting religious pictures, and was one of the best artists of the seventeenth century Roman school. He died in Rome in 1685.

The Baby lay a-sleeping,
    A-sleeping, a-sleeping,
The Baby lay a-sleeping
  In Mother Mary's arms.
The shepherds came with gentle tread,
And kneeled before the manger-bed;
And bowing with them there, behold!
The wise men bringing gifts of gold.
The rich and poor together came;
The Lord, He loves them both the same.

THE ADORATION OF THE WISE MEN

Saw you never in the twilight,
  When the sun had left the skies,
Up in heaven the clear stars shining,
  Through the gloom like silver eyes?
So of old the wise men watching,
  Saw a little stranger star,
And they knew the King was given,
  And they follow'd it from far.

Heard you never of the story,
  How they cross'd the desert wild,
Journey'd on by plain and mountain,
  Till they found the Holy Child?
How they open'd all their treasure,
  Kneeling to that Infant King,
Gave the gold and fragrant incense,
  Gave the myrrh in offering?

Know ye not that lowly Baby
  Was the bright and morning star,
He who came to light the Gentiles,
  And the darken'd isles afar?
And we too may seek his cradle,
  There our heart's best treasures bring,
Love, and Faith, and true devotion,
  For our Saviour, God, and King.
              —Cecil Frances Alexander.

GIVE HEED, MY HEART, LIFT UP THINE EYES

Give heed, my heart, lift up thine eyes,
Who is it in yon manger lies?
Who is this Child, so young and fair?
The blessed Christ-Child lieth there.

Ah, dearest Jesus, holy Child,
Make Thee a bed, soft, undefiled
Within my heart, that it may be
A quiet chamber kept for Thee.

My heart for very joy doth leap,
My lips no more can silence keep;
I, too, must sing with joyful tongue
That sweetest ancient cradle song.

Glory to God in highest heaven,
Who unto man, His Son hath given,
While angels sing with pious mirth.
A glad new year to all the earth.

— *Martin Luther*
Translation by Catherine Winkworth.

A BIRTHDAY GIFT

What can I give him,
　Poor as I am?
If I were a shepherd
　I would bring a lamb;
If I were a wise man
　I would do my part.
Yet what I can I give him,
　Give my heart.

— *Christina Rossetti.*

Holy Family

By Murillo, Bartolomé Estéban (1617-1682)
In the Prado Museum, Madrid, Spain

A CHARMINGLY natural air of life and happy humor breathes from this canvas. Tender and kindly in spirit, the warmth and comfort of this home-scene has a touch of delightful playfulness. Called the Holy Family "del Pajarito"—with the bird—it has a pleasing radiance, a sweet serenity, a liveliness, that is at once intensely human and beautiful.

The boy Jesus smiling, happy, is shown during a moment of play with his little white dog. He holds a bird, whose wings are almost fluttering in his hand, up out of the dog's reach. He leans back against his father, in full confidence and security of affection. So very alive does he appear that we expect him, any minute, to put down his arm and continue his romp. Murillo wanted to show Jesus as a lively boy who loved and played with pets just as other boys do.

The dog, with its lifted paw and nose, is one of those attractive and humorous figures both of children and of animals that abound with such charm in Murillo's pictures.

Here, are four different types of figures, all appearing to live and breathe just as in real life; all harmonious with the others, yet each with his own individuality and particular movement.

The playful gestures of the boy are quicker, more lively, than the larger, comprehensive gestures of his father; while the mother, in the shadowy background, is more calm.

The wicker clothes basket is like those we still have today, and in the back is a winding-reel for yarn.

Murillo did not always aim to present Mary enhanced by deep spirituality or grandeur. Here he shows her a simple loving mother, as she may have lived and moved in the humble home of Joseph, the carpenter of Nazareth.

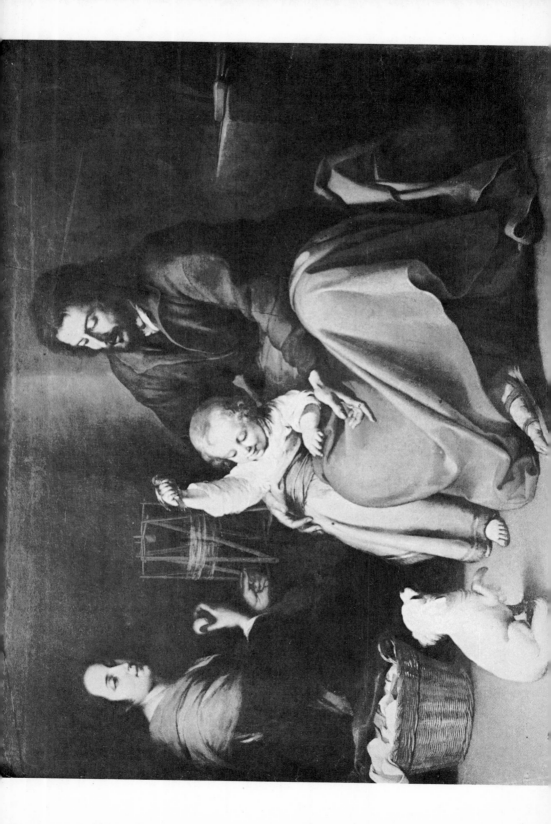

Remains of the Antonia Fortress in Old Jerusalem, Showing the Street Leading to St. Stephen's Gate (Lion's Gate)

From International Publishing Co.

THE ancient city of Jerusalem is built high on the hills of Judea, and has always been a natural place of defense. It was held by the Jebusites before the conquest of Canaan in Joshua's time, and one of its highest places, Mount Zion, was captured by David and his mighty men. Despite its extensive fortification with high walls all round about the city it was captured and destroyed several times by invaders such as the Babylonians and the Romans. Much of the old wall and fortifications have been rebuilt over the centuries, such as the walls of the Antonius Fortress pictured here. It was built by Herod during the days of Jesus. Of Jerusalem, the Psalmist sang: "Walk about Zion, and go round about her: tell the towers thereof. Mark ye well her bulwarks, consider her palaces; that ye may tell it to the generation following. For this God is our God for ever and ever: he will be our guide even unto death" (Psalms 48:12–14).

CRADLE HYMN

Hush, my dear, lie still and slumber;
   Holy angels guard thy bed;
Heavenly blessings without number
   Gently falling on thy head.

Sleep, my babe, thy food and raiment,
   House and home, thy friends provide;
All without thy care, or payment,
   All thy wants are well supplied.

How much better thou'rt attended,
   Than the Son of God could be;
When from heaven He descended,
   And became a child like thee!

Soft and easy is thy cradle;
   Coarse and hard thy Saviour lay,
When His birthplace was a stable
   And his softest bed the hay.
                — *Isaac Watts.*

THE BOY JESUS ON A JOURNEY

"THE JOY OF THE WHOLE EARTH IS MOUNT ZION"

When the boy Jesus was twelve years old, he took a very important journey. Nazareth, where they lived, was several days' journey from Jerusalem, but Joseph and, when she could, Mary, his mother, used to go there every year. They went, not to buy or sell, nor to see the sights, but to worship God. Every Sabbath at home they went to the synagogue, where they heard the word of God read, and joined in the prayers which they all said together; but at Jerusalem was the temple. It was the greatest place of worship in all the land. It was a great, splendid building, made of white stone. The worship in it was very impressive. The courts were full of people and there were great choirs of singers, and priests with rich garments. There were three great gatherings each year, and if the people could, they went to one or more of them. But the little children were left at home.

If Jesus ever asked to go with his father and mother, they said, "Wait, my boy. When you are twelve you may go."

KEEPING THE LAW

The reason they promised that he might go at twelve was that when he was twelve a Jewish boy must begin "keeping the law." He must be careful not to touch certain things. He must walk only so far on the Sabbath, and when he went to the synagogue he must wear a certain dress and must join in the prayers with the men. These and other things the boy was always proud to do. It made him feel that he was a man.

At last the time came when Jesus was twelve and he could go to Jerusalem and share in the worship there.

ON THE ROAD TO JERUSALEM

You can fancy how excited he was. He never remembered being so far away from home. When at last the bread was baked for the journey, and all the preparations were made and they were actually started, he could hardly keep his feet on the ground. He ran ahead till his father told him to save his strength for the hills later. He picked flowers in the meadows, for the trip was made in the springtime when all the hills are bright with blossoms. Sometimes he played with the young lambs beside the way, while the shepherds walked along and talked with his father. Sometimes he, too, walked gravely by them and

Joseph and Mary and Jesus on the Way to Jerusalem

Painting by Otto Gabriel Mengelberg (1817-1890)
Location of Original Painting Unknown

HERE are Joseph, Mary and Jesus on their way to Jerusalem to attend the Passover feast. Once before, they had come to Jerusalem to the temple, and there had presented the infant Jesus to the Lord; as we would say, had entered his name in the Church book. During the years that followed in Nazareth "the child grew and waxed strong in spirit, filled with wisdom: and the grace of God was upon him." (Luke 2:40.) When Jesus reached the age of twelve, it was necessary, according to the custom of his people, for him to begin to "keep the law." He must study and practice the many religious customs of the Hebrew people. He must also begin to learn a trade. The time to "put away childish things" had come.

We see the travelers as they are nearing the city. Jesus is talking while Joseph and Mary are listening and pondering. After reading the story on pages 201-206, study the picture and try to imagine what Jesus is saying. Is he asking questions about the city? Is he asking to be told again the meaning of the Passover?

The artist, Otto Gabriel Mengelberg, was born at Düsseldorf, Germany, in 1817. He studied painting first in Düsseldorf Academy and then with several famous teachers in other art centers. When thirty-one years old, he returned to Düsseldorf to live. Here he taught and painted, devoting nearly all of his life to representing religious subjects. Here he died in 1890. Many of his canvases are in churches and museums in his native country.

It is interesting to compare this portrayal of the twelve-year old Jesus with the picture by the nineteenth century French painter, Théodule Ribot, given on page 208.

SCHOOL AT SHUNEM

This picture shows the native teacher and his school in the neighborhood where Elisha was so hospitably entertained. The children are evidently not anxious to have their pictures taken. They are afraid perhaps of the "evil eye" of the Westerner's camera.

listened to their talk. Every now and then he ran up and put his hand in his mother's and she smiled at him; and they were all as happy as springtime and love could make them.

CAMPING BENEATH THE STARS

Then at night they gathered with other little parties also going to Jerusalem, and lit a fire by the road in the twilight, and ate their supper of bread and figs, and talked together until the stars were bright above. Then they all wrapped their cloaks about them and lay down; and Jesus looked up into the twinkling stars and thought how his mother had said that God who made all the stars loved us like a father. I think he must have whispered a little prayer, "O Father which art in heaven, show me how to be a good son."

"OUR FEET SHALL STAND WITHIN THY GATES, O JERUSALEM"

At last they came to Jerusalem. They found lodging with friends. and every day spent long hours in the temple. What Jesus was doing and thinking all the time the story in the Gospel of Luke does not tell.

There are times when some great thing comes into life, and a person grows a great deal in a short time. Such a period came to Jesus at the feast. How do we know? Because of what happened at the end.

A STREET IN JERUSALEM

A group of the little children of Jerusalem are gathered by the door of an old stone building.

THE HOMEWARD JOURNEY

Jesus must have been greatly trusted by his parents. They did not try to know where he was all the time. When the feast was over, the people who had come to Jerusalem made ready to go back home. Mary and Joseph started in company with a large group of friends. In the East there is always great confusion when a large caravan begins a journey. No one knows where any one else is. They do not go far the first day, and at the stopping place for

Jesus and the Learned Men in the Temple

By Théodule Ribot (1823-1891)
In the Museum of the Luxembourg, Paris, France

ALMOST everyone who has read the story of the twelve year old Jesus going up to Jerusalem with his parents on his first big journey has probably tried to imagine how He looked and what He did there. The Bible tells us one important incident, and the artist has pictured it for us. It is Jesus in the temple questioning with the learned men.

In the picture we see a gentle, bright-eyed boy in peasant's clothing surrounded by earnest men. See how these teachers and others talk among themselves wonderingly, and gaze at the boy and question him. It is true that "all that heard him were astonished at his understanding and answers." You will find the rest of this story on page 210. In Volume 7 on page 51 is the story as told so beautifully by Luke.

The artist, Théodule Ribot, was a very poor young Frenchman who painted mirror frames all day long to earn a living. At night, by the light of a candle, he taught himself how to paint people and scenes, in short, to paint pictures. Perhaps this working by candle light accounts for his preference for dark, shadowy backgrounds, such as in this picture.

At first Ribot painted the scenes around him, women at their household and kitchen tasks. Later, when he began to paint religious pictures he continued to put his characters in everyday dress and ordinary surroundings. This was in sharp contrast to the pictures by the school-trained artists of Ribot's day such as Dubufe, page 280, and Bouguereau, page 314. The people, when they first saw Ribot's pictures, thought them irreverent. But is was not long before they saw the deep sincerity and simple grandeur of them. Today Ribot is considered a master among nineteenth century French artists.

the night order begins to come out of the confusion. It is not strange, then, that Joseph and Mary should have started off without seeing Jesus. If Mary asked where he was, Joseph said, "Oh, I suppose he is somewhere around among our friends."

THE LITTLE BOY JESUS CANNOT BE FOUND

But when they camped for the night they tried to find him, and he was not there! You can fancy how worried they were all night, and how bright and early the next morning they went back to the city to find him. They went to the house where they had stayed, but he was not there. They hunted out the boys he had been with, but they knew nothing of him. Every day for three days they hunted and every night they were more puzzled. This was not like their thoughtful, obedient boy.

JESUS IN THE TEMPLE

Meantime, where do you think he was? Why, he was in the temple where the learned men were talking to the people who came, and were answering their questions. Jesus took an active part in the discussions, listening to all that these religious leaders had to say and asking them further questions. But Jesus quickly showed that he was no ordinary boy, for the Scriptures tell us that he displayed an understanding beyond that of a normal boy of twelve, as He himself in turn gave answers to their questions which amazed them and all who heard. So absorbed was he in this that he missed all of the preparations for returning home. Every day he came to the temple. Every day their amazement increased, at the way this bright-eyed boy with the loving ways understood God and the truths of God.

IN MY FATHER'S HOUSE

At last, when they had looked everywhere else, Joseph and Mary came to that part of the temple where the teachers sat; and there was their boy!

"Son," cried his mother, "why have you treated us so? We have been hunting for you, and been so anxious!"

The boy opened his eyes wide. "Why, mother!" he said, "where could you expect to find me except in my Father's house?"

I think he would have been glad to stay longer, but Mary and Joseph said it was time to go back, and he cheerfully went.

There was hard work to be done in the home at Nazareth, and Jesus did his share of it, thinking always that God was his Father.

"And Jesus increased in wisdom and stature and in favor with God and man."

—Now read the Bible text in Vol. 7, pp. 51-54.

QUESTIONS

What journey did Jesus take when he was twelve?

Why was it an exciting journey?

If you had lived in Nazareth why would you have enjoyed a journey to distant Jerusalem?

Why did Jesus not start home with his parents?

What part of the story shows his obedience to his parents?

Is God your Heavenly Father?

JESUS AND JOHN THE BAPTIST

While Jesus was growing up in Nazareth, "increasing in stature and in favor with God and man," another little boy was growing up in the hill country of Judea and we may be sure that he also, as he increased in stature, grew also in favor with God and man. This little boy's

John the Baptist at the Beginning of His Ministry

By Murillo, Bartolomé Estéban (1617-1682)

In the Prado Gallery, Madrid, Spain

THE child John the Baptist is shown here, in the desert, with a deeply-moved, serious, expression. The divine call is coming to him, telling him the needs of the world and its sorrows. He carries a cross, and the lamb looks up at him anxiously, as if it too, felt the importance of this occasion.

The artist who painted this scene also had a serious boyhood, full of hardships. Born in Seville, in 1617, Bartolomé Estéban Murillo was to become seventeenth-century Spain's leading religious painter, while his protector and fellow-Sevillian, Diego Velasquez, became Spain's chief court artist.

Little is known of Murillo's early life except that his parents are reported to have died when he was only eleven. The boy, having apparently already shown skill in drawing, was then apprenticed to the painter, Juan del Castillo, said, by some writers, to have been his uncle.

Castillo moved to Cadiz in 1640, leaving Murillo, at twenty-three, in needy circumstances, and without friend or advisor in Seville. To get money for colors and food, he began painting for the "Feria," or weekly street-fairs, held in the broad street facing the Church of All Saints.

To be an "artist of the Feria" was by no means a compliment, then. There, amid the pavements littered with indifferent meat and vegetables, cheap crockery and second-hand clothes, the artist had to "hawk" his wares. The buyers, usually of the lowest class, delighted in rough, showy pictures, garish colors, and "popular" subjects—the more familiar saints, gaudy flowers and fruits. The artist kept his paints beside him, ready to hastily make all alterations the customers wanted, even to changing a St. Catherine into a St. Anthony!

You may read more of Murillo's life with his second picture of John the Baptist, in Volume 7, page 282.

name was John and he was a relative of Jesus. His father was an old priest of the temple, Zacharias. His mother's name was Elizabeth. She was a cousin of Mary, the mother of Jesus, though much older than Mary. When the little baby who was born to them was taken to the temple to receive his name, a strange thing happened. The officials supposed that he would be called Zacharias after his father, but Elizabeth said, "No, his name is John." The old father had not been able to speak aloud for some time. They made signs to see what he wished and he wrote on a tablet, "His name is John." Then his voice came back to him and he praised God for all his goodness and especially for sending the little boy, John, to gladden the hearts of his wife and himself.

We do not certainly know that Jesus and John met and knew each other during their boyhood days, but it is extremely likely that they did. While their parents lived some distance apart, there is no reason to suppose that they may not have visited each other and they must certainly have seen each other at the Passover. The old artists have made such supposed visits the subjects of very charming pictures, such as "The Children of the Shell." It is very interesting to study all these pictures.

When John the Baptist grew to manhood he knew that he was a messenger from God and had a special work to do. He went into the pasture lands, the "wilderness" of Judea, and beneath the stars, amid the silences of the desert, completed his preparation. Then he came to the Jordan River and began to speak like one of the old prophets. Some of the people thought that he was one of the old prophets Elijah or Isaiah, come back to life. Crowds of people came flocking to hear him, rich men in their chariots, soldiers, priests, merchants, shepherds. He told them all alike that they must repent and, in this way, he began his own work. When Jesus was baptized, John said, "Behold the Lamb of God, which taketh away the sins of the world." In the old pictures of John, you will see that he carries a slender cross which has a scroll on which are these words in Latin, "Ecce Agnus Dei." The words mean in English, "Behold the Lamb of God." A voice from heaven was heard also saying, "This is my beloved Son in whom I am well pleased."

When Jesus began his great work, John felt that his own task was drawing to a close. "He must increase," he said of Jesus, "but I must decrease." John was seized by Herod, the wicked king, put into prison and beheaded.

HOW JESUS SPREAD THE GOOD NEWS

SEA:—The Sea of Galilee, not the ocean. In Jesus' time it was also called the Lake of Tiberias.

Jesus wanted all the people to hear the Good News about God. He wanted them to know that God was ready to help them, and that they could help God by their love and obedience.

How was he, a poor carpenter from Nazareth, to speak so that they could hear?

He was not rich nor learned. What the great teachers at Jerusalem said to their scholars was repeated to others, but he was not a great teacher at Jerusalem. He could not put it in a book. The few books were slowly copied by hand, and cost far too much for most people to own.

He could not publish his Good News in the papers; there were no papers.

He could not hire a hall and call a meeting. There were no halls to hire and he had no money for it if there had been.

The Children of the Shell

By Murillo, Bartolomé Estéban (1617-1682)
In the Prado Gallery, Madrid, Spain

YOU remember that Jesus had a cousin John, a little older than he, who was later to become known as John, the Baptist. Painters often pictured the two children playing together, as we see them here.

The picture shows Jesus, thoughtful of others, just as he was in later life, holding a shell filled with water so that John may drink. His sweet, happy-natured face shows his pleasure in doing a kind act. From the shell the painting gets its title, in Spanish, "Los Bambinos del Concho."

The pennant on John's cross, bears the latin words, "Ecce Agnus Dei" or "Behold the Lamb of God." The woolly lamb, looking up at the two boys, is a symbol of the Saviour.

Through the bright opening in the clouds peer two baby angels, looking as if they wanted to come down to play, too. These winsome, plump little cherubs again and again float and frolic across Murillo's paintings, touching them with gaiety, freshness, and joy. Round and light as the fluffy clouds they rest on, these tiny, lovely beings breathe out a poetic, fragrant charm; they "seem to have fed on roses." Here, one angel has just clasped his chubby hands together, while the other, with a whimsically thoughtful expression, purses his lips as he looks down at the world.

Murillo uses his "vaporoso" or "misty" style, in which he was remarkably skillful for his angel scenes. We see them diffused in a soft, misty radiance; delicate and transparent, as if a dream-like vision of heaven really had opened up before our eyes. No wonder Murillo was called "el pintor del cielo" or "the painter of the heavens."

More of Murillo's cherubs are seen in the pictures of the Madonna and of the Holy Family in Vol. VI, on pages 102 and 293.

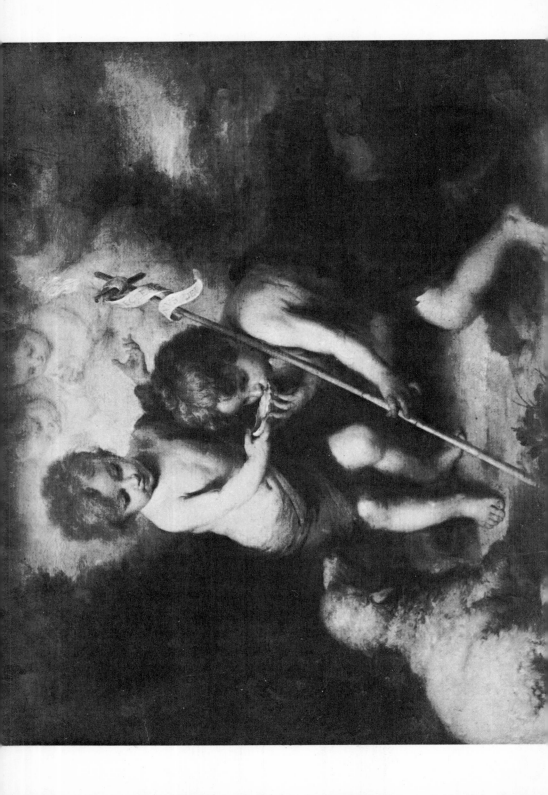

What did he do? Why, he first simply went about and talked with the people. And what he had to say was so new, and he himself was so full of love and good will and helpfulness that those who had heard him once wanted to hear him again.

HOW THE NEWS WAS SPREAD IN JESUS' DAY

While there were no newspapers, yet the people were all eager to get the news. They had tongues and ears, and they used both of them. If two travelers met on the road they sometimes sat down under a tree and exchanged all the news they had with each other. If a man went to the next town on business he was sure to be asked,

"What news have you brought?"

The women passed it on when they gathered to draw water at the village well, and the old men sat at the gates of the towns and told anyone who came and sat down by them all they had gathered from the travelers passing in and out. So the news spread all over the country very rapidly.

A NEW TEACHER HAS COME

Very soon, in Capernaum and Bethsaida and all the other towns along the Sea of Galilee, and then back in Nain and Nazareth and the hill towns, and before long, away off in the great city of Jerusalem itself, people were telling about that wonderful man named Jesus, who was talking in a new way about God and the Kingdom of God.

And hundreds of people said, "We will go and hear him."

IN THE TOWNS

So they came, till they crowded the houses where he stayed and the narrow streets. But there was a way of getting around that. Jesus began to go out of the towns.

He walked out of the little narrow, crooked streets, and all the people followed him. Then, when he was out in the great, wide spaces of all-out-doors, with the sunshine overhead and the green hills about and the little birds flitting past, he stopped and talked with the people.

BY THE SHORE OF THE SEA

Once he was by the seaside when they crowded about so that those a little distance off could not see or hear. Then he noticed that a little fishing boat was drawn up on shore. He had it put in the sea and got into it and went out a little way on the water. Then the people all sat down on the sandy beach or stood about as he talked.

Once he went up on a hillside and sat down and talked to them as they sat below.

He talked with them very simply. He was a working man, like them, and he knew just what they thought and how they talked.

He told them stories or parables to make his meaning more clear. They did not always understand the truth he was trying to teach, but they would remember the parable and later might see what it meant.

THE LOST COIN

He knew how a woman searched in all the corners of her dark little rooms if she had lost a coin; so when he wanted to say that God cares even for sinful people, he told a little story about a woman and her lost coin, and how when it was found she ran to her neighbors to tell them the good news. So God, he said, searches for sinners and is glad to find them.

When you read that Jesus "preached," it means that he talked with people, sometimes a few, sometimes a great company.

Fig Branches in Palestine

From International Publishing Co., Ltd.

GOD described the Promised Land to Moses as "a good land, a land of brooks of water, of fountains and depths that spring out of the valleys and hills, a land of wheat and barley, and vines, and fig trees . . ." (Deuteronomy 8:7–8). Figs are a delicacy that delight the taste and also a necessary food. They are delicious when eaten fresh, and very nourishing when dried and preserved. The fig tree was a symbol of peacefulness and prosperity. The prophet Micah spoke of the day when "they shall sit every man under his vine and under his fig tree, and none shall make them afraid." (Micah 4:4)

MADONNA AND CHILD

By Bodenhausen, C. (b. 1852)

IN THIS picture the mother of Jesus seems to stand upon the clouds. Her long hair floats in the wind. Glory streams through a rift in the clouds above. The mother is clothed all in white. Compare the modern picture with those of the Italian masters.

IN THE SYNAGOGUE

On the Sabbath Jesus went to church. The synagogue, as the church was called, was a building where the people gathered each Sabbath for a service. There were prayers and the reading of a selection from the old Scriptures, our Old Testament. Then, if the leader of the service wished, he might speak to the people, or invite any one in the audience to speak. Sometimes Jesus was invited, and when he spoke the people said afterward, "How different from our teachers! He speaks as though he knew what he was talking about himself, and had not merely learned it from others."

Another thing which Jesus did drew a great many people to him, but it was always being so misunderstood that he even sometimes told people not to talk about it, and that was the healing of the sick.

HEALING THE SICK

Jesus was so anxious to help people that when he saw suffering he always wanted to relieve it. He had the power of healing.

When people found that Jesus was willing to cure the sick the news spread very fast. They brought the sick to him and laid them out in the streets before the house in which he was. People came kneeling to him and begging that he would help their sick friends. Once when a house was crowded, the friends of a sick man opened a hole in the flat roof above and let the sick man down before Jesus. They were so anxious to bring their friend to the healer!

All these things together soon made Jesus the best-known teacher in the land. But he did not neglect to teach his disciples. He spent as much time alone with them as he could.

SOME PEOPLE TURN AWAY

There came a time later when those who had come simply because they were curious to see and hear a new man dropped away and the crowds were not so great. Some had come to him hoping that he would say he was the Great King, and raise an army to free the people from Rome. They soon saw that he would not do this, and they did not come to hear him any more.

Jesus continued to spread the Good News in the same way. He went about from place to place with his band of companions, the apostles, and talked with any who came to him. People sometimes invited him to dinner, and he went. Sometimes he and his friends ate by the roadside. He was never too tired to talk with people. They brought the sick, and he healed them. They brought little children to him, and he took them into his arms and gave them his blessing.

There is a verse in the gospels which puts in a few words how Jesus spread the Good News:

"He went about doing good."

QUESTIONS

What did Jesus want to tell the people?

What ways which we could use did he not have?

How did he spread the Good News?

Why did he use stories?

What are the different ways in which the people in your church help to spread the Good News about God?

HOW JESUS CHOSE HIS COMPANIONS

TAXGATHERER:—In some European countries taxes are even now collected in this way. As the farmers or harvesters enter a town the taxgatherer collects a tax from the produce or goods which they bring.

People never can get along alone in the world. If they do any work worth doing, they must have help. That was true of Jesus. He needed his helpers, even though they did not understand all he was trying to do.

At first he went about among the people alone. Very soon, however, he had gathered enough friends so that he could choose his helpers from among them.

He called them his disciples, which means learners. They were also called the apostles, which means those sent out, because Jesus later sent them out to be his messengers. There were twelve of them. They stayed with him, traveled with him, helped him when the crowds gathered about, were messengers to tell the people what he was trying to do, and later, after he left them alone, they were the leaders of the churches— except one, who proved to be so false that he betrayed Jesus in his greatest time of need.

We are told in the Gospels about how Jesus chose some of these followers.

CHOOSING THE DISCIPLES

One day Jesus was walking by the shore of the Sea of Galilee. The little lake is about twenty miles long, but there were many towns along its shore and all the country west of it was filled with villages and swarming with people. There was good fishing in the lake, and at certain times in the day the water was dotted with fishing boats, throwing nets and drawing them in. Jesus lived for a time in a town on the shore, and some of his friends were fishermen.

RUINS OF THE SYNAGOGUE AT CAPERNAUM

The Synagogue at Capernaum was very often visited by Jesus. It has been excavated and the great stones from the ruins are shown in the picture.

SIMON AND ANDREW

As he walked along the shore this day and watched the fishers out on the sparkling water, he saw one boat near the shore with two brothers in it, friends of his, Simon and Andrew. They were throwing their net into the water, then slowly drawing it in and taking out the fish from it.

Jesus stood and watched them. He knew that they were earnest and honest. They were sometimes blunt and outspoken—especially Simon—and sometimes they acted before they thought. But Jesus had learned to love them and he knew they were willing to trust him. He wanted them for his companions.

The boat drifted near shore. He called to them, and perhaps they talked a little while with him as they neared shore after their fishing trip. Perhaps they talked about the fishing, and about the Good News Jesus had come to

WHERE THE JORDAN FLOWS INTO
THE SEA OF GALILEE

Rushing down, down, down from Mount Hermon in the north, the River Jordan flows into the sacred Sea of Galilee. Passing through this Sea, the Jordan flows on through its deep gorge, till it falls into the Dead Sea.

But here after dawn, where the River Jordan flows into the Sea of Galilee, these fishermen rest their oars near this flowery bank.

Found in the Temple

By James J. Tissot (1836–1902)
Photographed by Three Lions, Inc.

In painting this event in the life of Jesus, the artist shows its effect on those individuals sharing in it.

Jesus had come from Nazareth to the Passover in Jerusalem with Mary and Joseph. He had talked with the great teachers in the temple and became so absorbed He forgot to join His family for the trip home. Missing Him on the way home, they returned and found Him.

The face of the Boy Jesus shows wonder. Was He still feeling amazement at sitting with the great teachers, asking them questions and listening to their answers? Did He have a feeling of sadness that His parents did not realize there were things He should be doing for His Heavenly Father?

Mary shows her anxious affection and the sadness she feels, at what, to her, was her son's disobedience. Joseph is puzzled, yet he wants to be fair. He strokes his beard and considers the matter.

The teachers had been so astonished at the young Boy's wisdom that they followed the family to the Temple Gate. As they stood at the steps, they must have been saying, "We can expect to hear more from this boy as he grows up." One teacher's face shows concern as to how the parents may discipline the Boy. Another looks as if he would like to follow and lay a hand of approval on Him.

What follows this scene? Luke tells us: "And he went down with them and came to Nazareth, and was subject unto them; but his mother kept all these sayings in her heart. And Jesus increased in wisdom and stature, and in favour with God and man." (2:51-52)

First Miraculous Catch of Fish

By James J. Tissot (1836–1902)
Photographed by Three Lions, Inc.

THE MIRACLES of Jesus were an important part of His ministry. Not only did they reveal His Divinity, but He used them to further His work on earth. Thus, the first miraculous catch of fish resulted in the calling of His first four disciples.

At this moment, Peter is kneeling before Christ because he feels too sinful to be in the presence of his Lord. Jesus reaches out His hand, telling him not to be afraid. And that Peter can help Him in His work with men, which is much better than catching fish.

Now fishing was Peter's occupation. It was also the occupation of his brother, Andrew, and his friends—James, John and their father, Zebedee. All had been out fishing the night before and caught nothing.

Jesus had been speaking to the crowds on the shore of the Sea of Galilee. He had used Peter's empty boat as a pulpit so the people could more easily see and hear Him. When the sermon was over, Jesus turned to Peter and suggested that he row into deep water and let down his net. Peter, thinking of the night before, hesitated. "We have fished all night and caught nothing," he explained. Then he added, "But at thy word I will let down the nets."

As Peter and Andrew began to haul in the nets they realized they were going to need help. They beckoned for James and John to bring their boat near and all were astonished as the catch of fish filled both boats.

The miracle had impressed the other three as it had Peter. For, ". . . when they had brought their ships to land, they forsook all, and followed him."

Teaching by the Sea of Galilee

By James J. Tissot (1836–1902)
Photographed by Three Lions, Inc.

Here tissot recreates an often repeated scene—
Jesus teaching by the Sea of Galilee. It was an
ideal place. The quiet waters, the towering mountains, and the blue sky above suggest an atmosphere of humility and tranquility. The Teacher
sits, as was the custom in that day. He gestures
with His hands to explain His words. The faces
in the crowd seem to indicate that His listeners
are receiving the message in different ways.

There is a boy in the picture, listening intently, suggesting that Jesus is telling a story.
To the left is a serious group with heads bowed
in thought. Their hearts may be the "good
ground" where the seed of Jesus' teaching would
bring forth fruit.

To the right stands one man who seems to be
critical, possibly a Pharisee in whose heart the
thorns of pride and prejudice will choke the
truth which he hears. Near the Pharisee, three
men sit discussing what has been said. Are they
the ones whose hearts Jesus speaks of as "stony
ground" where the seed withered away because
it had no moisture?

All these people are hearing words that have
come down to us in the Gospels. And to each of
them Jesus is saying, "He that hath ears, let him
hear."

The headdress of the men reminds us of the
need for protection from the hot sun. The boy,
too young for such a turban, wears a skull cap.

It is a satisfying picture. The face of Jesus is
serene. No wonder many people said, "He taught
as one having authority, and not as the scribes."

The Sermon On the Mount

By James J. Tissot (1836–1902)
Photographed by Three Lions, Inc.

NEAR THE SHORES of the Sea of Galilee, the mountains rise up close by the water's edge. For the background of this picture, the artist has chosen a spot on the side of one of these mountains. It is not far from the port of Capernaum and one can see the blue water in the distance.

Here, Jesus preached the greatest of all sermons. In the picture, the people are coming in groups to hear Him; multitudes from Judea, Samaria, Phoenicia, and the seacoast towns of Tyre and Sidon. Some sit in the shade, almost under the ledge of rock. Those seated near Him may be the disciples.

Perhaps, as Jesus began to speak, He was thinking not only of the people present but of people of all places and all centuries—even you and me. He spoke of great truths like those stated in the Beatitudes and in the Lord's Prayer. Yet, He illustrated His teachings with talk of things from everyday life—salt, a rusty treasure, a lily in bloom, a blade of grass, a bird pecking at a grain of wheat.

Even today the truths of this sermon are helpful in meeting the problems of everyday living—of anxiety about food and shelter and clothing—of how to treat other people, even enemies.

The Sermon on the Mount is not just a list of individual truths. It is a revelation of the true Christian—his heart and his life. There is something for everyone.

The group on the mountainside that day found it so, too.

Instructing the Twelve Disciples

By James J. Tissot (1836–1902)
Photographed by Three Lions, Inc.

THE MEETING pictured in this scene took place more than a year before the dark day when Jesus laid down His life to save the world which He loved.

Jesus had been preaching in the cities and villages of Galilee. Moved with compassion, He had healed many people. His efforts took Him into homes, fields, streets and even synagogues— any place He could bring help, comfort or understanding to the people.

He realized that more people needed His gospel so He asked his disciples to help. First, He called the twelve together to give them instructions.

The painting shows them in a quiet place where a tree shades them from the heat and a ledge of rock gives them privacy.

The gesture of His hands seems to indicate He is telling them of the many needy people who are without a leader or shepherd. He gives them authority over unclean spirits, to cast them out, and to heal all manner of disease and all manner of sickness. He commands them to make no charge for teaching nor healing and, on their trips, to take no money, no food, no extra clothing, "for the workman is worthy of his meat."

Jesus assures the twelve of the Heavenly Father's care for them. "The very hairs of your head are all numbered," He said.

The faces of the listeners reveal both faith and eagerness to learn. Their Master is trusting them to share in His work. They must not fail Him.

Blessing the Little Children

By James J. Tissot (1836–1902)
Photographed by Three Lions, Inc.

Once again, the artist tells a well-known and much-loved story. A careful look at the characters in the painting reveals their emotions as they realize Jesus loves every one of them.

The great Teacher had been talking about the holiness of married life, reminding the people that God himself was the Creator of man and Founder of marriage and the family, where "children are an heritage of the Lord."

His talk brought a group of mothers with their little ones, seeking the prayers of the Master for their children. Each hoped that He might touch her child.

Jesus did more than that. He called the children to Him, took them in His arms, laying His hands upon each of them. It was a great moment for mother and child.

Jesus is blessing a little girl, while a little brother, on his mother's shoulder, waits his turn. Perhaps this is the whole family. A larger boy with another child in his arms is patiently waiting.

At the extreme right of the picture a mother holds her child. Both seem happy. Evidently this child has already felt the tender touch of the Master's gentle hands.

Some of the onlookers are sitting down. A few have climbed the steps for a better view. All of them show interest and approval.

Two disciples in back of Jesus, seem to be trying to send the mothers and children away. Their action displeased Christ. We can almost hear Him saying, "Suffer the little children to come unto me, and forbid them not, for of such is the Kingdom of Heaven."

Zacchaeus in the Sycomore Tree

By James J. Tissot (1836–1902)
Photographed by Three Lions, Inc.

THIS PAINTING of a man in a sycomore tree, with its wide-spreading branches makes one curious why a grown man is up in a tree.

The man is Zacchaeus a wealthy citizen of Jericho. He was the much disliked chief tax collector, whose opportunities for wrong doing had given him a bad reputation.

Jesus and a group of pilgrims are going to Jerusalem for the Passover. It was the custom for people to gather in the streets as a welcome when an important group passed through. Jericho was crowded that day. There were many who wanted to see Jesus of Nazareth, about whom they had heard so much.

Zacchaeus did too, but he soon realized this would be impossible, for he was short, and the crowd pressed close. He decided to run ahead and climb a sycomore tree that he remembered grew along the way.

As Jesus passed under the tree, He surprised everyone by saying, "Zacchaeus, hurry down, for today I will stay at your house."

Zacchaeus must have almost fallen out of the tree. He couldn't understand such friendliness, but it gave him much joy. The crowd was confused. "Jesus gone to be a guest in the home of a sinner!" they said, hardly believing it.

Standing before the Master, Zacchaeus, for the first time, saw his real self and decided to change. He vowed to pay back, four times over, any amounts he had taken unjustly and to give the poor half of his possessions.

Hear, as the people did that day, Jesus' words, "This day is salvation come to this house . . . For the Son of man is come to seek and save that which was lost."

Healing the Lame and the Blind

By James J. Tissot (1836–1902)
Photographed by Three Lions, Inc.

This scene, in the Court of the Gentiles, on one of the porches of the great Temple in Jerusalem, is quite different from a few hours earlier. Then, there had been tables for exchanging money because the priests demanded that offerings be in Jewish coin, rather than Roman. In booths, merchants had sold animals for sacrifice at far above market prices, keeping the excessive profit for themselves and the high priest.

The clamor and cheating had so angered Jesus that He had driven out the merchants and money changers to restore the sacred atmosphere of the Temple.

News of what He had done soon spread to a very different group. It included poor, sick, lame and blind people who gathered each day at the gates of the Temple, hoping that some worshiper might toss a coin their way. "The great Healer has come again," they reasoned. For they remembered that once He had been there and made many people strong and well.

In this picture, we see the people crowding the Temple Court. The outstanding figure is the busy Healer who has again come to Jerusalem. Before Him kneels a man both lame and blind. His face displays faith in the healing touch of the Master.

Behind Jesus, some of His followers look on in wonder. The group across the Court, withdrawn from the needy people, is antagonized and frustrated by the miracles. These men, already enraged by the cleansing of the Temple, hear the voices of children singing, "Hosanna to the son of David." No wonder Jesus said, "Out of the mouth of babes . . . thou hast perfected praise."

bring. Perhaps Jesus called himself a fisherman, catching men for God.

However that may be, before they had come to the shore, Jesus said to them,

"Come with me, and I will make you fishers of men."

And they, who had learned to love this young man from Nazareth, took his offer of companionship. They brought their boat to the land and left it, and through all the rest of Jesus' travels they went with him and were among his most trusted friends.

JAMES AND JOHN

Jesus' mind must have been full that day of the thought of gathering a group of companions. A little way farther along the shore there was another company of his fisher friends. They were two brothers, James and John, with their father Zebedee. They all sat in their boats, tied up close to the shore, busy mending their nets. Jesus stopped to talk with them. Perhaps he asked them also to become fishers of men, along with their friends, Simon and Andrew.

At least, he invited them to come with him, and they accepted. So five men walked on down the shore of the little lake: Jesus and four friends who loved him so well that they were willing to give up other things and go about with him.

These four, Simon and Andrew, James and John, always remained Jesus' closest friends; and John became known especially as "the disciple whom Jesus loved."

PHILIP AND NATHANIEL

Two more of the disciples were friends before Jesus chose them, Philip and Nathaniel. In the Gospel of John we are told how Jesus called them.

At one time Jesus was again among the people to whom John preached. Philip and Nathaniel were also there. They also were among those who were looking for their coming Messiah. Jesus may have had long talks with Philip. In some way he came to feel that he knew him and could trust him.

When the time came for him to go back to his home he hunted up Philip and said, "Come with me"; and Philip consented. But before they started he went off to find his friend Nathaniel.

"I have found the man of whom the prophets wrote!" exclaimed Philip.

Now Nathaniel felt, quite rightly, that when any one, even his good friend Philip, made such a claim as that he had best be cautious.

"Indeed?" he said. "Who is he?"

"Jesus," Philip replied, "who comes from Nazareth, the son of Joseph the carpenter."

"Nazareth!" said Nathaniel. "That town! Can any good thing come out of Nazareth?"

"Come and see," Philip answered. "Don't take my word for it. Come and see for yourself."

So Nathaniel came, doubtful of the enthusiasm of his friend Philip.

To his surprise, Jesus knew him already.

"This is a true-hearted Israelite," Jesus said.

Nathaniel opened his eyes in astonishment.

"How do you know me?" he exclaimed.

"I saw you praying under the fig-tree," answered Jesus.

What that meant between the two neither Jesus nor Nathaniel ever said, but in some way it showed Nathaniel that Jesus knew what he supposed was secret in his own heart.

Nazareth

(Photographed by Three Lions, Inc.)

NAZARETH of today is much larger than the village in which Jesus grew up as a boy, and where He learned to be a good carpenter. It is located in the hilly country between the Mediterranean and the Sea of Galilee. It was here that Jesus preached His first sermon, in which He declared that He has been anointed to preach the gospel to the poor and was sent to heal the broken hearted. Some of His listeners took objection to His message, "and thrust Him out of the City, and led Him unto the brow of the hill whereon their city was built, that they might cast Him down headlong. But He passing through the midst of them went His way . . ." (Luke 4:29-30).

Nazareth still has its narrow streets and flat-roofed houses as when Jesus lived there. From its hillside one can see much of the province of Galilee; and almost always the sky overhead is blue and radiant in the sunshine.

Philip findeth Nathanael, and saith unto him, We have found Him of whom Moses in the law, and the prophets, did write, Jesus of Nazareth, the Son of Joseph. And Nathanael said unto him, Can there any good thing come out of Nazareth? Philip saith unto him, Come and see. (John 1:45-46.)

CITY OF TIBERIUS
This is one of the important towns on the Sea of Galilee.

"Philip is right. You are the Messiah," he said.

"Do you believe because of this?" Jesus said. "You shall see greater things yet."

In time, both Philip and Nathaniel became members of Jesus' group of disciples.

We have the story of how Jesus called one other man to this group, Matthew, a taxgatherer.

THE DESPISED TAXGATHERERS

Among all the people of the Hebrews none were so despised as the taxgatherers. This was partly because the taxes were gathered for a foreign government. Everybody felt that it was a thing no patriot would do, and they despised any man who did it as a traitor to his nation.

The taxgatherers had a bad name also, because so many of them were dishonest. The government did not ask for a certain tax from each person in proportion to his

property, as governments do now. They demanded a
certain amount from a town or a group of villages and
left the taxgatherer free to collect that, and as much more
as he could. The people expected the publican, or taxgatherer, to be dishonest and oppressive, and he usually
was.

THE GREAT CARAVAN ROAD

There was a great road passing through the towns
near the Sea of Galilee. Along it went shepherds, driving
their flocks to market; country people, with donkey loads
of wheat or straw or firewood; pilgrims going to Jerusalem
to the feasts, as Jesus did when he was twelve; people of
all kinds passing from one town to another. Sometimes
a caravan of slow-stepping, long-necked camels came
by, bearing goods of merchants from far-distant lands.
Sometimes a courier galloped past on his horse, carrying
messages to the governors from distant Rome. Now and
then a band of Roman soldiers marched past, their short
swords by their sides and their shields and breast plates
gleaming in the sun.

THE TAXGATHERER AT CAPERNAUM

Where the road left the city of Capernaum, was a
table with low seats beside it. Here sat the taxgatherer
and his assistants. No merchant could carry any goods
in or out of the city without paying a tax. How people
hated the Jew who sat there collecting the taxes for
Rome! Many a black look he got from his own countrymen as he sat there day after day.

But one man never gave him black looks. He went
in and out of the town, for he lived in it a while with his
mother. Occasionally he even sat down in the shade of
the tree and chatted with the taxgatherer, whose name

BEAUTIES ON THE GALILEE SHORE

What a wonderful experience to rise early and watch the sun come up over the Sea of Galilee to scatter the night! As we walk along some of the beaches, we tread on myriads of tiny pearl-white shells. In the fields, spring flowers of every color nestle in the green grass, and we may pick the big scarlet anemones —the Syrian windflowers—said to be the "Lilies of the Field."

All these beauties of the Galilee shore, the Lord Jesus saw when he dwelt here.

Read Matthew 6:28-34.

was Matthew. Matthew, or Levi—he bore the two names —perhaps told Jesus, as they sat talking there, how lonely he was in spite of the fact that he had a house in town and plenty of money. Nobody wanted to speak to him, and when they dared, they sneered at him and always they turned their faces away when they passed.

"Oh well!" perhaps he said, "I wish the Great King would come. I would like to collect taxes for a Hebrew government."

Then perhaps Jesus said, "God will not pass you by. He cares for you."

And so a friendship grew up between Jesus and the taxgatherer.

THE CALL OF MATTHEW

There came a day when Jesus walked out of the city gate, walked straight up to Matthew, held out his hand and said, "Come with me."

Matthew knew what Jesus meant, for already some of his friends had been gathered. It was astounding that Jesus should call him, whom the rest so despised. But he had no hesitation. If Jesus wanted him, he would come, and all his life long he would follow the man who dared to make friends with the taxgatherer.

He rose up, left his table with its moneys and accounts in the hands of the men sitting with him, and went with Jesus.

We do not know how Jesus called the others, but we may be sure that they were each drawn to him because they had come to love him for his kindness and sympathy.

JUDAS THE MAN OF KERIOTH

They were all from Galilee except one, Judas Iscariot, that is, Judas the man of Kerioth, a town in Judea, in

CHRIST AT AGE OF 30
A painting by H. Hofmann

the south of the country. He was the man who so misunderstood Jesus that at last he proved a traitor to him
and betrayed him to his enemies. At first there must
have been something good in him, or Jesus would not
have chosen him.

Jesus had selected his friends one by one, but he wished
to set them apart publicly, so that all might know they
were his special followers.

THE SOLEMN CALL TO SERVICE

One day, when a great crowd had gathered, he went
up on a little hillside and sat down. Then he began calling
these men by name, one by one, and they went up on the
hillside with him. It was a great, solemn day when he
made choice of them. They were the first ministers of the
Christian church. To this day the work of the ministers
is the same as theirs: to try to understand Christ, and
then to get the people to understand him also.

The names of those whom Jesus called to be apostles
are as follows:

THE COMPANY OF THE APOSTLES

Simon, whom he called Peter; that is, the Rock.
Andrew, his brother.
James, the son of Zebedee.
John, his brother.
Philip.
Nathaniel, his friend, also called Bartholomew.
Matthew, the Publican.
Thomas.
James, the son of Alphaeus.
Thaddeus.
Simon, the Zealot.
Judas Iscariot.

QUESTIONS

What does "disciples" mean?
How did Jesus call Simon and Andrew to be disciples?
Who was Matthew before he became a disciple?
How many disciples were there?
Can you be a "learner" of Jesus?

JESUS IN HIS OLD HOME

THE OLD FRIENDS AT NAZARETH

Jesus had not been long in his work before he began to wish to see his old home, Nazareth, and to tell his Good News to his old friends there.   So he planned a visit.

He must have had many friends in Nazareth. There were men with whom he had played when they were boys together, householders and farmers for whom he had made tables and ox-yokes, old men whom he had heard read the Scriptures in the synagogue on the Sabbath, boys and girls whom he had watched grow up since they were little toddlers playing about the door of his carpenter shop.

A STREET OF NAZARETH

This is a street in Jesus' old town of Nazareth. Perhaps the Roman soldiers marched along this paved street in Jesus' time.

He wanted to attend the synagogue once more, as he had for so many years, ever since he could remember. Perhaps he wanted to introduce his new friends who were traveling with him to the old friends of his boyhood. Above all, he wanted to tell them about the Kingdom of God and how they could enter it.

A HOCKEY GAME IN PALESTINE

The children of Palestine have little time for playing. These boys are playing a game somewhat resembling hockey.

Games of children are not very often mentioned in the Bible but we may be sure that the little girls had dolls and that the children played in the streets as they do now. Jesus referred to some game of children when he said, "I have piped and ye have not danced."—*Luke 7:32*.

Jesus loved his old home and the people who lived there. He sometimes was very tired, with the crowds and the people constantly coming and going. As he came up the long hill toward Nazareth he must have thought,

"Now I can have some rest."

He must have enjoyed seeing all the friends of the old days. How long he stayed there and how much rest he had we do not know. The end of his visit was a sad break with the town he loved so well.

IN THE OLD HOME CHURCH

When the Sabbath came, Jesus went to the synagogue, just as he always had done. Sometimes when people have been long away from a town, the thing they want most is to go to church once more in the same old church they went to when they were children.

Palestinian Cart Drawn by
a Pair of Oxen

From International Publishing Co., Ltd.

OXEN were beasts of burden from earliest times in Palestine. Oxen are strong and patient, and were invaluable to the Palestinian farmer. The Bible tells that the patriarchs, Abraham, Isaac, and Jacob, had oxen in that far-off day. The Israelites brought oxen with them from Egypt. These were used both for carrying burdens and also for sacrifices. Proverbs 14:4 indicates the importance of oxen to the farmer for it declares, "Where no oxen are, the crib is clean: but much increase is by the strength of the ox." Oxen are still a familiar sight in Palestine.

VIRGIN'S WELL AT NAZARETH

These women have been to the well just as Mary must have gone when she lived at Nazareth. They are balancing the water jars on their heads.

It must have seemed home-like to be within the old familiar walls, and hear the old familiar voices read the Scriptures and lead in the prayers, which they all recited together. Then came the reading of a portion from the prophets. This was not so formal a part of the service as the first reading. Any one might be asked to do it, and, if he wished, to speak.

Every one knew that this young Galilean had been talking to crowds everywhere. It was known also that he had cured sick people. It was told that he, who had worked for years in a carpenter shop right in this town, declared God had sent him to speak to the people.

The leader of the service beckoned to whom he would to come up on the platform and read the Scriptures. Every one wondered what would happen if he beckoned to Jesus; and they were not surprised when he did.

Jesus took the book, which was a roll, in his hands, unrolled it till he came to a certain passage in Isaiah, and read

"The Spirit of the Lord is upon me, because the Lord hath anointed me to preach good tidings unto the meek; he hath sent me to heal the broken-hearted, to proclaim liberty to the captives, and the opening of the prison to them that are bound; to proclaim the acceptable year of the Lord."

Then he gave the book to the attendant and sat down in the teacher's seat.

All the church was quiet. Everybody was hushed, looking to see what he would do. Would he presume to speak from the chair where teachers, so much older than he, had so often spoken in his hearing?

Yes—he was about to speak. Would he tell them not to be discouraged? That at some time in the future this prophecy will surely be fulfilled?

They were not prepared for what he did say.

"This day is this Scripture fulfilled in your ears."

As he went on speaking, they looked at each other in wonder at the words he was speaking.

"IS NOT THIS THE CARPENTER?"

"Is not this the carpenter?" they whispered to each other. "How can he talk of the great day of God having already come? That day means wealth and glory to Israel. If he had a little wealth and glory himself, we could listen better. We know how poor and obscure he is."

Someone muttered loud enough so that he could hear, a proverb, "Physician, heal thyself."

Another person said boldly, "We hear of wonderful works away off in Capernaum. Do some here among us."

Then Jesus looked sad and stopped talking about the wonderful day of God.

He began with another common proverb:

"No prophet has honor in his own country. Do you remember that in the stories of Elijah and Elisha it was not their own people that were benefited, but others? It was a Syrian, not a Hebrew, cured of leprosy; a widow of Sidon, not of Israel, helped in a famine."

Then a growl of anger began to arise. Who was this young carpenter that he should talk that way to them?

THE ANGER OF THE MOB

In less time than it takes to tell it this church-full of people, gathered for worship, had become a mob insane with anger. They pulled him out of the teacher's chair, hustled him out of the building and dragged him toward the brow of a cliff just outside the town.

When a crowd becomes a mob it sometimes does the most cruel things, things that the people would never think of doing at other times. Perhaps nobody in the town really wanted to kill this kindly man whom all knew and many had loved for years, yet that is just what they would have done in a few moments more if their sudden fury had not been stayed.

WELL OF THE APOSTLES

This spring is the only well between Bethany and the Jordan valley. It is called the Well of the Apostles because they must have often stopped to drink from the well on their journeys.

JESUS SORROWFULLY LEAVES HIS OLD HOME

Then something happened. What it was they themselves did not know. They saw Jesus walking back, and the mob fell apart to let him pass. He went down the street, out of the city gate, and they went home, ashamed, let us hope, that they had so profaned the Sabbath Day.

It was a sad end to Jesus' visit. He never came back there to live. One hopes that some of his old friends went to him in other places, and that they listened to what he had to say.

He never had a home again. To the end of his life he was known as "Jesus of Nazareth," in spite of the fact that his own town had driven him out.

"Behold, I stand at the door and knock. If any man will open the door, I will come in and sup with him and he with me."—Read in Vol. 7, p. 77.

QUESTIONS

Why do people like to go back to their old homes?

What in the story shows that Jesus was accustomed to go to church?

What happened when he went to church at his old home?

Why were the people angry with him?

If the people had treated him differently, what could he have done for them?

THE SERMON ON THE MOUNT

HOW JESUS ONCE PREACHED A GREAT SERMON

On one occasion there was a very large crowd around Jesus. They had come from all the towns and villages on both sides of the Sea of Galilee and even from Jerusalem, far off in the South, and from the cities of the seacoast, Tyre and Sidon, far off in the north.

It was at this time he went up on a hillside and publicly chose his apostles. Then he came down a little lower on the hillside, where the people could all hear him speak, and gave what is called

Head of the Madonna — Detail from Madonna del Cardellino

By Raphael Sanzio (1483-1520)
In the Uffizi Gallery, Florence, Italy
Color Photograph by Alinari Brothers, Florence

THIS detail is from the beautiful MADONNA DEL CARDELLINO or MADONNA OF THE GOLDFINCH. The entire painting contains the three figures of Mary and the holy children, Jesus and John the Baptist. The Christ child is stroking a goldfinch which the infant John holds, hence the name of the picture. From this photograph we can appreciate the indefinable charm and delicate religious feeling of the characterization. The quiet and beauty of the landscape but echoes the divinely human loveliness of the mother of our Lord.

This picture was painted about 1506 by Raphael as a wedding present for a Florentine friend, Lorenzo Nasi. Raphael was then twenty-three years old and had been in the great art-center of Florence for two years. Two years later, 1508, he was called to Rome by Pope Julius II, who was then employing Michelangelo. There his genius expanded to its full measure. Yet this painting from Raphael's early days in Florence ranks among his most perfect creations.

The spirit of gracious charm and serenity that speaks to us from Raphael's paintings, early and late, is the same that characterized his life. For once in the history of the human race, Plato's dream was realized, and the world saw a painter whose own beautiful nature was in perfect harmony with his art. His creations, "like a healthgiving breeze from a purer region, draw the soul insensibly into likeness and sympathy with the beauty of reason." Michelangelo's stupendous creations may impress us more profoundly. The magic of Leonardo's art may attract us by a more subtle spell. But Raphael, by his genius for assimilating the best around him and for transforming it into a language all could understand, appeals to the whole of mankind.

THE SERMON ON THE MOUNT

He began with the Blessings, or Beatitudes:

"Blessed are the poor in spirit: for theirs is the kingdom of heaven.

"Blessed are they that mourn: for they shall be comforted.

"Blessed are the meek: for they shall inherit the earth.

"Blessed are they that hunger and thirst after righteousness: for they shall be filled.

"Blessed are the merciful: for they shall obtain mercy.

"Blessed are the pure in heart: for they shall see God.

"Blessed are the peacemakers: for they shall be called the children of God.

"Blessed are they which are persecuted for righteousness' sake: for theirs is the kingdom of heaven.

"Blessed are ye when men shall revile you, and persecute you, and say all manner of evil against you falsely, for my sake.

"Rejoice, and be exceeding glad: for great is your reward in heaven: for so persecuted they the prophets which were before you."

HOW TO BE HAPPY

People often ask, "How can I be happy?" These blessings are Jesus' answer. You are not made happy by what you get, but by what you are. The key to a blessed life lies in your heart! It is not having money or the things money will buy. It is being merciful and pure in

heart. Even he who suffers because he has done right
is blessed.

Jesus went on to say how real righteousness is not
merely doing what is right, but thinking what is right.
He said, "You have heard it said, 'You must not mur-
der.' I say, 'You must not be angry. You must not be
revengeful. You must love every one, even your enemies.'"

"LOVE YOUR ENEMIES"

Jesus said some things in this sermon that make
people stop and think. "Love your enemies" is one of
them. How can any one love an enemy? How can he
love a person who hates him and does him wrong?

When you love any one, you want the best things for
him. You are willing to help him to the best things. Now
instead of wanting the worst things to happen to those
who do you wrong, you can want the best things to happen
to them. That is what Jesus did. When he was crucified
he prayed for those who were killing him, "Father, forgive them." You can do that for your enemies.

Jesus gave the golden rule in this sermon:

THE GOLDEN RULE

**"Whatsoever ye would that men should do to
you, do ye even so to them."**

He spoke of prayer and fasting, which was a part of the
worship in his time. He said that worship was not a
show, to be seen by men, but was just between God and
man. All righteousness was a matter of a man's own
heart.

This faith leads to trust in God. Look at the flowers
and the birds. God takes care of them. If one will seek
first the Kingdom of God, then God will take care of him.

MOUNT OF THE BLESSINGS

Perhaps wild flowers of all colors were growing thick on this daisy bank beside the Sea of Galilee on the day when the Saviour, seeing the multitudes, went up and sat on a mountainside, and, opening his mouth, taught them many blessings.

Do you know The Blessings, or The Beatitudes? Can you recite them? Some people say that this is the very mount upon which the Saviour sat, and they call it the Mount of The Beatitudes. See page 249.

Read Matthew 5:12, Volume 7:93-95.

So that the people would know how to pray, Jesus gave them a model prayer. It is called the Lord's Prayer.

THE LORD'S PRAYER

Our Father, which art in heaven,
Hallowed be thy name,
Thy Kingdom come.
Thy will be done in earth,
   as it is in heaven.
Give us this day our daily bread.
And forgive us our debts,
   as we forgive our debtors.
And lead us not into temptation,
   but deliver us from evil:
For thine is the kingdom, and the
   power, and the glory, forever.
Amen.

Even though this is a perfect prayer, it is not enough just to speak the words. As we are praying we must think what the words mean and wish the things for which the prayer asks.

Notice that the prayer begins with three requests about God. Next, it asks four things for ourselves and then returns to God for the ending thought. This is a good example to follow in all our prayers.

You can read it from the Bible text in Volume 7, page 100.

BETHPHAGE

The Lord Jesus on that first Palm Sunday came here to Bethphage, on a slope of the Mount of Olives. And from here, on "an ass and a colt the foal of an ass," he "King of Kings and Lord of Lords," in lowly state rode down the Mount of Olives to a gate in Jerusalem's wall.

LITTLE WORD PICTURES

Jesus said things in this sermon in a way to make people remember them. He drew little pictures in words. He said: "A city that is set on a hill cannot be hid"; "Men do not gather grapes from thorns, or figs from thistles"; "If your boy asks for bread, will you give him a stone?"

He put his thoughts in pictures. He said, "Don't take revenge," but this is how he said it: "If any one hits you on the right cheek, turn the left to him. If any one makes you go a mile with him, go two."

But still he knew that some would listen to him and go away and forget it all; and that some who remembered what he said would not try to act on it. So he closed his sermon with the story of the two builders, one wise and one foolish.

THE TWO BUILDERS

"Every one, therefore, that heareth these words of mine and doeth them shall be like a wise man who built his house upon a rock;

And the rain descended
And the floods came
And the winds blew
And beat upon that house,
And it fell not, for it was founded upon
    a rock.

"And every one that heareth these words of mine and doeth them not shall be like a foolish man who built his house upon the sand;

And the rain descended
And the floods came
And the winds blew
And beat upon that house,
And it fell; and great was the fall thereof."

—Now turn to Vol. 7, p. 93 and read the full text.

QUESTIONS

Why is this sermon called the Sermon on the Mount?
What kinds of people did Jesus call blessed?
What is the way to be happy?
How can people love their enemies?
Why is one who does Christ's word like a house built on a rock?
Give the Golden Rule.

BAKER OF PALESTINE

Interior view of a bakery shop in Palestine. The round flat loaves of bread are ready to be put into the oven.

HOW JESUS RAISED A LITTLE GIRL FROM THE DEAD

WAILING:—It was the custom in the East for friends and people hired for the purpose to wail loudly for the dead.

Jesus was talking to a great crowd, as he often did. There were so many people that he had taken them, as he so often did, out on the shore of the Sea of Galilee.

They were listening eagerly to him when there was a movement at the back of the crowd. Someone was trying to push his way through.

Perhaps some said, "Hush. Keep still. Be quiet. The Master is talking."

THE MAN WHO PUSHED THROUGH THE CROWD

But still the man pushed on through the crowd till he came to Jesus. Then he fell down at his feet and began to plead with him.

SERMON ON THE MOUNT
A painting by Robert Leinweber

"Come to my house," he begged. "Come quickly. My little daughter is very sick. She is at the point of death. Come quickly. Come and lay your hands on her. She will live if you only come."

The poor man was almost distracted with his grief.

Now Jesus was always ready to help. He said, "I will come."

So without waiting to finish what he was saying to the crowd, he arose and went with the father.

The man was the minister of the synagogue. Perhaps this was the synagogue at Capernaum where Jesus had attended. Once he had healed a palsied man there, and the minister had seen it. Perhaps Jesus knew him, and had seen the twelve-year-old daughter near his house in the city.

The crowd saw him start off and followed to see what would happen. When they got into the narrow streets of the town, they pressed and crowded about Jesus. Jairus, the father, was impatient to get home. He could hardly wait. His little daughter might be dying now.

THE WOMAN WHO TOUCHED JESUS IN THE CROWD

Then Jesus stopped and turned about in the crowd.

"Who touched me?" he said.

"Master," said the disciples, "the crowd are all about you, pressing on you. Let us go on."

"Some one touched me," said Jesus. "I know that the healing power went out from me to some one."

"I touched you," said a poor woman, frightened and trembling. "I have been sick for years, and have spent all I had on doctors but got no better. I thought if I could only touch the edge of your robe I should be cured."

Jesus said, "Go in peace; be cured of your disease."

Jesus Teaching from a Boat

By Heinrich Hofmann (1824-1911)

In the National Gallery, Berlin, Germany

THIS picture helps us to visualize that time when Jesus walked the countryside of Galilee and, by the beauty of his compassionate personality and courageous teachings, drew crowds of interested listeners wherever he went. At times people came in such numbers that Jesus had to speak from a hillside or, as here pictured, from a boat.

The setting is a rocky, grassy shore of the Sea of Galilee, near a wooded grove. Little children, men, and women make up the company to whom Jesus is speaking. The scene is full of rich variety and human drama.

The most striking figure is that of Jesus. He stands, full of repose and compassion, his open arms including everyone, inviting all to share his wisdom and his love.

In the boat, at the Master's feet, sit two men. These are disciples. The one, young and trusting, is John; the other, older and full of fiery energy, is Peter. Within arm's reach of John is a group of three of whom the kneeling mother is the center. Next we notice the shepherd lad, with his flute and dog, and then the central group of men and women, some seated, some standing. What rapt interest and worshipful love all these individuals reflect as they gaze upon the face of Jesus!

Behind the women is a white-haired man with sightless eyes being guided toward Jesus by a boy. Mark the contrast between this old man's eagerness and the whispering withdrawal of the couple behind him. Likewise what a vivid difference there is between the troubled, suspicious reserve of the Scribes and Pharisees and the restful, loving faith of the women and the disciples. But the Great Teacher speaks to all, promising, "Unto you that hear shall more be given."

Jesus Healing the Sick, another painting by the well-known artist Hofmann, is on page 290.

Winnowing at a Threshing Floor in Palestine

From International Publishing Co., Ltd.

WHEN grain was harvested in Palestine it was brought to the threshing floor where the grain was separated from the chaff by flailing or by being tossed into the air so that the lighter chaff would be blown away from the heavier grain. It was at the threshing floor of Boaz that Ruth made request for Naomi's land (Ruth 3). King David bought the threshing floor of Araunah on which the Temple in Jerusalem was built (II Samuel 24:18–25). John the Baptist saw the judgment as the winnowing of wheat, saying, "And he will thoroughly purge his floor, and gather his wheat into the garner; but he will burn up the chaff with unquenchable fire" (Matthew 3:12).

Meantime the minister stood impatiently waiting. If only this delay would be over and Jesus go on to his house!

Then from down the street came one of the friends whom he had left at home.

"It is too late," he said. "Don't trouble the Teacher any further."

"Oh," thought Jairus, "if we only had not been delayed!"

Jesus turned to him and said, "Come. Only believe."

THE LITTLE GIRL IS DEAD!

It was a sad-hearted man who walked on with Jesus. Jairus could not help being glad the woman was cured. He tried to rejoice with her, but the thought of his little daughter lying dead at home would keep coming in. If they had not been stopped by the woman, perhaps they would have been in time. To be sure, Jesus was coming now, but what was the use?

When they entered the house, the mother and her friends were wailing loudly, as people do in the East after a death.

Jesus said quietly,

"Do not mourn. The little girl is not dead, only sleeping."

THE LITTLE GIRL HEARS THE VOICE OF JESUS

Then he turned all the others away, called Jairus and his wife and three of his disciples, Peter and James and John, and together they went into the room where the little girl lay.

He went up to the bed, took her hand. and said gently, "Little daughter, get up."

She opened her eyes and got up.

Jesus led her to her mother, and while they all stood in amazement, not knowing what to think, he said quietly, "Give her something to eat. She is weak and hungry."

QUESTIONS

Why did the minister of the synagogue come to Jesus?

What was his name?

Why did he want Jesus to hurry?

What happened at the house?

What do you think the minister and his wife said to their friends about Jesus?

STORIES ABOUT THE KINGDOM

TARES:—Weeds.

LEAVEN:—Yeast to make the bread rise.

TREASURE:—People in those days had no safes or banks in which to keep their valuables. In time of war it was the natural thing to hide treasures in this way.

Jesus always had difficulty in making the people understand what he meant by the Kingdom of God.

They meant by it a great empire like the Roman Empire, with a king and a court and soldiers to make other nations submit by force of arms.

He meant the rule of God in the hearts of men, with God the king of life and thought. He meant the willing submission of men to God, because they loved him.

He tried by many ways to help them to understand.

Once he told a group of stories about the kingdom. Let us see if we can tell what he meant by them.

THE ENEMY WHO SOWED TARES

The Kingdom of God is like a man who sowed good seed in his field. At night, while he was sleeping, an enemy came and sowed tares. When the wheat grew

Jesus Healing a Little Child

By Gabriel Cornelius Max (1840-1915)
At National Gallery, Berlin, Germany

HERE Jesus, the Great Physician, gently places his restoring hand upon the head of a sick child. Through the mother's faith the child will be made well. "Freely have ye received" of his kindness, "freely give" of your faith.

The painter of the scene is Gabriel Cornelius Max, a modern German artist. Max was born in Prague in 1840 and died in Munich in 1915. His father, a well-known sculptor, directed his son's early artistic training. The lad was deeply musical by nature but was also early attracted by the beautiful old pictures treasured in the neighboring churches.

His formal artistic studies were begun in 1859 at the Academy of Vienna. Here young Max found his own ideas in conflict with the traditional teachings of the Academy and he remained much by himself. During this period the musicians and painters of the locality were very interested in the artistic problem of interpreting each other's work. Max's natural love of music and this problem of interpreting music in painting gave the young artist the inspiration for his first notable work, a series of twelve sketches illustrating the compositions of Beethoven, Mendelssohn and Liszt. Shortly after this, in 1864, Max became the pupil of Piloty, teacher and director of the Munich Academy. Toward middle age Max withdrew more and more from public life. As time progressed, he developed a melancholy turn of mind and rarely left the quiet of his homes in Munich and Ambacher.

Max was a prolific painter and illustrator and his pictures may be seen today in many galleries of Europe and America.

WOMEN CARRYING BRUSH

These women can hardly be seen under the huge bundles of brush which they are bringing in for fuel.

up, there were the tares, too, growing as fast as the wheat.

The servants of the man said, "Master, your wheat-field is all full of tares. Shall we pull them up so that the wheat will have a better chance?"

The master said, "No. You would pull up the wheat with them. Let them both grow till the harvest. Then I will say to the reapers, "Gather the tares and tie them in bundles and burn them, but gather the wheat into my barn."

He meant that God was not to bring his kingdom by force, coming in and pulling up the evil. That would do more harm than good.

"Be patient," he said to them. "The world contains much evil. Do not think that God will root it out now. That is not the way the Kingdom of God comes."

Then he told them another story. They all knew the mustard plant, which grew very fast in the long summer. Sometimes it became eight or ten feet high, and when the seeds were ripe in the fall the little birds came to eat them.

STAIRWAY STREET IN JERUSALEM

Some of the streets in Jerusalem are so steep that it is necessary to make them into stairways. These are interesting people who are coming down the street in the sunshine. In the foreground is a man who is a merchant, and well-to-do, for he has a warm coat trimmed with fur. He is like the "merchant man" of whom Jesus speaks, who sold all his possessions to buy the pearl of great price.

THE MUSTARD SEED

"The Kingdom of God," Jesus said, "is like the mustard seed, which a man sowed in his field. It is a very small seed, a tiny little speck by the side of a grain of wheat. But when it is sown, the plant from it grows until the birds sit on the branches."

Jesus meant that the Kingdom of God begins like a tiny seed, hidden in the ground, not like a conquering army. He was again trying to make the people see that they should not expect a great king with splendor and much parade. God's kingdom grows hidden in the heart, as a seed grows hidden in the ground.

Then he taught the same thing in another way.

THE YEAST IN THE FLOUR

"The Kingdom of God," he said, "is like leaven, which a woman hid in three quarts of flour till the whole of it was leavened."

Jesus Blessing Little Children

By Bernhard Plockhorst (1825-1907)

THE Bible story which inspired this idyllic painting and the lovely children's song "That Sweet Story of Old" (see Volume 9) is found in Matthew 19:13-15 and in Mark, as given in Volume 7, page 206. The artist has laid the scene at a water-trough in a wooded, grassy place which overlooks a river valley and the rising hills beyond.

Jesus is seated on the stone curb of the trough holding a curly-headed little fellow who has just climbed into his lap, and is laying his hand on the nearer of two children who have run forward eagerly to share the caress. A shy little dark-haired girl still stays close to her mother, but will soon join the others. Just behind this central group, another mother stands, holding on her shoulder her infant son who reaches out baby-fashion, impatient to do what he sees others doing.

In the left foreground, a beautiful, young mother listens to her little boy, who asks her consent to give the kindly man some of the flowers they have gathered. His sister, whose profile only can be seen, is looking up, fascinated by the gentle Stranger. In the left background we see the faces of two disciples, touched by the lovely scene which they had almost prevented from happening.

If you look carefully behind Jesus, you will see a flock of sheep at the watering place. Only the elbow of their shepherd is visible. In the near distance, a woman carrying a water-jar on her head is coming toward the spring. This story-within-a-story is meant to remind us of the work-a-day world in which Jesus moved and taught. The sheep and the shepherd are also symbolical of the loving care that God takes of his people, as explained in the section "Sheep and Shepherds," beginning on page 31.

Another well-known picture by Plockhorst is on page 342, Volume 7.

But because the Kingdom is not the great, splendid empire they had looked for, they were in danger of thinking it worthless. He knew how people are apt to value a thing by the show it makes.

He tried to show them that to have the rule of God in the heart is more valuable than anything else.

THE TREASURE HID IN A FIELD

"The Kingdom of Heaven is like a treasure hid in a field, which a man finds," he said. In those days people often hid their money or jewels in a hole in the ground. Then sometimes they died and did not tell where it was. Years passed and when it was found no one knew to whom it belonged. Sometimes men did find a treasure in a field just as he said.

"Then the man hides it again and goes and sells everything he has and buys the field."

THE PEARL MERCHANT

Again he said, "It is like a merchant seeking fine pearls. At last he finds one, but it costs a great sum. He does not have enough money at hand to buy, but he wants it so much that he goes away and sells everything he has to buy that pearl."

THE KING OF LOVE

Jesus knew that if he had put on the armor of a soldier, and buckled a sword at his side, and sent a trumpeter before him crying, "Make way for the king," hundreds of people would have left their work and joined his army to fight, and perhaps to die. They would have given all they had for the kingdom, if only it had been something they could see.

When Jesus said, "Let God be the king of your hearts and rule over your lives," they were not willing to pay the least price for that.

Are people at present ever like that?

—Read in Vol. 7, pp. 124-130.

QUESTIONS

What did the people mean by the Kingdom of God?
What did Jesus mean?
What was the story of the man with good seed?
What is the story of the mustard seed?
Why is the Kingdom like treasure hid in a field?
What does it mean to have God the king of your heart?

WHO IS THE NEIGHBOR?

PENNY:—A small silver coin.

The people who listened to Jesus fell into the habit of calling him the "Teacher."

One day a learned man stood up in the crowd when Jesus was speaking and said,

"Teacher, what shall I do to win eternal life?"

Perhaps Jesus had been speaking of eternal life. Once he said that God had sent him that men might have eternal life through faith in him their Messiah.

The man asked his question not because he cared to know. He was sure he knew much more about it than Jesus did.. He asked because he hoped that Jesus would say something which the people themselves would think displayed his ignorance.

Jesus answered him very wisely.

"What does the Scripture say?" he replied. "What do you read there?"

The Scripture was what the man was supposed to know best, and he answered readily enough,

"It says, 'Love God with all your heart and your neighbor as yourself.' "

The Good Samaritan

By Rembrandt van Rijn (1606-1669)

THE story of the Good Samaritan, which Jesus told to illustrate the meaning of "Love thy neighbor as thyself," is retold on pages 272-78. Here we see a great artist's interpretation of this beautiful lesson in neighborliness, painted for his countrymen in a familiar setting so that they might immediately perceive its application in their own lives.

The Samaritan and the wounded man have just arrived at the inn. The Samaritan, in turban and long travel cloak, pauses in his conversation to watch the two servants carrying the sick man toward the inn. Another servant, holding the Samaritan's horse, stands on tiptoe to see, while curious guests look out from the window of the inn. Notice, too, the action of the animals: the horses turning to watch the men, the hen fluttering over to protect her chicks. A quiet, mountainous countryside and walled city are seen in the distance.

Do you feel the spirit of compassion pervading this scene? Do not the interested, helpful actions of the peasants, the sympathetic face of the Samaritan, and the kindly curiosity of the onlookers emphasize both the helplessness of the injured man and the nobility of these acts of human kindness?

Thus does the great Dutch artist, Rembrandt, reveal not only his penetrating understanding of human emotion, but also the spiritual significance of Jesus' teaching. How very simple and sincere is Rembrandt's interpretation in contrast to the aristocratic splendor or sentimentality characterizing the religious pictures by other seventeenth century artists, such as LeBrun, Van Dyke, and Rubens (Volume 7:36, 60, 376). Rembrandt, in thus choosing his settings and characters from the life about him, anticipated later artists' approach to their subjects (see pages 208, 318). Another of Rembrandt's beloved pictures is in Volume 7, page 278.

These were very familiar words to all the people.

Jesus said, "That is right. Do that and you will win eternal life."

The answer was so simple that it made the question the learned man had asked seem silly. Some of the people were ready to laugh at him. He felt that he had made himself ridiculous, and tried to save his dignity by asking another question. "Yes, but who is my neighbor?"

Then Jesus answered by telling a story. To understand it you must know two things. One is that a certain road in the land, from Jerusalem to Jericho, was one much traveled but much haunted by robbers. It went down steep hills, with no towns or villages. On the sides were high rocks and deep valleys where robbers could easily hide, and the road had sharp turns which made it easy for the robbers to come close to the travelers without being seen. Not only in the time of Christ, but for many hundreds of years before and after, the road was famous for the robberies of innocent travelers.

The other thing to know is that the Jews and Samaritans hated each other. The reason went back a long time before the days of Jesus — so long that most people did not stop to ask the reason at all. They both worshiped the same God; but the Samaritans, who lived in the city of Samaria, once the capital of a part of the country, were not allowed to come to the temple at Jerusalem.

As usual when people dislike each other, both sides were to blame; but all that has little to do with the story. The whole story rests on the fact that both hated each other, and never did a kind deed or said a kind word to each other if they could help it.

Here is Jesus' story:

A MAN FALLS AMONG THIEVES ON THE JERICHO ROAD

A man went down the road from Jerusalem to Jericho, and fell among the robbers. They stripped off his clothes and knocked him down and pounded him, so that he could not follow them; and then they went off, leaving him lying on the road half-dead. Now see what happened.

THE PRIEST PASSES BY

A priest came along, going up to take his part in the temple worship in Jerusalem. When he saw the wounded man lying in the road, he said to himself, "There are robbers about. If I go near him he will see me and call, and the robbers will hear him and attack me, too. I will slip by without his seeing me." So he went by as far on the other side of the road as he could.

THE LEVITE LOOKS AND PASSES BY

Then came a Levite, also going up to Jerusalem.

The Levites assisted in the temple worship. Some of them sang in the choir, and some cared for the temple and its contents. This man was on his way to worship God.

When he saw the wounded man he said, "Poor fellow! I will see how badly he is hurt." And he came and looked at him.

"Oh," he said, "It is too bad. I cannot take time to help him. I should be late at Jerusalem if I did"; and he went on, leaving the wounded man in the road.

THE GOOD SAMARITAN

The next person who came was a Samaritan.

Did he say, "Ah! A Jew hurt! Good enough for him"?

CHILDREN OF JERUSALEM
The boy at the right has a tray of flat cakes of bread which he has for sale.

BOY SCOUTS IN PALESTINE
This group of Boy Scouts is composed of boys who have now gone back from America to Palestine. The building is a Jewish school. Many Jewish people returned to the home land with something of the spirit of the exiles from Babylon in Nehemiah's time, to build up the "old waste places," to restore the land to its old beauty and to save it from destruction. This Zionist movement has been greatly strengthened by the change from Moslem to Christian rule. "The wilderness and the solitary place shall be glad for them: and the desert shall rejoice and blossom as the rose."—*Isaiah 35:1.*

Not at all! He got off his beast, took the wounded man in his arms, bound up his bleeding wounds, lifted him on his beast, and walked by his side, holding up the wounded man.

Suppose the robbers came around the turn of the road now! He could not defend himself, and they could take his beast and all his money, and leave both the men helpless on the road.

"IF THINE ENEMY HUNGER, FEED HIM"

Slowly and painfully they went along till they came to an inn. Here the Samaritan got a room for him and took care of him through the night. The next morning he paid their bill and then took out two pence, and said to the inn-keeper, "Take care of that poor fellow. Do what is necessary for him. If you spend more than this I will repay you when I come back."

"Now," said Jesus, "who was the neighbor of the man who fell among the robbers?"

The learned man did not like to say, "The Samaritan"; so he said, "I suppose it was he who helped the man."

Jesus said, "Go and do likewise."

Thus Jesus showed that he was truly worthy to be a teacher, and the people saw it.

What does it mean to be a neighbor to-day?

—Bible text in Vol. 7, pp. 174-176.

QUESTIONS

What question about eternal life did a learned man ask Jesus?
Can you repeat the Scripture he repeated?
Why did he ask, "Who is my neighbor?"
What story did Jesus tell in reply?
How did the story answer the learned man's question?
To whom are you neighbor?
Can you be neighbor to people in Europe or India or China?

THE PRODIGAL SON

One day Jesus told this story.

A certain man had two sons. He loved both of his sons very much. He shared everything he had with them and the two sons worked for their father. But the younger son was not happy. He wanted to go away from home. Finally, he said to his father, "Father, give me my share of the family money now."

The father was sad, but he gave his son the money. In a few days the boy was on his way to a far-off country. There he spent his money to have a good time. He spent it on many foolish things.

As long as he had money, he had friends that were happy to share it with him. But when his money was all gone, his friends left him, too. He could not even buy food for himself. He became very hungry.

There was a famine in that country. There were not many jobs. The only work the boy could find was feeding pigs for a farmer. The boy was so hungry that he wanted to eat the food that the pigs ate.

One day, as the boy sat there with the pigs, he suddenly realized how wrong he had been. He said to himself, "My father's servants have more than enough to eat, and here I am starving! I am going home right now! I will ask him to let me be one of his servants. I am not good enough to be his son."

So the boy started for home at once. His shoes were worn out and his clothes were ragged. He even wondered if his father would let him in the house.

When he came close to home, he saw someone running toward him. It was his father! The father threw his arms around the boy's neck and kissed him. How surprised the boy was!

PRODIGAL SON

By Louis Edouard Dubufe (1820–1883)

This picture shows the prodigal feasting with his boon companions; again he is a swineherd, and the third picture shows him coming back to his father's house, a kneeling penitent, before his aged father.

"Father," he said humbly, "I have sinned against God and against you. I am not good enough to be your son any more. Let me be one of your servants."

But the father did not listen. He called to his servants, "Bring my son the best coat you can find. Put a ring on his hand and shoes on his feet! We will have a fine dinner for my son. We will eat and enjoy ourselves. My son, whom I thought was dead, is home again alive."

So they had a fine dinner and invited all the neighbors. How good the boy felt to be home again!

The older brother was out in the field working and did not know his brother had come home. When he came close to the house, after work, he heard music and the voices of many people. When he found out that his younger brother had come home, he was jealous. He would not go in to the dinner.

So the father came out and said, "Come in and eat with us. Come in and enjoy the dinner."

But the older son said angrily, "All these years I have worked faithfully for you. I never disobeyed you. And yet you never gave me a dinner so that I could have a good time with my friends. As soon as my brother comes home, after wasting all your money, you give him a fine dinner."

The father answered, "Son, you are always with me. All that I have is yours. You can have a dinner any time you like. But your brother is home now and we should celebrate and be glad. I thought he was dead, but he is alive. I thought he was lost, and now he is found."

Jesus also said, "Just so is there joy in Heaven over one sinner who comes back to God."

—Read the Bible text in Vol. 7, pp. 193-4.

THE BOY WITH THE LUNCH BASKET

Two Hundred Pennyworth:—A large sum. Perhaps as much as $200 of our money.

There was a time when Jesus sent his disciples two by two to tell people what he had been teaching. He knew that no matter how great the crowds were, there were many people so busy at home that they could not come to hear him.

When the disciples came back, they had much to tell Jesus, and he had much to say to them. But they found no time for talk because the crowds about were greater than ever, and they found no leisure even to eat.

JESUS AND THE DISCIPLES GO AWAY TO REST

"You need rest," he said to them. "Come away into a desert place for a time."

So he sent away the crowd and took a fishing-boat — for this happened on the shore of the Sea of Galilee — and went straight across the lake to a place without houses on the opposite shore.

CHILDREN AT THE MARKET

These children in their patched clothes are looking eagerly into the open window of a shop. What do you suppose they see? Perhaps it is a bake-shop. They are all probably very hungry.

But the crowd was not to be left that way! It was rather thoughtless of them, when they knew Jesus and his disciples wanted to be alone, but crowds are apt to be thoughtless.

THE CROWD FOLLOWS

They could see where the boat was pointed — a spot just around the upper end of the lake.

Some one said, "If we hurry we can get there as soon as they do."

Some one else said, "Let's go." So all the crowd started up the shore of the lake, across the ford of the shallow river at the upper end, and along the bank on the other side. And sure enough, by

THE SEA OF GALILEE

the time the boat arrived, there was a crowd waiting for them on the grassy slope above the lake.

And so their day of rest was spoiled, and the long quiet talk together was never held.

Perhaps the disciples were annoyed and wanted Jesus to send them back to the other side of the lake again. It was selfish of the people to intrude in this way.

"SHEEP WITHOUT A SHEPHERD"

But Jesus said, "No. I pity them. They are like a great flock of sheep without any shepherd."

Then he went out of the boat and sat down on the grass with them and talked to them. Some of them had brought sick friends, and these he healed.

The disciples were tired and could not get over their disappointment. They said nothing till the sun began to get low and the shadows grew longer. Then they came to Jesus and said, "Isn't it time to send them away now? See how late it is getting. They ought to go around the lake and get their supper. They can buy nothing here. Some of them have come a long way and have no food. They will faint with hunger before long."

They were saying one word for the people and two for themselves, because they wanted the crowd to go and let them rest. But Jesus, instead of taking their side, simply said,

"Give them something to eat yourselves."

They were amazed at his reply. "Shall we go across the lake and buy two hundred pennyworth of bread for them?" they asked. Jesus was asking the impossible.

"How much food have you? Go and see," said Jesus.

THE LITTLE BOY WHO BROUGHT HIS LUNCHEON

"There is one boy here," said Andrew, "who has five little loaves and two small fishes, but what is that for so many?"

What indeed! The little loaves were thin, like rolled-up pancakes, containing not much more than a large biscuit, and the little dried fish were a relish to eat with them.

To their surprise, Jesus treated it very seriously.

"Bring the food to me," he said, "and seat all the crowd in groups up there on the grass."

So they arranged the company in groups of fifty and a hundred, and they looked like a flower garden, with their bright robes against the green grass.

"Give us your food," said Andrew to the boy with the lunch basket.

He did not know what to think of that. He did not want to lose his supper, but if this wonderful teacher had sent for it!

Then his eyes grew big with surprise. The Teacher had the little loaves and fishes in his hands, and was standing, looking up to heaven, and praying God to bless this to the feeding of the people.

> "'TWAS SEED TIME WHEN HE BLESSED THE BREAD
> 'TWAS HARVEST WHEN HE BRAKE"

Then the Teacher began to break the food in his hands and give it to the disciples, and the disciples gave it to the people, and the contents of the boy's lunch basket fed all that crowd—twelve thousand of them.

The boy could not understand it at all. So many people fed out of his lunch basket! He was glad he

WINE-PRESS

This is a stone wine-press where the grapes are trodden out. The elderly proprietor has ridden up on his little donkey to oversee operations.

"There was a certain householder, which planted a vineyard, and hedged it round about, and digged a wine-press in it."—*Matthew 21:33*.

brought it along! Then it occurred to him, what if, as he had been tempted to do, he had refused to let the man have his food, and had kept it for himself! Well, perhaps some one else in the crowd would have let the Teacher have a lunch basket, but then he would have lost the satisfaction of feeding the multitude. Anyway, he was glad he had been thoughtful enough to bring a lunch and not too selfish to share it.

THE FOOD THAT WAS LEFT

Soon the supper was over. The men with Jesus were gathering up what was left in baskets. Andrew came to the boy and said, "Here is some of the food left," and to the lad's surprise, Andrew put down by him more bread and fish than the boy had in the first place!

And now Jesus was standing up with his arms stretched out over the people, and asking God to bless them and be their shepherd. Then he sent them away so that they could get to the towns on the other side of the lake before dark.

But instead of doing as he told them, they did a strange thing.

You remember how the people of Jesus' time expected a Great King, a Messiah, who should free them from the Romans and then make a great Jewish Empire. That was the only picture they could form of the Kingdom of God, about which Jesus so often spoke.

Now people all over the country had been questioning if Jesus himself might not be this Great King; and all the crowd had heard it said that he might be.

While they were eating, some one had said, "How convenient it would be if he were the Messiah! He could raise an army to fight the Romans without thinking of how he should feed them!"

CHRIST WALKING ON THE WATER
A painting by Robert Leinweber

The word had spread among the crowd, till by the time the supper was over, everybody was ready to believe that this man was the Messiah.

"BE OUR KING!"

When Jesus dismissed them, instead of going, they all began to shout, "Be our king!" "Be our king!"

Now Jesus had no intention of being a king of that sort. It only showed how they had misunderstood him. But the more he refused, the more they crowded about him, till they were ready to carry him off by main force.

He had to tear himself away from them, and only after he had gone up the steep hill behind them did they quiet down and turn back to the towns on the other side of the lake.

Poor people! They were indeed sheep without a shepherd.

When they were gone, Jesus sent the disciples back in the boat. The hoped-for day of rest had gone, and there was no use in keeping them there any longer.

As for himself, he felt the need of a quiet talk with God, and he went up into the mountain alone to pray.

—Read the complete story in Vol. 7, pp. 150-151; 318-319.

QUESTIONS

Why did Jesus try to go away from the crowd?

When they followed him, what did he do?

How does the story show that Jesus was unselfish?

What food did the boy with the lunch basket have?

What did Jesus do with it?

If you had been the boy with the lunch basket, would you have given it away?

How much was left after the people had eaten?

What do you have that you can share with others?

Why did the people wish to make Jesus king?

Why did he refuse?

Jesus Welcoming the Children

A painting by Robert Leinweber

THERE is a touching incident in the Gospel narrative which inspired this lovely painting. It is recorded in Matthew 19:13-15 and again in the Gospel of Mark in these words:

> "And they brought young children to him, that he should touch them: and his disciples rebuked those that brought them. But when Jesus saw it, he was much displeased, and said unto them, 'Suffer the little children to come unto me, and forbid them not: for of such is the kingdom of God. Verily I say unto you, whosoever shall not receive the kingdom of God as a little child, he shall not enter therein.' And he took them up in his arms, put his hands upon them, and blessed them." MARK 10:13-16

The disciples thought that children were not important enough to claim the Master's attention, but Jesus taught them a never-to-be-forgotten lesson! The child nature is presented by Jesus as the ideal for his kingdom because of its dependence on others, its receptiveness, its capacity to develop, and its freedom from self-consciousness and worry.

Small wonder that the artist should choose this important incident as the subject for his painting.

HOW A POOR WOMAN MADE A GREAT GIFT

MITE:—A very small copper coin, the smallest in use.

She was a very poor woman, and she lived a long time ago in a famous city in the Bible land, called Jerusalem. In that city there was, as you know, the great temple where the people went to worship. All about the temple were open spaces where the people stood and walked about and talked, when the service was not going on.

THE CONTRIBUTIONS OF THE PEOPLE

By the side of one of the doors of the temple were boxes with openings in the top. They were for the contributions of the people. They took the place of the contribution plates that are passed in our churches. Each one stepped up to the great box and put his money in; and some people liked to make a show of it, so that everybody would know that they were giving, and others dropped their gifts in when nobody was looking.

There was one time in the year when much money was given. It was a festival called the Passover, a thanksgiving for the deliverance of the people from bondage. The people, at this festival, remembered how God had cared for their fathers in the time long, long ago, and thanked him for what he had done for them. For days before the Passover, people from all about crowded to the city, for if they could they always came to Jerusalem for the Passover. The open space before the door of the temple was crowded all day, and clink, clink, clink, dropped the money in the great box at the door.

THE POOR WOMAN TO WHOM TROUBLE HAD COME

The poor woman had always been accustomed to give her offering with the rest, but this year it was

going to be harder than ever. Her husband had died,
and the tears came into her eyes when she thought
how last year they had saved and planned together to
make their thank offering, then had gone up to the
boxes together and dropped it in — each of them two
coins, and each coin all the earnings of the man for
two days. They had been glad that they could give so
much to thank God for his good gifts to them. This
year she had not even one of those large coins to drop
in and hear clink in the box. She had not been able to
work much, and, when she did, it was little enough that
she could earn. When she had paid for flour to make
bread and for a handful of dates and for a few sticks of
wood to build a fire, she counted what she had left. It was
only two little coins, which would not have bought five
cents' worth of food: "two mites which make a farthing."

ONLY TWO LITTLE COINS!

But she wanted to say "Thank you" to God.
People are never so miserable but that they can find
something happy, if they look for it. She was a brave,
cheery woman, and she could think of a great many
reasons to thank God. So she wanted to put some
money in the box, just as she always had done. But
it was so little! She would be ashamed to have anybody see her putting it in. She would have to slip up
when nobody was about and hold her hand carefully
so that no one could see how small her gift was!

Then she thought, "No. I am giving what God
has given me. I will not be ashamed even if I am so
poor that my gift is small. I do not think God would
like to have me ashamed of my gift to him."

So the next day she went to the temple. Many
people were there, walking about and talking, and there

The Widow's Mite

By Alexandré Bida (1813-1895)
Lithograph Illustration for the Bossuet
Translation of The Four Gospels

A ND Jesus sat over against the treasury, and
beheld how the people cast money into the
treasury; and many that were rich cast in much. And
there came a certain poor widow, and she threw in
two mites, which make a farthing.

"And he called unto him his disciples and saith unto
them, 'Verily I say unto you, that this poor widow
hath cast more in than all they which have cast into
the treasury.' For all they did cast in of their abundance; but she of her want did cast in all that she
had, even all her living." (Mark 12:41-44.)

The artist, Alexandré Bida, was born in Toulouse,
France. He was a pupil and follower of Delacroix, a
famous teacher in Paris. Between 1844 and 1855 Bida
made three trips to Palestine, and there learned to
depict the life and scenery of the country with great
power. Bida's illustrations of the Gospels, of which
this is one, are well-known and are considered among
his best work. Many of his scriptural scenes are unsur-
passed in force and directness by other contemporary
painters. Bida died at his home in Vosges mountains
near Toulouse in 1895.

In Volume 7, page 86, is another illustration of a
Gospel story by Bida.

was almost a line going up to the boxes. Clink, clink, clink, dropped the money. Sometimes the coins were heavy and the clink was loud, and sometimes the coins were light and the clink was so small you could hear it only a little way.

THE RICH MAN'S GIFT

Here was a rich man in a silken robe going up. He was talking with a group, and he took out a handful of great coins, holding them so that every one could see them, and dropped them in one by one. Clang, clang, clang, they went, and all the people turned to see who was giving so much.

THE RICH WOMAN'S OFFERING

Here was a woman who lived in a fine house not far from the poor widow. She went up with her head high and her new robe rustling about her feet. She waited till others came up, and then she dropped a large silver coin — clink — into the box. And her new robe cost twenty times the great silver coin.

TWO GOLD PIECES FROM THE MERCHANT

A great merchant who had come from a far-away city with a train of camels and servants and taken all the best rooms at the inn, put in two gold pieces, and went away talking about how much money he had made in the last year.

Right after him came the poor widow. She had to wink hard to keep the tears out of her eyes when she thought of how little her gift was, but she walked up bravely, saying to herself, "I will not be ashamed to give as God gives me."

She dropped her two tiny little coins into the box. They were so small that no one except the poor woman herself could hear their clink as they fell to the bottom. Then she drew her old cloak about her — she had not had a new one since she was there a year ago — and hurried away. "No one noticed me," she thought. "I am glad of that."

But some one had noticed her.

Jesus and his friends had come up, with the others, to spend the Passover in Jerusalem. At that very moment he was in the space in front of the temple door. He had been talking with his friends, but had stood quiet a little while and watched the people putting their gifts in the box. He saw the rich people giving much, and he saw the poor widow drop in her tiny little gift.

THE GREATEST GIFT OF ALL

And he saw that her gift was the greatest of them all. He turned to his friends and said, "That poor widow has given more than any of the rest. They have given a little out of their riches; she, out of her poverty, has given all she had."

This is how the Bible tells the story:

THE BIBLE STORY

"And Jesus sat over against the treasury, and beheld how the people cast money into the treasury; and many that were rich cast in much. And there came a certain poor widow and she threw in two mites which make a farthing.

And he called unto him his disciples, and saith unto them, 'Verily I say unto you that this poor widow hath cast more in, than all they which have cast into the treasury: for all they did cast in of their abundance; but she of her want did cast in all that she had, even all her living.'"   —Mark 12:41-44.

The Triumphal Entry

By Bernhard Plockhorst (1825-1907)

THE first Palm Sunday, which this painting helps us to visualize, is described on pages 299-304. The Bible story recorded in Matthew, Mark and Luke, is given in Volume 7, pages 217-8.

For some time preceding this eventful day, Jesus and his twelve disciples had been making a teaching tour, starting in the north and gradually coming south towards Jerusalem. Day after day, many people came to hear the Master's wonderful teachings and many were healed of their illnesses. So, by the time the little company had reached Bethany, two miles from Jerusalem, the whole countryside was clamoring for Jesus to be their king.

Jesus perceived that the people misunderstood; he was not their earthly king, but their spiritual king. However, inasmuch as it had been prophesied: "Thy king cometh, meek, and riding upon an ass," in this manner would he enter Jerusalem, proclaiming to all men his Messiahship. This was a great day and all Jesus' friends gathered "to rejoice and praise God . . . saying, 'Blessed be the King that cometh in the name of the Lord.' "

Here is pictured the moment when the triumphal procession enters the gates of Jerusalem. The Saviour advances on a white ass, the animal which Oriental rulers always rode, raising his hand in a gesture of blessing. Doves of peace hover overhead. Jesus is gazing straight ahead, beyond the joyous children, the worshiping friends, the "sore displeased" scribes, and with gentle sadness, is thinking of how much more needs to be accomplished before God's Kingdom is established on earth.

Plockhorst, who painted many well-known religious pictures and traveled in Palestine, settled in Berlin, where he lived to the age of eighty-two.

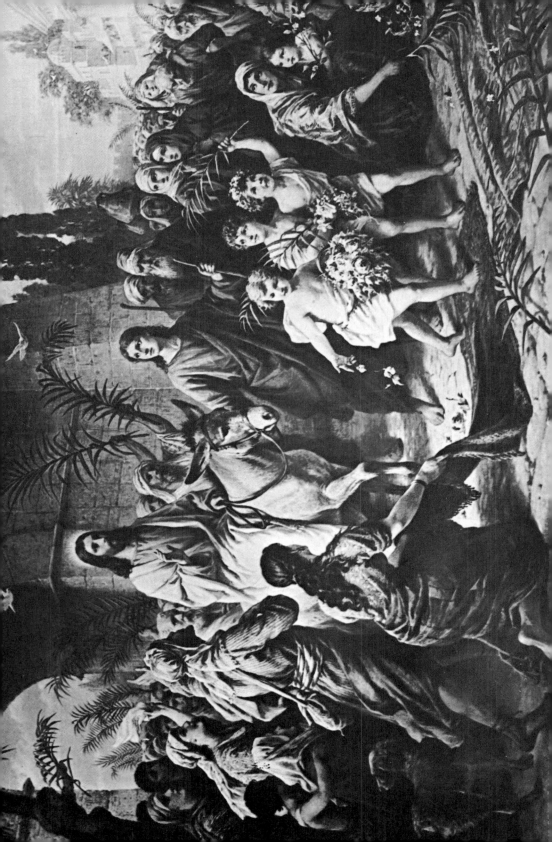

THE TRIUMPHAL ENTRY

THE GREAT FEAST

Jesus had come to Jerusalem. Many others had come, too, for it was a great feast, called the Feast of Passover. It was a time when all who could, came to the services in the temple. Jesus himself was brought to the feast by his parents when he was twelve. Jews who lived in other countries came when they were able.

Thousands of people were there. Some were friends of Jesus. More knew only a little about him. Some had never heard of him.

Jesus was not staying in Jerusalem, but with friends in a village outside the city, called Bethany.

One morning he said to two of his disciples, "Go over into the village close by, and you will find an ass tied, with a colt near by. Bring it here. If any one asks what you are doing, say it is for me, and they will let it come."

The disciples went and brought the ass to Jesus at Bethany. They spread their robes on it for a saddle and Jesus mounted and started for Jerusalem.

In those days soldiers and officers of the government rode on horses, but people who were going on business usually rode on asses. In the ancient times the kings of Israel had ridden asses, so that it was natural for Jesus to go to the city in this way.

"THY KING COMETH"

Some of his disciples remembered that in one of the old books of the Bible there was a promise of a future king of Israel: "Thy king cometh, meek, and riding upon an ass."

One of them whispered the words to another, and said, "See! He is to be the Great King."

Soon they were all saying to each other,

"He is the King."

"At last! We have waited so long!"

"He wouldn't be the King before. Now he is ready."

"Here in Jerusalem! That is how it should be. Here in our old city, where the kings used to reign!"

As Jesus rode on, his friends called to their friends,

"Come follow the King of Israel!"

ON THE ROAD FROM BETHANY

The crowd grew greater as they passed out of Bethany. They were greatly excited. Now, at last, Jesus would claim to be the King they had so long waited for.

Jesus knew how they misunderstood him. Just now he cared less for that than for their love and friendship.

Meantime he had friends also among the people who had come to the feast and were staying in Jerusalem. They had been asking about him.

"Will he come to Jerusalem?" they asked each other.

"I heard he had started," said one.

"They say he came through Jericho, on the way here," said another.

By and by came one, a friend of Jesus, who had come early from Bethany.

"He stayed in Bethany yesterday," he said. "He will be coming into the city this morning."

It ran through the crowd like wild-fire.

"He is coming into the city this morning."

"He must be on the way."

"He will be in the city this morning."

Then another word went through the crowd. "Let us go out and meet him."

And all his friends were soon saying, "Come. We will meet him."

THE CROWDS POUR OUT TO MEET HIM

Out of the city gate they poured, down into a valley, up the hillside beyond, men and women and little children who had heard him speak near their homes. One said, "I heard him say, 'Come unto me and I will give you rest.'"

And another, "I saw him heal a lame man once."

And another, "I was sick and he made me well."

And another, "He took my little Rachel in his arms, and I want to see him again."

All these were strangers who had come for the feast; but some of the people of the city saw the crowd go out and went along to find out what would happen.

Some one in front called out, "I see him in the road up the hill! What a crowd is with him! We must hasten if we wish to see him."

One of those with Jesus looked down the road at the same time and said, "There come friends of ours up the hill. They must be coming to meet the Master."

The two companies met on the hillside. Many of them knew each other, and there was great rejoicing. Most of all they rejoiced that they were taking their Master to the city to be the Great King.

They honored him in every way they knew how. Some of them spread their loose robes on the road for him to ride over. Some broke off the great leaves of the palm-trees and strewed them in the way. Some

VIA DOLOROSA

Along this street went Jesus on the day of his crucifixion carrying his cross. That is why it is called "Via Dolorosa," "Street of Sadness." At different points on this street, localities are marked and they are called stations of the cross. At one point Simon of Cyrene took the cross from the shoulders of Jesus. At another point Pilate said, "Ecce Homo," "Behold the Man," and so on, until the dark hill of Calvary was reached.

carried the palm leaves before him, as though he were a great conqueror come from a war. And the crowd that went before him and that followed shouted and sang.

"Hosanna to the son of David! Blessed is he that cometh in the name of the Lord! Hosanna in the highest!"

And all the little children who had come with their parents jumped and ran about and shouted, "Hosanna," so that some said to Jesus, "Tell the children to stop."

But he refused to tell them to stop.

"If they stopped, the very stones would shout," he said. This was a day of joy, and he would do nothing to make the joy less.

INTO THE CITY OF DAVID

So Jesus rode on, with the shouting crowd about him.

They came into the city. The people stared at these strangers.

"Who are they?" they asked.

"ECCE HOMO" ARCH

"Some fishermen and farmers from Galilee," was the reply.

"Who is the man riding?"

"A carpenter's son, who has been teaching among them. They think he is to be the Great King!"

There was not room for a crowd in the narrow streets, and soon it fell away. Jesus went into the temple with the others, and later returned to Bethany. So this was a day of happiness and triumph for Jesus. The church has always remembered it and in later years it has celebrated this day, and called it "Palm Sunday."—Read the Scripture text in Vol. 7, pp. 217-218; 360-362

QUESTIONS

How did Jesus come into Jerusalem?
Why were so many people there?
What did his friends wish Jesus to do?
Can you tell why he did not do it?
What did the children do?
What is Palm Sunday?

HOW THE LEADERS OF THE PEOPLE KILLED THEIR BEST FRIEND

THE HATRED OF THE LEADERS

Some of the people loved Jesus very much. Some of the leaders of the people disliked him. At last the dislike grew more and more till they planned to kill him. Why should they have disliked so good a man?

It was partly because they misunderstood him. Like his friends, they thought he would try to be king. They thought he was not the rightful king, but was only leading the people astray. If he claimed to be king, he would, they thought, gather an army and try to free the Jews from Rome. Then the Romans would come and destroy the city and the nation. It was better that he should die before he brought all this trouble on his country.

They did not know that Jesus had no wish to be a king of that sort.

Then, too, Jesus taught things which did not agree with their teaching. He did not come to learn of them. He dared to differ from them. He told the people that the righteousness they taught was not enough. When the people flocked to Jesus, the teachers and leaders of the nation feared they would lose their influence.

All this made the leaders jealous of Jesus. Jealousy is very bad, and makes people willing to do very wrong things.

So the leaders went to the Roman governor and told him that Jesus was plotting against the government, trying to make himself king.

The governor gave them a band of soldiers to arrest Jesus. They wanted to do it quietly, so that his friends would not make trouble.

THE TREACHERY OF JUDAS

Here comes one of the sad parts of the story. One of Jesus' disciples, named Judas, proved himself to be such a terrible traitor that he was willing to help arrest him.

After Jesus came out from the last supper he went to a garden with great trees, called Gethsemane, and prayed. Judas knew that Jesus sometimes went there, and he came with a band of soldiers. As he expected, he found Jesus there. He went to him, greeted him, and kissed him. That was a sign to the soldiers, and they came up and arrested Jesus.

AT THE HOUSE OF CAIAPHAS

It was late at night, for Jesus had been talking long with his disciples, but he was allowed no rest. First he was hastened to the house of Caiaphas, the high priest.

Among the Jews there was a council which judged the cases of criminals. Messengers were sent out to the members of this council saying,

"Come quickly, Jesus has been taken."

Before the day dawned the judges gathered. In the flickering light of the torches they gathered about him and asked him questions, trying to find something against him. They sought for people who had heard him say something wrong. They did not try to be fair. They tried to find some way of condemning him; but they were not able to find it.

VIA DOLOROSA—PILATE'S ARCH

Jesus had two other trials. Both were before noon on that day. Both were unfair.

THE TRIALS BEFORE HEROD AND BEFORE PILATE

One trial was before a ruler named Herod, who ruled over Galilee, where Jesus lived. The other was before the Roman governor, Pilate, who was the ruler of Jerusalem and the country about.

THIS IS THE MAN
A painting by Robert Leinweber

Pilate wanted to release Jesus. He saw that the Jews had accused him of being an enemy of Rome only because they were jealous of him. He talked with Jesus, and then went out to the Jews and said,

"This man is innocent. I will release him."

By this time the enemies of Jesus had gathered a great mob, who stood before the governor's door with the Jewish leaders.

THE MOB DEMANDS THE DEATH OF JESUS

When they heard Pilate say he would release Jesus they all shouted,

"No! No! Crucify him! Crucify him!"

Some one in the crowd called out, "This man wants to be king. If you let him go, you are no friend of the Roman Emperor."

Pilate was afraid as he watched the angry mob. He saw they were bent on Jesus' death, and he did not dare to displease them. They might report to Rome that he was not doing his duty, and he would lose his office. He cared more about keeping his office of governor than he did about doing right; so he gave in to them, did what they wanted, and sent Jesus to be crucified.

PILATE WASHES HIS HANDS BEFORE THE MOB

But he wished them to know he believed Jesus innocent. He did a curious thing. He brought out water and a wash basin and washed his hands before the mob.

"This is to show you," he said, "that I am not responsible for the death of this man. You must take the blame."

"We will take the blame," shouted back the mob.

Jesus was taken out of the city and crucified at a

place called Golgotha, "The Place of the Skull." Two robbers, who had also been condemned to be crucified, were taken and put, one on his right side and one on his left. So Jesus died between two criminals.

Crucifixion was a most painful, cruel, and shameful death. Jesus had told his disciples how he would die, and in the Old Testament, too, we read of the coming of the Messiah, "the Redeemer," to atone for the sins of all mankind in his death.

THE UTTERANCES OF THE SAVIOUR ON THE CROSS

In the four gospels will be found the records of seven utterances of Jesus during the time he hung on the cross (see Volume 7: 402.) Significant of the supreme purpose of his death were his words to the penitent thief, "Today thou shalt be with me in Paradise," and his prayer for those responsible for his execution, "Father, forgive them, for they know not what they do." Thus died Jesus the Messiah, the Son of God, and the world's Saviour.

QUESTIONS

Why did the leaders dislike Jesus?
How was Jesus arrested?
Who was Caiaphas?
Who was Pilate?
Did Jesus have a fair trial?
What did Pilate think of Jesus?
Why did he order him to be crucified?
What did Jesus say, on the cross, about his enemies?
How can we be like Christ?

—Read the full record in Vol. 7:244-264; 372-401.

THE GLAD STORY OF THE RESURRECTION

JOSEPH OF ARIMATHAEA

Not all the council of the judges had agreed to the condemnation of Jesus.

One of those who did not agree was a man named Joseph, who lived at a village, Arimathaea, near Jerusalem. He was one of the people waiting for the kingdom, and hoped that Jesus would be the king. He had been a friend of Jesus, and his friendship did not fade away because Jesus' enemies had killed him.

He went to the Roman Governor, Pilate, and asked to have the body of this crucified man.

Pilate cared little what became of the body of a criminal. If Joseph was a friend and wanted to give burial, he might.

THE TOMB IN THE ROCK

Outside Jerusalem were tombs carved out of the rocks. Some of them were like little rooms, with places on the sides where bodies were laid. Often the door of the tomb was a round wheel of solid stone which could be rolled before the opening. Such tombs were costly, and only rich men could afford them.

Now Joseph had such a tomb near Jerusalem. It was newly carved in the rock. A few days before, Joseph would have laughed with scorn had he been told that the first body to lie in the tomb would be that of a man who had died the disgraceful death of crucifixion, but now he reverently prepared the body of Jesus for burial, wrapping it in cloths as the Jews always did, and laid it in his own new tomb. He was not ashamed to let it be known that he loved and honored Jesus.

JESUS CARRIED TO THE SEPULCHRE
A painting by Robert Leinweber

The friends of Jesus knew where he was buried. It was then late on the day before the Sabbath.

The Jews kept the Sabbath very strictly; and the friends of Jesus would not even visit the grave on that day. They were very sad. They had believed firmly that Jesus was to be the Great King — and now he was dead! All their hopes were gone.

They did not know that God was going to make Jesus honored far more than if he had been King of the Jews. They thought everything was over.

But they still loved Jesus; and loving is often more important than knowing.

So after the sad Sabbath, some of them went out to the tomb very early on the next morning.

THE STONE IS ROLLED AWAY FROM THE TOMB

They found the stone rolled away from the door, and an angel sitting by it.

"You seek Jesus," he said. "He is not here, he is risen."

IT WAS JESUS HIMSELF!

They hurried away to tell the rest of his friends; but one, a woman named Mary, waited. Soon she saw some one coming toward her.

She said to herself, "Here is the gardener," for the entrance to the tomb was in a garden.

"Sir," she said, "if you have taken him away, tell me where you have put him."

"Mary," said he.

Then she knew his voice. It was Jesus himself!

He sent her to tell his disciples that he was risen.

At first they did not believe it, but Peter and John came to the tomb to see, and, sure enough, the tomb was open and the body of Jesus gone.

Women at the Tomb

By William Adolphe Bouguereau (1825-1905)

In the Museum of Antwerp, Antwerp, Belgium

THE story of this Resurrection morning scene is found on pages 310-2 and the Bible text, in Volume 7, page 271. The artist has followed Mark's account. We see the two Marys and Salome, dressed in deep mourning, at the opening of the sepulchre. One, holding the basin of "sweet spices," kneels and peers intently into the lighted tomb, while another kneels, and the third stands, supporting herself against the sidewall.

After the tumultuous emotions of the last few days, all are overcome with this awesome discovery that their Master's body is gone. What does it mean? The young angel, "clothed in a white garment," greets them with uplifted arm and comforts them with his immortal words: "Be not affrighted: Ye seek Jesus of Nazareth which was crucified: he is risen; he is not here."

The artist, Bouguereau, was born in La Rochelle, France. He had to begin supporting himself at an early age, but the desire to study art was so intense that, finally, in spite of his father's opposition, he went to live with an uncle in Bordeaux. Here he attended evening drawing classes and soon became the best draughtsman in the class. In 1846 young Bouguereau went to Paris to study with the famous teacher Picot. He worked indefatigably and early found the artistic line which he wished to follow, that of traditional, classical art, and never swerved from it throughout his long and honored career.

In 1850 Bouguereau won the coveted Grand Prix de Rome of the Ecole des Beaux Arts, which gave him four years of study in Italy. The Italian influence is evident when one compares this picture with that of his contemporary, Barabino (Volume 7:132). Although Bouguereau was well-known for his mythological and allegorical decorations, his meditative temperament found its truest expression in religious subjects. He died in his native city in 1905.

THE WALK TO EMMAUS

That afternoon two of the friends of Jesus were going to a village called Emmaus, over the hills about five miles from Jerusalem. Their minds were full of sadness over what had happened, and they talked of it as they walked along.

A stranger joined them, and asked what made them look so sad.

"Have you been in Jerusalem," they asked, "and do not know the things which have happened?"

"What things?" said he.

"About Jesus of Nazareth," they replied. "We had hoped he would be the Great King, and now he is dead."

Then the stranger began talking with them, and tried to show them that Moses and the prophets had predicted in the Old Testament how the Messiah must suffer and die for man's sin, and rise again from the dead. And they began to see, as they had never seen before, that the triumph of God's great plan need not be with bloody battles or gleaming swords, but may be found in humility and suffering.

At last they came to Emmaus. "Stay with us and tell us more," they said.

The stranger seemed to want to go on, but they urged him, and he stayed.

Till supper time they talked, and then, as they sat at table, the stranger took some bread in his hand and looked up to heaven and asked God's blessing on their supper —

Then they knew him! It was Jesus their Lord!

They looked at each other in astonishment, and when their eyes turned to him again — he was no longer there.

"Ah," they said to each other, "how our hearts burned as he talked with us on the way!"

Back they started for Jerusalem that very night, to tell the rest that they had seen Jesus. When they came to the others, the first thing they heard was,

BEGGAR BOY

This is one of the sturdy beggars who abound all over the East. This boy certainly looks able to be at school or at work.

"Jesus is risen! Peter has seen him."

He appeared to others of his friends, so that they all came to realize that Jesus was not dead, after all. Death could not hold him. "He is risen, as he said!"

The disciples of Jesus went out to tell others of him, not as a man who had been defeated and killed, but as a man whom God had raised from the dead, and who ever lived with God. Christ never can be defeated.

Christians called the day of Christ's resurrection, Easter.

Easter is a day of joy and thanksgiving for all the world, for it means that Jesus is stronger than death. The disciples went out after Easter to tell the good news of the resurrection.

"And he led them out as far as to Bethany, and he lifted up his hands, and blessed them.

"And it came to pass, while he blessed them, he was parted from them, and carried up into heaven.

"And they worshiped him, and returned to Jerusalem with great joy: And were continually in the temple praising and blessing God. Amen." —Turn to Vol. 7 and read pages 267-279.

The Visit to Emmaus

By Léon Augustin Lhermitte (1844-1925)
In the Boston Museum of Fine Arts, Boston
From a Copley Print, Copyright by Curtis and Cameron

THE scene here represented is the high point of that beautiful story called The Walk to Emmaus which begins on page 315. We read that the risen Christ in the guise of a fellow traveler whose identity is not known joined two of his followers on the afternoon of Resurrection Day as they were walking from Jerusalem to Emmaus. Finding that they were dismayed over the death of Jesus and did not understand why it had happened, the Stranger explained to them its inner meaning and showed how the Scriptures had foretold it. When they came to Emmaus, the men asked this unknown friend to rest and sup with them. At the table, Christ suddenly revealed Himself in that moment when He broke the bread and offered thanks to the heavenly Father. The Saviour then disappeared and the two hastily returned to Jerusalem to tell the disciples there the glad news of what had taken place and the new understanding and hope that the Master's words had brought them.

To picture this moment in all its vivid earnestness the artist has chosen toil-worn, humble peasants like those in his native village in northern France; a modern setting for an event which happened long ago. We see the two wayfarers just when "their eyes were opened," sitting spellbound with devout emotion. The woman and boy serving them are not aware of what is happening. The Saviour sits opposite with head lifted reverently offering thanks. "And it came to pass, as he sat at meat with them, he took bread, and blessed it, and brake, and gave to them. And their eyes were opened, and they knew him; and he vanished out of their sight."

You will find another fine picture by this artist in Volume 7, page 99.

The Followers of Jesus

HOW JESUS' FRIENDS WENT TO PRISON

BEFORE his death Jesus had said to his friends that he would be with them. When they realized that he was not dead but raised again, they were very happy, and believed that he was with them to help them, even though they could not see him.

They knew now that he was the Great King, the Messiah, and that he would come to take his kingdom whenever God was ready to declare him as their king. Meantime it was their duty to make the people see that he was the Messiah.

They never lost a chance to say what they believed and to try to win friends for Jesus.

The disciples stayed on at Jerusalem instead of going home to Galilee. In Jerusalem was the temple, the great church where the people loved to worship God better than in any other place in the land.

One morning Peter and John, who were, you remember, two of the disciples of Jesus, were going into the temple. It was about nine o'clock, when many of the Jews went to the temple for prayer.

THE DISCIPLES HEAL A LAME BEGGAR

At the door of the temple which was called the Beautiful Door, lay a beggar. He was not beautiful. He was so lame that he could not walk at all. Every day friends brought him to this door, and he sat there all day and said to those who went in, "Give to the lame man." "Give to the lame man."

319

In those days there were no hospitals or homes for the blind or the lame, and those who could not work had to beg for a living.

This poor beggar saw Peter and John coming up and reached out his hand to them. Peter said, "We have no money, but we will give you what we have. In the name of Jesus, walk"; and he took hold of his outstretched hand and lifted him up.

The man felt that his feet and ankles had strength in them, and he stood and walked and leaped and loudly thanked God.

The crowd gathered and stared to see the lame beggar whom they had known so long, well and walking. Every one was amazed.

He caught hold of Peter and John. "Here are the men who did it," he shouted. And all the people crowded about, wondering greatly.

Then Peter spoke.

"Do not stare at us so," he said, "as if we had done this by our might or power. God gave Jesus to you, but your rulers would not hear him, and killed him; but God raised him up again. Jesus healed this man. We worked in his name. He is speaking to you in this way, calling to you to repent and let him bless you."

PETER AND JOHN IN PRISON

But soon the officers came to see what all the crowd was about. They were not pleased to hear Peter talking about Jesus, and arrested Peter and John, and put them in prison till the next morning, when they would bring them into court.

That was the first time any of the followers of Jesus had ever been put in prison because of their loyalty to him.

The next morning the court gathered. It was not one judge, but a group of the wisest and greatest of the leaders of the people. It was usually called the Council, and was much reverenced by the people.

The prisoners were brought in and questioned.

BOLD AS LIONS

Then a strange thing happened. Instead of being frightened and humbled by the night in jail and the presence of this great council, they were as bold as lions. Peter began to speak as if, instead of being a fisherman, he had talked to courts of law for years. He knew that very council had condemned Jesus to death. He dared to say that this Jesus, whom they had condemned, was the Great King, and that there was no other way for them to find God except through him.

The council saw that these men knew nothing about the law, but that they had been with Jesus.

They said to the jailor, "Take them out." When the council was alone, they said, "What shall we do? We can't have them talking to the people about Jesus like this. Let us tell them they must not speak of Jesus any more, and let them go."

So they called them in and told them not to speak nor teach in the name of Jesus.

But Peter and John said, "No, we must speak. We cannot but speak of the things we have seen and heard about Jesus."

The council did not dare to put them in jail again, for all the people knew that they had done a good deed to a lame man. So they let them go, and Peter and John and the rest went on telling the people about Jesus.

What do you suppose became of the lame man? The story in the Bible does not say, but I think he, too, must have become a follower of Jesus.

QUESTIONS

If Jesus was the Great King, what did the disciples think they ought to do?

What happened to the lame beggar at the temple gate?

Why were Peter and John put in prison?

What did Peter say when the council told him not to talk about Jesus?

What do you suppose became of the lame man?

—This story in Bible language is found in Vol. 7, pp. 458-463.

CAPERNAUM

PETER AND JOHN HEAL THE LAME MAN
A molding by D. Mastroianni

HOW SAUL CHANGED FROM AN ENEMY TO A FOLLOWER OF JESUS

A JOURNEY TO DAMASCUS

One time a man set out on a long journey. He was going from Jerusalem to a city called Damascus, several days' journey away. But there was no railroad to carry him, nor any wagon, nor any roads on which wagons could go.

He and the men who went along with him made slow progress. They traveled one day, and another day, and yet another. They saw caravans of merchants with great, slow-moving camels. They met messengers of the government riding on swift horses. They saw men going to the towns from the little villages of farmers, with grain and fruits on their donkeys. Every night they stayed in some inn, where the courtyard was filled with the camels, horses, donkeys, and baggage of all kinds of travelers.

Saul was not a merchant nor a government messenger nor a countryman going to market. Why was he making the journey?

SAUL, THE ENEMY OF THE FOLLOWERS OF JESUS

It was not many years after the death of Jesus. The followers of Jesus were still few and without influence. Most of the leaders of the nation were opposed to them. Saul had been in Jerusalem. He was a young man, who had come to Jerusalem to study, and had joined the persecution of the followers of Jesus. One of these, named Stephen, had been killed, and Saul had been glad it happened. He wanted to put them all in prison because he thought that they were harming his nation.

That was why he was going to Damascus. In that city, so he had heard, friends of Jesus were winning followers and he wanted to stop it. So he had got let-ters from the heads of his nation in Jerusalem, and was on his way to Damascus to bring back the believers in Jesus as prisoners to be tried in Jerusalem by the Great Council.

As he went on, day after day, he had much time to think. He must have thought about Jesus. He had heard about how kind he was, how loving, how he had taught about God, and how he had helped the sick and comforted the sorrow-ful. And now he was going

STREET IN THE ANCIENT CITY OF DAMASCUS

to put in prison the followers of this teacher! Perhaps he wondered if he was right. Perhaps every day he was a little less sure that he was right.

WHAT HAPPENED ON THE WAY

Then, one day something happened. Here is the Bible story of it.

"And as he journeyed, he came near Damascus: and suddenly there shined round about him a light from heaven: and he fell to the earth, and heard a voice saying unto him, 'Saul, Saul, why persecutest thou me?'

"And he said, 'Who art thou, Lord?'

"And the Lord said, 'I am Jesus whom thou persecutest: it is hard for thee to kick against the pricks.'

"And he, trembling and astonished, said, 'Lord, what wilt thou have me to do?'

"And the Lord said unto him, 'Arise, and go into the city, and it shall be told thee what thou must do.'

"And the men which journeyed with him stood speechless, hearing a voice, but seeing no man. And Saul arose from the earth; and when his eyes were opened, he saw no man; but they led him by the hand, and brought him into Damascus. And he was three days without sight, and neither did eat nor drink."

SAUL BECOMES A FOLLOWER OF JESUS

In Damascus a follower of Jesus, named Ananias, came to Saul and laid his hands on him, and his sight came back.

For some days Saul stayed at Damascus. He went among his people and announced that he, too, was a follower of Jesus! The people were astonished, for they knew why he had come to Damascus. He came to arrest the followers of Jesus, and now he said he was one himself! They could not understand it.

Here was the secret! Saul had been brought to see that he was wrong. He was a brave man, brave enough to say that he had been wrong, and to do all he could to make it right!

Saul lived many years after this, and traveled in many lands, trying to get other people to believe in Jesus.

In time he was called by another name, Paul. He wrote some letters to the churches, which are now in

THE HOLY LAND THROUGH WHICH PAUL TRAVELLED

the New Testament. Do you know the name of any of them?

Who was Saul?

Why did he go to Damascus?

What great thing happened to him on the way?

Why was it a brave thing for Paul to become a follower of Jesus?

When one believes a thing is right, what is the brave thing to do? —Read the Bible text, Vol. 8, pp. 23-27.

HOW PAUL WAS TAKEN FOR A GOD

Paul and a friend, Barnabas, were on a long journey. They had gone to another country, as missionaries do now, to tell the people about Jesus. They had crossed the sea from Antioch to the large island of Cyprus, which you can find on the map. Then they had crossed again to Perga, on the southern coast of Asia Minor. From here they had gone right inland. They had climbed up a long, steep road over a range of mountains. The way was known to be dangerous because of robbers, who hid behind the rocks and caught people in the narrow valleys. Probably they went through these mountains with some band of merchants.

THE PEOPLE BEYOND THE MOUNTAINS HEAR OF JESUS

Beyond the mountains lived people of another race. Some of them could speak the language of Paul and Barnabas, but most of them spoke their own language. Here Paul and Barnabas stayed and taught the people about Jesus. Some of their own race lived there, but the greater part of the people were of other races.

In one of the cities, Lystra, a lame man sat by the street. He had never walked, and all the people knew

THE COLOSSEUM, ROME

CONTRARY to general belief, the great Colosseum of Rome was not built in the early days of the Roman Christians. It was not here that the earliest Christians were martyred. This huge building was built very early in the Christian era, in 72 A.D. The Emperor Vespasian built as far as the third row of arches, and the work was completed by Titus, after his return from the conquest of Jerusalem. It is said that 12,000 captive Jews were employed upon the work, so that it is a relic of the third captivity of the Hebrew people. It was used for gladiatorial combats, and Christians were martyred here after the days of Paul.

him as the lame beggar. Paul passed by him one day,
when he doubtless begged for a gift from this man of a
foreign land.

Paul stopped and said, "Stand up!" The man stood
up and walked. The people on the street saw it. Soon
the news ran about the streets, "The stranger has made
the lame beggar walk!" Everybody ran to see what
had happened. A crowd gathered, and in the middle of
the crowd was the lame man, who had never been known
to stand up before, telling what the stranger had done.

ARE THESE STRANGERS GODS?

The people looked at each other in wonder. Who
were these strangers? Then they answered their own
questions.

"The gods have come down to us in the likeness of
men."

They said Barnabas must be Jupiter; and Paul,
Mercury, because he did most of the speaking, and
Mercury was the messenger of the gods.

Near the city was a temple of Jupiter, where they
offered sacrifices to the god. A priest lived near who
had charge of the temple. Somebody told him what
had happened, and he brought oxen with garlands
about their necks, as they decorated them for sacrifice,
and all the multitudes crowded to the city gates to
sacrifice to these gods in the form of men.

This talk about Paul and Barnabas being gods had
been in the language of the people, and Paul and his
friend had not understood what was said. But when
the preparations for sacrifice began they knew what it
meant.

Perhaps some one dropped on his knees before them
and bowed his head to the ground and prayed.

NOT GODS BUT MEN WITH GOOD NEWS

Paul and Barnabas ran to the multitude who were crowding out to the temple of Jupiter, and called to them, "Sirs, why do you do these things? We are men like you. We have come to bring you good news, to ask you to turn from such things to the God who made the sky above and earth below and the sea. It is he who gives you rain and fruitful seasons, and fills your hearts with joy and gladness. Worship him, not us."

They spoke earnestly and long, and only with difficulty did they persuade the people not to offer sacrifice to them.

All the rest of that day, as they walked down the streets, they must have passed little groups of people who were discussing, in their own language, whether Paul and Barnabas were not, after all, gods who for some reason wanted people to believe they were men.

Paul had many other strange experiences in his travels, but never again was he taken for a god.

—The Bible text of this story is found in Vol. 8, pp. 42-43.

QUESTIONS

Who was Paul?
Why were he and Barnabas on a journey?
What happened at a city called Lystra?
Why did people take Paul and Barnabas for gods?
What did Paul and Barnabas say?

HOW A GREAT MOB TRIED TO HINDER PAUL

EPHESUS:—A great commercial city of Asia Minor which has now completely vanished. Only a few ruins of its theater and two columns of the temple are left.

Paul traveled through many lands and lived in many cities, telling the people about Jesus.

Once he lived for two years at a famous city called Ephesus. He made many followers of Jesus there and gained many friends, so that all the city came to know about him and the things he taught.

Now Ephesus was famous for several things. There was a great theater, an open-air place with rows of raised seats about, where thousands of persons could sit and see what was going on in the center.

THE FAMOUS TEMPLE AT EPHESUS

There was also a famous temple at Ephesus, with an image which people said had fallen down from heaven. Once a year there was a great feast at the temple, and, all the time, people brought gifts and offerings. They liked to buy something and take home, somewhat as people now buy postcards and mementos of places they visit.

The most common things they bought were little silver copies of the image of the temple. So many of these were used that making them was a great business, employing many men. These workmen watched Paul's teaching with jealousy. Paul taught that God was not made in workshops or worshiped by images. If that teaching went on, where would they be?

THE MOB OF SILVER WORKMEN

One day a leader among the silver workmen, named Demetrius, called the workmen all together.

"You know," he said, "how we all get our wealth. And you hear this man Paul, who teaches that gods that are made are not gods at all. There is danger to our business. There is danger, too, that this temple of our great goddess, Diana, will lose the visitors who flock here from all the world."

As he kept on talking the men became excited. Some one shouted, "Great is Diana of the Ephesians!" Then the crowd took up the cry, and they all shouted, "Great is Diana of the Ephesians!"

They rushed toward the theater. The crowd gathered on the way. They all poured into the great open theater, shouting at the top of their voices, "Great is Diana of the Ephesians!"

If one asked another what it was all about, and why they had come there, the only reply he got was, "Great is Diana of the Ephesians!" for most of them had not the dimmest notion of what the gathering was for.

Paul heard what was going on, and, brave man that he was, proposed to go to the theater and talk to the crowd. But his friends said, "No. You could do no good. They would not listen."

A Jew in the audience tried to say something to them, but when they saw him raise his hand to get their attention, they only shouted the louder, "Great is Diana of the Ephesians!" and not a word could he speak to them. For two hours the theater was filled with a confused, shouting mob. It was not a pleasant thing, and not quite safe. In their excitement they might go out on the streets and break into houses or kill people.

THE MOB BECOMES QUIET

After a while one of the high officials of the city came, and tried to speak. When they saw him, they gradually became quiet.

PAUL TENTMAKING IN CORINTH
A molding by D. Mastroianni

He made a little speech, advising them to go quietly away. "If this man Paul has done any wrong," he said, "Demetrius and his friends can take him to the courts and the judges will do justice. There is no reason for a riot like this." And so he dismissed them, and they all went home; and they had only succeeded in making Paul and his teaching better known than they had been before.

This is only one of the many times when Paul roused great opposition, but he went on doing what he knew to be right in spite of it all.—Read in Vol. 8, pp. 82-87.

QUESTIONS

Why was the city of Ephesus famous?
What did Paul do in Ephesus?
Why were some of the workmen opposed to him?
What did the crowd do?
Who was "Diana of the Ephesians"?
Did the opposition hinder or help the spread of the Good News?
How does the story show Paul as a brave man?

HOW PAUL WENT TO ROME

SHIP:—The ships of Paul's day were very small compared with our own. Paul's ship could be carried on the deck of one of our great steamships.

THE CAPITAL OF THE WORLD

In the New Testament time the greatest city was Rome. It was the capital of a great empire, covering all the lands of the New Testament story, and many more.

Paul traveled in many lands and taught in many cities, but he had never been in Rome. He had planned to go there, and tell about Jesus, but one thing and another had kept him back.

At last he thought he saw his way to go. He wanted first to go back to the city where Christianity started, where he himself once lived—Jerusalem. Then, he said, he would go to Rome. There were already a few Christians at Rome, and he had written them a letter, and near the end of it told of his plan to visit them. This letter is in the New Testament, and is called "The Epistle to the Romans."

Then at Jerusalem Paul's enemies had him arrested and put in prison. For two years he was kept in prison. His case had not been tried, and yet he was not released.

PAUL APPEALS TO THE EMPEROR FOR TRIAL

At last he became tired of waiting, and he asked to be sent to Rome and tried by the emperor himself. He had a right to ask this, and the officers sent him to Rome.

So at last he went to the great city, but as a prisoner.

He did not go alone. Several other prisoners were taken. A captain and a band of soldiers went as guards, and a few of Paul's friends were allowed to sail on the same ship.

They went nearly all the way by water. But there were no great steamships to carry them. All the ships were sailing ships, with great oars to row when the winds were light. They did not run at certain times, nor have agencies where one could buy tickets, as at present. Each ship was independent, and went when it could get a cargo; and passengers made what arrangements they could.

So the captain found a ship, and the party all set sail on it. They went only part way on this, then had to find another ship. They found one carrying wheat to Rome, and set sail again.

In fine summer weather, with good winds, the sail across this sea, the Mediterranean, is very fine. The water is sometimes smooth and beautiful; the wind gentle and steady; and the ship moves on, day after day, under cloudless skies. But Paul and his party were going in the late fall, and storms and uncertain winds were not uncommon at such times.

From the first the voyage was uncertain. The winds were contrary. They had to anchor the ship in a little harbor of an island for a time. Paul advised not to go on, but they did.

A TERRIBLE STORM ON THE MEDITERRANEAN

Then, after a little, a furious storm arose. They took down the sails and let the ship go as it would. The storm became worse. The heavy-laden ship rolled from side to side. They were afraid it would go under, and they threw overboard some of the wheat to lighten it. Day after day passed. The clouds hung low. They saw no sun or moon or stars. They did not know where they were, or which way they were moving. Any day they might be tossed on the rocks. They did not try to eat nor sleep, but only to lie in the ship and hold on to the ropes, while the salt spray blew over them and the waves dashed high above the sides of the ship. They were all helpless together — the sailors and the captain and the soldiers and the prisoners and the passengers.

"BE OF GOOD CHEER!"

But when every one had given up hope, Paul tried to cheer them up. He said, "And now I exhort you to be of good cheer: for there shall be no loss of any man's life among you, but of the ship.

A HEBREW GIRL

"For there stood by me this night the angel of God, whose I am, and whom I serve, saying, 'Fear not, Paul; thou must be brought before Caesar: and, lo, God hath given thee all them that sail with thee.'

"Wherefore, sirs, be of good cheer: for I believe God, that it shall be even as it was told me.

"Howbeit we must be cast upon a certain island."

Then one night about midnight the sailors, who knew the signs of the sea, thought that they were coming to land. They found that they were in shallow water. No one knew whether they were off a shore of sand or jagged cliffs, and in the black night there was danger if they struck the rocks. Everybody was awake now. Everybody was alert.

They must stop the ship from going aground, if possible. Over with the anchors! Everybody helped lift the great iron anchor — the captain and Paul and the prisoners and the soldiers and all. Splash! It was over! Then another anchor on the other side; then another and another — four great anchors to hold them in the sands. The ropes tightened, the anchors held, the ship was at last safe for the moment! But it was not safe for long.

PAUL BECOMES LEADER

In times like this the men who lead are the really great men. Paul, the prisoner, not the captain nor the master of the ship, became the leader. There were about two hundred and seventy-five people on the ship As they crowded together, listening to the roar of the sea dashing on the shore, Paul spoke. "For fourteen days we have been in the storm, and you have had little food. Eat something now. It will be for your safety."

Then he took food himself, and thanked God for it before them all and ate. And they, cheered by his example, also ate.

SAFE ON SHORE AT THE ISLAND OF MALTA

By this time it was almost morning. When the day dawned they saw a bay with a beach, and decided that they could drive the ship on the sand there. So they cut the ropes that held the anchors, and steered for the beach. But on the way they ran into cross-currents, and could not bring the ship where they planned. The bow plunged into the sand and stuck fast. The stern was out in the water where the waves beat on it, and the great planks snapped and the stout old ship began to go to pieces. Some leaped into the sea and swam for the shore; the rest, some on planks and some on other things from the ship, floated ashore.

And so it came to pass, that they all escaped safe to land. The land was the island of Malta, a small island in the midst of the Mediterranean.

It was months after, that Paul at last reached Rome; but not one of all the people on the ship was lost in the great shipwreck.

—The full Bible text of this experience is found in Vol. 8, pp. 123-136.

QUESTIONS

Why was Rome important?

Why could not Paul go to Rome as he had planned?

What happened on Paul's journey to Rome?

Where was he shipwrecked?

What were some of the things Paul suffered because he was a follower of Christ?

Why does it pay to suffer for the right?

The Story of the Hebrew People

THIS short story of the Hebrew People is intended as a review of the stories which have been given in this volume and as a preparation for the stories which will be told in the volumes which follow. Some of the characters you have learned to know well. Others no less interesting you will come to know well in the other volumes.

Long, long ago there was a group of shepherd tribes living on the hills in the land of Canaan. There were cities and towns in the land, but the shepherd tribes lived in very few of them. For the most part they lived in black tents on the hillsides, and pastured their flocks on the slopes of the hills.

Yet they said, "The land is ours. Our fathers lived here, and their God gave them the land."

Then the children asked, "Who were our fathers? If God gave us the land, why is it not ours?"

And these are the stories the children were told, as God had instructed.

STREET SCENE IN HEBRON

This interesting city is older than Damascus. Abraham, Isaac, and Jacob all lived here for many years, and they were all buried here.

The Story of the Hebrew People

THE STORY OF ABRAHAM

ONCE, long ago, the father of all our people lived away off on a wide plain in the North. He was a great man, with flocks and herds, but he had no son; so his nephew was a son to him and his wife. His name was Abraham; his wife's, Sarah; and his nephew's, Lot.

For a long time he and his nephew lived on the wide plain, and tended their flocks, and took the wool of their sheep to Haran, a town near by, to sell to the merchants, who came on camels from far away.

All of that land worshiped false gods, but Abraham believed in the true and living God. And God called him to take all his flocks and tents and servants and Lot and Lot's wife and go into another land. 'They came to these hills of Galilee and Judea, where we now live.

But he and Lot had many sheep and cattle, and the hills could not give pasture for them all; so Lot went down into the rich land of the Jordan valley, and Abraham stayed on the hills. One night as he lay sleeping, God spoke to him and said,

"Your descendants will be more than the stars in the heavens, and to them will I give all this land."

THE STORY OF ISAAC AND JACOB

Abraham became greater and greater, till he had many cattle, and many servants, and the kings of the land made treaties with him. He now had two sons, Ishmael and Isaac. Ishmael went off to live in the

344

lands to the south. The descendants of Ishmael became the roving tribes of the desert, the Arabs. Even down to the present time they live in tents and they have changed very little from the days of Abraham. Isaac was a home boy, and stayed by the flocks of his father.

When Isaac became the head of the camp, he also was the friend of the great chiefs of the land. He in turn had two sons, Jacob and Esau, and they were as unlike as could be. Esau was a bold lad, who liked nothing better than to go off on a hunt. Jacob loved the flocks and stayed about the tents. Esau was the favorite of his father; Jacob, of his mother.

Now Esau was the older and by right should have

THE SHEPHERD PRINCES OF ISRAEL

"And I will make of thee a great nation, and I will bless thee, and make thy name great; and thou shalt be a blessing:

"And Abram took Sarai his wife, and Lot, his brother's son, and all their substance that they had gathered, and the souls that they had gotten in Haran, and they went forth to go into the land of Canaan; and into the land of Cannan they came.

"And Abram passed through the land unto the place of Sechem, unto the plain of Moreh. And the Canaanite was then in the land."

been given the chief place in the family; and so his father intended. But his mother stole it away from him for her favorite, Jacob.

"Wait till my father is dead, and then we will see!" said Esau.

So his mother, who had come from the great plain in the North where Abraham had lived at first, sent

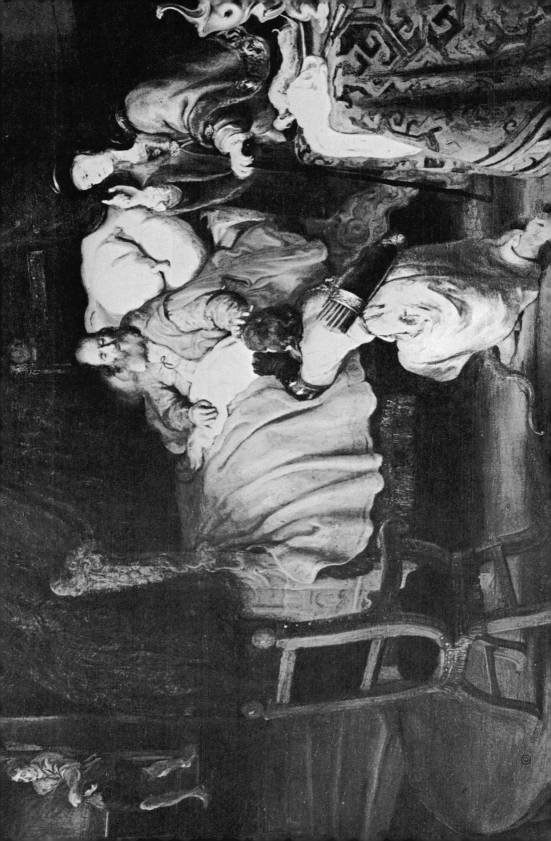

Jacob to her relatives, out of the way of his brother. She hoped he need stay only a short time; but it was many years before he came back again. When he did, he was himself the head of a great camp, with flocks of his own, and men to care for them, and twelve sons, whose names the Hebrew tribes bear.

Like his mother, Jacob had his favorites in the family, and that always makes trouble. One son, Joseph, he loved better than any of the others. Then, what do you suppose the older brothers did? They caught him one day a long way from home and sold him to a troop of merchants going with their camels to Egypt, a land far away to the southwest. His father had given him a fine coat, far too fine for a shepherd boy. They took it off, killed one of the many kids in the great flock, dipped the coat in the blood and took it to their old father.

"Here," they said to him, "is a coat we found. You can see if it is Joseph's."

"It is my son's coat," said the old man. "Some wild beast has killed Joseph."

ABRAHAM

"And the Angel of the LORD called unto Abraham out of heaven the second time,

"And said, 'By myself have I sworn, saith the LORD, for because thou hast done this thing, and hast not withheld thy son, thine only son,

"'That in blessing I will bless thee, and in multiplying I will multiply thy seed as the stars of the heaven, and as the sand which is upon the sea shore; and thy seed shall possess the gate of his enemies;

"'And in thy seed shall all the nations of the earth be blessed; because thou hast obeyed my voice.'"

ISSAC BLESSING JACOB
A painting by Gerbrandt Eeckhout

After many years had passed, and the sons were now men with children of their own, there came a famine in that land. In all the camps, up and down the hills, the children were crying with hunger, and the men and women were growing thin and hollow-eyed. But away off in Egypt, so they said among the tents, was food in plenty.

Jacob called his sons together and said, "Go to Egypt and bring food for us before we starve."

It was a long way to Egypt, but the shepherds went and bought food from the greatest man in Egypt, next to the king of the land.

And lo and behold, that man was their own brother Joseph, whom they had sold into slavery years ago!

They did not know him, but he knew them. At first he pretended to be very stern with them. He told them they were spies, and put one of them in prison while he sent the others back with food. When they came back for more food he was still more harsh with them, till he made sure that they had learned to love their old father. Then he told them who he was and sent for Jacob and all the camp to live in Egypt.

THE DECEPTION OF JACOB

"And Jacob went near unto Isaac his father; and he felt him, and said 'The voice is Jacob's voice, but the hands are the hands of Esau.'

"And he discerned him not, because his hands were hairy, as his brother Esau's hands: so he blessed him.

"And he said, 'Art thou my very son Esau?' And he said, 'I am.'"

THE STORY OF MOSES

While Joseph lived everything was happy. By and by, when Joseph and all who knew him were dead, a king arose in the land who made slaves of the Hebrews. For a long time their lot was hard. They cried to their God for help, and no help came.

Then God raised up a great leader, the greatest the people ever had in the old days, Moses. When he was a baby there was a law that all the Hebrew boy-babies should be killed; so his mother had put him in a little basket and fastened it at the edge of the river. The king's daughter found it and brought the baby up as her own.

THE FINDING OF MOSES

"And the daughter of Pharaoh came down to wash herself at the river; and her maidens walked along by the river's side: and when she saw the ark among the flags, she sent her maid to fetch it.

"And when she had opened it, she saw the child: and, behold, the babe wept. And she had compassion on him, and said, 'This is one of the Hebrews' children.'"

But when Moses was grown he wanted to help his own people and not to live in luxury as an Egyptian. After many adventures he tried to persuade the king to allow the people to go free. No indeed! The people were worth too much as laborers for that.

"If you will not," he said, "our God will send troubles on you."

"What is your God that we should care for him?" answered the king.

Then troubles, indeed, began to come to the people of Egypt! Flies, always many in Egypt, became a very plague. The cattle died of disease. Swarms of locusts ate all the growing crops. Great storms, with lightning and hail, swept over the land. After every disaster, Moses came to the king and said, "Can we go now?"

Each time the king said, "No." Then at last came a night when in every Egyptian house one of the family died; but no one among the Hebrews.

"Let the Hebrews go," cried the frightened Egyptians.

The king called for Moses, in the middle of the night, and said,

"Take your people and all that belong to them and go, as quickly as you can, before we are all dead."

Then all the people gathered their cattle and their goods, and hastened to leave the land, starting under the starlight before the break of day.

But the Egyptians repented that they had let their slaves go, and marched after them to bring them back; but God opened up a way for them right through the waters of a narrow sea that shut off their path, and so they got out of Egypt safe and sound.

For a whole generation they lived in the country south of Canaan. It is half a desert, and they had to fight for the right to hold springs of water for themselves and their flocks. But they were growing strong in all those years, and learning how to live in a wilderness and endure hardship. Moses was their leader in it all, the greatest, wisest and best man who ever led the Hebrew people. Then they came from the south of Canaan around to the east, and took some of the land on the east side of the deep valley of the Jordan. Here some of the Hebrews settled, content with the

CAMEL AND DRIVER IN DESERT
SOUTH OF CANAAN

rich pastures which looked so luscious and green after the gray desert. Here Moses died. He went up into a mountain where he could look over to the hills west of the Jordan, and he never came back.

God himself had buried him, said the Bible.

THE STORY OF JOSHUA

The old leader had appointed a successor, a vigorous young warrior, Joshua. This man led the people over the Jordan, and God opened the way as he opened the way through the sea.

And here the Hebrews were in the old land where their fathers, Abraham, Isaac, and Jacob, had lived. They were wandering shepherds, just as their fathers had been; but now they had grown to be a great people with many flocks. They must fight for a chance to live in the land. They met some of the people of the land in battle. They made treaties with others. They spread over all the country, but many of the cities were still held by the old inhabitants.

JOSHUA LEADING THE HEBREW PEOPLE

"And it came to pass, when the people removed from their tents, to pass over Jordan, and the priests bearing the ark of the covenant before the people;

"And as they that bare the ark were come unto Jordan, and the feet of the priests that bare the ark were dipped in the brim of the water (for Jordan overfloweth all his banks all the time of harvest),

"That the waters which came down from above stood and rose up upon a heap very far from the city Adam, that is beside Zaretan; and those that came down toward the sea of the plain, even the salt sea, failed and were cut off and the people passed over right against Jericho."

And so God had led them all the way till he brought them into Canaan.

This was the story of the olden times which the grandfathers told when the grandchildren said, "Tell us, please, where our people came from."

THE JUDGES

The people were not very united. Some lived far to the south, about Hebron and Beersheba, where Abraham and Isaac lived. Some lived much farther north; and between the two was a band of towns occupied by the old inhabitants of the lands. The people of the south and of the north had little to do with each other. Some lived on the eastern side of the Jordan, and the deep valley of that river almost cut them off from those on the western side. There was no single government to hold them together. When one part of the Hebrews were attacked by their enemies, the rest might come to their aid if they pleased—and they

GIDEON'S ARMY

"So Gideon, and the hundred men that were with him, came unto the outside of the camp in the beginning of the middle watch; and they had but newly set the watch: and they blew the trumpets, and brake the pitchers that were in their hands.

"And the three companies blew the trumpets, and brake the pitchers, and held the lamps in their left hands, and the trumpets in their right hands to blow withal: and they cried, 'The sword of the LORD, and of Gideon.'

"And they stood every man in his place round about the camp: and all the host ran and cried, and fled."

often did not please. No nation can become great while thus disunited. This was called the period of the Judges, from a group of heroes known as the Judges.

DEBORAH

One of the Judges was a woman named Deborah.

There was danger that the old inhabitants would overcome the Hebrews. A king had risen among them who gathered an army to fight the Hebrews. Deborah, with a chieftain called Barak, called all the northern Hebrews, "Come up to fight for your freedom." Some did not come, but those who did fought a battle on a plain, where the Canaanite army thought they would have an advantage. But in the midst of the battle a fierce storm broke. The rain and hail drove in the faces of the enemy, and the ground became a bog, and the Hebrews drove the enemy into a little river, now swollen with the rain, which flowed across the plain. They knew that God sent the storm to help them against the Canaanite king, Sisera. The Hebrews made a song about it, and sang how "The stars in their courses fought against Sisera."

GIDEON AND THE MIDIANITES

Once the Midianites, wild, rough desert tribes from the land east of the Jordan, found how weak the Hebrews were. They came over in harvest time with great troops of camels, put up their black tents, and robbed the people of the grain and other crops they had so carefully tended all the summer. Then the desert raiders went off, and the poor little Hebrew children had to live on whatever their parents could get for them. For several years this happened, and the Hebrews did not dare to fight the robbers.

Palestinian Village Well

From International Publishing Co., Ltd.

EVERY village in Palestine had its well of water, for without it there could be no sustenance for the people nor for the flocks and herds. The village well became a meeting place for conversation and friendship among the villagers. It was the responsibility of the women to draw water and carry it to their homes. It was at the well that the servant of Abraham met Rebecca and invited her to become the wife of Isaac (Genesis 24:11). At the well of Sychar the woman of Samaria met Jesus and learned about the water of Life (John 4:6–14). The shepherds brought their flocks of sheep and goats to the village well, and travelers paused to rest beside it and to drink its cool, refreshing water.

Then God called to the leadership of Israel a young man, Gideon. He gathered an army of thirty-two thousand men to war against the Midianites. A series of tests, reduced this army to three hundred. God promised Gideon victory to this army.

The victory of Gideon and his three hundred is one of the most remarkable of Hebrew history. Gideon gave each of his little band an earthen water pitcher and torch. They surrounded the camp of the Midianites during the night with torches hidden in pitchers. Under the direction of Gideon these three hundred men suddenly broke the pitchers and flashed the lighted torches and shouted, "The sword of the Lord and of Gideon!" The Midianites awakened in fright; the flashing lights and sounding trumpets gave the impression of vast surrounding armies. Confused, Israel's enemies ran away in all directions, fighting with each other in the darkness. Those who survived fled across the Jordan and the Israelites were delivered from the Midianite oppression.

THE PHILISTINES

During all these years another people were growing up on the shore of the Mediterranean Sea west of the southern hills. They were called the Philistines, and they were in some ways a stronger and more warlike people than the Hebrews. It was from them that the land of the Bible came to be called Palestine.

The Philistines, after they gained the plains by the sea, pressed back into the hills. For several generations they warred with the Hebrews, and it seemed likely that they would be masters of all the country. Many were the battles fought between the two little peoples, and for a long time the Hebrews paid tribute to the Philistines.

Once, when the Philistines came up to fight, the Hebrews took the most sacred thing they had into battle with them. It was called the ark of God. They thought God would go with this ark and give them victory. But the Philistines only fought the harder and took the ark off to their own land, after a sore defeat for the Hebrews. Later they sent back the ark, but they did not give freedom to the Hebrews.

The Philistines were more united than the Hebrews. The Hebrews began to think that if they were ever to win their freedom, they must be united also.

SAMUEL

At that time they had a Judge, an old man whom all the nation honored, named Samuel. When he was a boy, he had lived in the temple. You know the story: how one night the boy Samuel heard God call him and thought it was the old priest. He grew up to be a leader of the people. He had sometimes gathered them for battle against the Philistines, and had led them to victory, but had never been able to free them entirely. A Philistine army might at any time march up to a Hebrew town and say, "Give us fifty sheep and a camel's load of wheat," and the Hebrews had to give what was demanded.

The people became restless under this. They thought if they had a king they could all stand together. They began to say to Samuel, "Give us a king."

THE EARLY KINGS

SAUL

At last Samuel met a man, tall, strong, a fine, kindly man, named Saul. He was a farmer's son, and his

life out of doors gave him
the body of a warrior. Samuel talked with him and was
pleased with his good sense
and modesty. He told Saul
that some day he would
be king, and Saul went
back to his farm and said
nothing.

Sometime later messen-
gers ran breathless to all
the villages of the Hebrews.
They said that a Hebrew
town was besieged by
enemies; who would gather
an army and help them?

Then Saul showed that
he was worthy to be king.
He gathered an army, drove
back the enemy and re-
lieved the town; and all the
people said, just as Samuel
had done, "This is the man
to lead us."

SAUL ATTEMPTS TO KILL
DAVID

"And the evil spirit from the Lord
was upon Saul, as he sat in his house
with his javelin in his hand: and
David played with his hand.

"And Saul sought to smite David
even to the wall with the javelin; but
he slipped away out of Saul's presence,
and he smote the javelin into the wall:
and David fled. and escaped that night."

So the great, strong, quiet farmer became the first
king of the Hebrews. During all his reign he was trying to free the people from the Philistines. Sometimes
he chased their armies out of the hills, but they always
came back, and at last he died in battle with them.
His reign began gloriously, though the farmer-king
had no splendid court and no palace and no armed
guards about him, as did the kings of the great empires
of the world. Later on, his reign was not so glorious.
He became a moody, jealous man; at times he was

actually insane. He had a son, a fine, lovable young man named Jonathan.

DAVID AND JONATHAN

This son became the great friend of another young man, David, who had been a shepherd boy in Bethlehem. You know the story of David: how, in one of the Philistine wars, he killed a huge warrior, Goliath, with a stone from his shepherd's sling. This had made him a great hero among the people and he had been made an officer in Saul's army. But Saul was jealous of his popularity. He tried to kill him, and David had to go away and hide in the caves of the wilderness. Saul was angry that Jonathan remained his friend.

"Do you not see," he said, "that all the people admire him, and that he, and not you, will be king after me?"

And so indeed it fell out; but not because Jonathan and David quarreled. They remained to the end warm friends; and had Jonathan lived, he would still have been David's best and most loyal friend.

But in the same battle in which King Saul died, Jonathan was slain. David, chosen of God to be king many years before, now came to the throne of Judah and Benjamin. A few years later all Israel was ruled by him.

David's reign was long and prosperous. He finally drove back the Philistines and compelled them to stay at home on the plains near the sea. He captured the city of Jerusalem, up to that time still held by the old inhabitants, and made it his capital. In his time the Hebrews became a nation with whom other nations were willing to make treaties. No longer were they a mere disunited collection of shepherd tribes; and it was largely due to the energy and ability of David, the king who had been a shepherd boy.

SOLOMON

The next king, Solomon, the son of David, was able to do still more because he could begin where his father left off. He made alliances with the kingdoms about. He built palaces and a temple at Jerusalem. The Hebrews, who had seen no splendid cities, thought these buildings were very wonderful. The temple stood for over three hundred and fifty years, and every generation it grew dearer and dearer to the people.

David was a poet; and the people later loved to think that the most beautiful poems they had must have been written by him. Solomon, they said, was a very wise man, and they told of his wise sayings and clever judgments in court cases.

THE GREAT REVOLT

The great buildings and the splendid courts and the fine gifts sent by Solomon to win the friendship of other kings cost a great deal. The people paid heavy taxes, till they sometimes wished their king was not so

THE RETURN OF KING REHOBOAM TO JERUSALEM

"Then King Rehoboam sent Adoram, who was over the tribute; and all Israel stoned him with stones, that he died. Therefore King Rehoboam made speed to get him up to his chariot, to flee to Jerusalem."

splendid. They were proud of him and of all he did. But when he died, they came to his son, Rehoboam, who was the next king, and asked him to make their taxes lighter.

The young king was foolish enough to refuse. Then the people were angry. "To your tents, O Israel," they said. "Now see to thine own house, David." The whole northern part of the land, ten tribes, to count in the way of old Hebrew custom, refused the king. The smaller southern part, two tribes, accepted him. The northern part was called Israel; the southern, Judah, from the larger of the two tribes.

So the descendants of David continued to rule at Jerusalem over a much shrunken kingdom, and up north, in the land made famous by Gideon and Deborah and many other old heroes, a new king was chosen. Neither kingdom ever became as great as the old kingdom was. The northern kingdom, Israel, was the larger, and had the most fertile land and the most people; but it had a great many changes in its kings. There were wars, and new kings overthrew old, and the land was often in confusion. Both countries had some kings who were wise and some that were foolish; but none of them became so great or so famous as David and Solomon.

THE PROPHETS

There was another class of men during these long years who became more famous than the kings. These were the prophets. They were men who tried to lead the people to obey their God. They brought the message that God had given to them. Sometimes the people did not like it. Some of the rich people wished to oppress the poor. Others wished to cheat in business,

while the rulers wished to
take money for giving help
to those who came to them.
The prophets said all these
things were wrong. Some
of the people were unkind
and cruel. They thought
that if they gave a gift to
the temple God would not
care about the other things.

When the people would
not listen to them, the
prophets tried to get their
attention.

THE PROPHET

AMOS

One of them, named
Amos, was a shepherd. He
wanted to tell the rich
people they should not oppress the poor, but what rich
man would listen to him, a poor man in a shepherd's
coat? So he came out once when a great crowd was
gathered and began to speak. He began to say that
God would punish the countries around for their sins.
Now the Hebrews had been at war with the countries
about, and they were ready to listen when he said:

"For three transgressions of Moab, yes, for four,
God will punish that people.

"For three transgressions of Edom, yes, for four,
God will punish that people.

"For three transgressions of the Philistine city
Gaza, yes, for four, God will punish that people."

"Good!" the rich men must have said. "That
shepherd is talking sense. We will listen."

Then, when he had the attention of all the crowd, he thundered out:

"For three transgressions of Israel, yes, for four, God will punish YOU"; and he told them in very plain language what wrong they had done to the weak and the poor.

"Do you think," he said, "that you can do wrong and then come and worship God and have him pleased with you? No! Do right, be just to those who work for you, care for the poor widows and orphans, do not oppress the poor. That is what Jehovah wants."

ISAIAH

One prophet, Isaiah, was often in the king's court and tried to lead the king and the people to do what God had taught. In his day, Egypt, an empire south of them, was trying to urge them into a war with Assyria, an empire to the north. Isaiah was sure this was wrong and foolish. "Trust God," he said. "Do not trust Egypt." But the people would not listen.

So one day he came out on the street dressed very queerly. He had laid aside the rich robes of his court dress. He had on only ragged garments. Not a beggar in the street was dressed so poorly.

"Look at Isaiah!" said the people. "He looks as though he had been taken captive and was on his way to be sold as a slave."

Now that was just what he wanted them to think.

The next day he went on the street again in the same dress. Everybody in the city was talking about it now — how the rich man from the court, Isaiah, was going about the city looking like a captive of war.

They all knew Isaiah as a prophet of God and that his strange appearance was to give them a message that

DISTANT VIEW OF JERUSALEM AS SEEN
BY TRAVELERS COMING FROM BETHANY

God wanted them to hear. Perhaps the next time they came out they gathered around him to hear what he would say.

He said, "You wonder why I do this. I will tell you. This is a sign against Egypt. Her people promise you help if you will go to war. Egypt will not give that help. She will be captured. Her people will be led away captive, clothed as I am. You must not trust in Egypt but put your trust in the God of Israel." They listened to Isaiah and were not conquered until one hundred and fifty years afterward.

EZEKIEL

At a later time there was another prophet, named Ezekiel. In his day, the Hebrews had lost almost all their power as a nation, but some of them were saying, "Our capital city Jerusalem never will be taken by an enemy. God will not allow that. If it is taken, then we shall know that our God is very weak and we shall not worship him any more."

Ezekiel knew that if the city was taken by the enemy it would not be because God was too weak to prevent it, but because the people had done wrong. God would not try to save the city.

Ezekiel wanted to make them see clearly what God had told him. Perhaps they would not understand it if he only said it; so he acted it out.

Ezekiel took a clay tablet, like a large slate, and drew in the soft clay a map of the city. Then he put it down on the ground. All about it he built little mud forts, as though he were going to besiege the city. He took a sheet of iron and set it up between himself and the city. Perhaps those who watched him asked each other, "Has Ezekiel gone crazy? Why is he making mud forts, and playing with a map of Jerusalem on clay?"

It was not boy's play. It was an attempt to show them that, when the enemy came against Jerusalem and built forts, God would not help the city. He would be shut off from it as though a sheet of iron was between him and the city.

The people might forget what he said, but they would not forget what he did.

So the prophets tried to make the people remember their message. They differed in many ways, but they were all alike in one thing; they were all inspired of God to bring his word to the people. They were bold, brave men, not afraid to stand up for what they believed to be right. They did more for their nation than any of the kings who lived in the palaces.

ASSYRIA AND THE HEBREWS

During these long years there was one great nation, more powerful than any other. The name of the nation was Assyria.

The king of Assyria sent his army into Palestine, or any of the other countries of all that part of the world, and said, "Pay me a great sum, or I will destroy your land and burn your cities." Usually they did not feel able to resist, and the king of the little country brought out his treasures, made the rich bring in their money and the poor give up some of their sheep or goats, and so try to buy off the terrible Assyrian army. Then every year they had to send caravans of camels to Nineveh, the Assyrian capital, loaded with tribute, to satisfy Assyria and keep the cruel army away. Almost every year, somewhere in the wide empire, some small nation refused to pay the heavy tribute. That usually brought only worse trouble on them.

Israel sometimes refused to pay tribute. Finally Assyria sent an army, captured and burned the capital, Samaria, took away the king and thousands of the most prosperous people, and made them live in lands far away. In their place they brought in other people from distant countries, and put over them, not another Hebrew king, but an Assyrian governor.

"Now," they said, "we will have no more rebellion in Israel."

This was the end of the northern one of the two kingdoms of the Hebrews. The southern, Judah, lasted for about one hundred and fifty years longer.

Before the close of this hundred and fifty years Assyria became weaker. They had lived by robbing their neighbors, and that comes to an end after a while.

THE HEBREW PEOPLE GOING INTO CAPTIVITY

"And he carried away all Jerusalem, and all the princes, and all the mighty men of valour, even ten thousand captives, and all the craftsmen and smiths: none remained, save the poorest sort of the people of the land.

"And all the men of might, even seven thousand, and craftsmen and smiths a thousand, all that were strong and apt for war, even them the king of Babylon brought captive to Babylon."

THE CONQUEST OF JUDAH BY BABYLON

Then arose Babylonia, an ancient nation, old before the time of Abraham, which had been obliged to

Wailing Wall of Jerusalem

From International Publishing Co., Ltd.

THE wailing wall in Jerusalem has been for centuries one of the most historic and treasured places. Over the years of history Jewish pilgrims have come from all lands here to pray and to weep for the loss of the land of their fathers. The wailing wall is a part of the Second Temple which was built by Ezra and Nehemiah after the return of the Jews from the captivity in Babylon, and on the site of the first Temple built by Solomon. Scholars are certain that the five lowest courses of stones here pictured are from the Second Temple which was destroyed by the Romans when they conquered Palestine. At the present time the wailing wall is within the Hashemite Kingdom of Jordan and therefore no longer available to the Jewish pilgrims.

see Assyria for long centuries more powerful than itself. When Assyria became weak, Babylonia attacked her, and Assyria fell with not a friend in all the world to mourn her loss. That was the result of being cruel and trying to get all she could from others.

Then Babylonia began to send out her armies and demand tribute, just as Assyria had done. Judah paid for a time, then revolted and refused to send any more money or goods to Babylon, the capital city of the empire.

Babylonia sent a great army to Judah, took Jerusalem, burned the houses, broke down the walls, killed many of the people, and sent many of the rest to live in the villages in Babylonia.

It was a sad time for the people. They saw their old homes burned and many of their neighbors killed. They were marched away by stern soldiers to a strange land.

So ended the kingdom of Judah. Every king since David's time had been of his descendants, but that was all over now. There were no more kings in Jerusalem.

If you ask what right Assyria and Babylonia had to demand tribute from smaller and weaker countries, you are raising a question they never asked. They were strong enough to do it, and that was enough. But it is not true that "might makes right," and nations ought to meet God's standard of righteousness.

AFTER THE EXILE

The time when so many of the people lived in Babylon was called by them the exile. An exile is one who is away from his home or his native land. Some of them longed to get back to the green hills of Palestine again. They remembered their God, and on the Sabbath Day came together to pray to him.

At last Babylon fell, in turn, before a new, strong empire, Persia. The Persian king was named Cyrus. When he asked his generals how it was that they had been able to conquer so strong a kingdom as Babylon, probably one said, "It is because our armies are so strong."

But a wiser man said, "It is because the Babylonians were so weak."

"But what made them weak?" Cyrus must have asked.

"I will tell you," said some wise man. "In the villages of Babylonia are thousands of people who are not Babylonians. They have been brought here from other countries. They hate Babylonia. They were glad when the empire fell. No country can be strong with so many discontented people in it."

"We do not wish Persia to be weak in this way," said Cyrus. "Send these people back to their homes."

The Hebrews were very glad and rejoiced that God had put this thought into the heart of Cyrus.

Those who could went back; but many had business or families so that they could not go, and for hundreds of years many Hebrews lived in Babylon.

Those who went back to Jerusalem had a hard life for a long time. There were years when the harvest was poor, and sometimes they had hardly enough to eat. They tried to rebuild the old city, but those who came back and those who had never gone away were all together so few in numbers that they could not rebuild the old city. After sixteen years they built a temple, but it was almost a hundred years before the walls of the city were built.

Then Nehemiah, a man who had been in the court of the Persian king, gave up his life in the court and

came back to Jerusalem to
help his own people. He
put some of his own courage
into the rest of the people,
and they worked with a
will, till the wall was built
again.

They had learned one
lesson,—not to rebel against
a great empire. They were
almost always friends with
Persia, and every day
prayers were offered for the
empire.

THE MACCABEES

In time Persia passed
away, and troubles came
again to the Hebrews. At
one time they were under
a king who tried to make
them forget the religion of
their fathers. Then they

NEHEMIAH REBUILDS THE
WALLS OF JERUSALEM

"Moreover the old gate repaired
Jehoiada, the son of Paseah, and Me-
shullam, the son of Besodeiah; they
laid the beams thereof, and set up the
doors thereof, and the locks thereof,
and the bars thereof."

felt that they must fight for freedom to worship God.
They were led by a very skilful leader, Judas Maccabeus,
and by his brothers after his death. The nation became
free for the first time since the old days of Assyria.
But those were the days of great empires, not of small
kingdoms; and Palestine soon became part of the great
empire of Rome, the Province of Syria ruled by native
kings, but only under the direction of Roman governors.
Later, in 64 A.D., Palestine rebelled and Jerusalem was
totally destroyed by the Emperor Titus after a terrible
siege of two years.

During all the five hundred years after the days of Babylon, the important thing was not who sat in the governor's palace at Jerusalem, or what nation ruled over them. Rather, it was the question of what the people were thinking. They were thinking of God. They could not understand how he could love the nation and let other nations rule over it. But they did not give up trusting him. They knew that some time God would give them a kingdom again, with a great and good king of their own. This king they called the Messiah, and when Jesus came, some of the people thought he would be the Great King. But God planned something better for the world than even a great Hebrew kingdom.

Hebrew children still asked their parents to tell them about the old times. But now they were no longer a group of shepherds on the hills of Palestine. They lived in many cities in many lands. Some were still in Palestine. Some were far west in Rome, the capital of the great empire; some, far east in Babylon the ancient. Some lived in Egypt, where the Hebrews had been slaves long ago, and some were in cities far north of Egypt, cities of Greece and Macedonia. Wherever they were, they still told the children the old stories of Abraham and Joseph and Moses, and taught them to love God and to keep his law.

That is the long story of the Hebrew people in the Bible times.

QUESTIONS

The Story of Abraham

Who was Abraham?
What long journey did he take?
Who was Lot?

RIDING DOUBLE ON A DONKEY,
THE COMMON BEAST OF BURDEN IN PALESTINE

The Story of Isaac and Jacob

Who were Isaac and Jacob?
Which one stayed at home?
What sons did he have?
Which of these stayed at home?
How did Jacob get the chief place in the family?
How did Jacob suffer for having done wrong?
Who was Jacob's favorite son?
What happened to him?
What did Jacob suppose had happened?
Where did Jacob's sons go to buy food in famine?
Who sold them the food?
What did Joseph do for his father?

The Story of Moses

Who was Moses?
How was his life saved when a baby?
What did he want to do for his people?
Why did the Egyptians object to the Hebrews leaving Egypt?
Why did they consent at last?
Where did the Hebrews live for a time after leaving Egypt?
Who died alone on a mountain?

The Story of Joshua

Who appointed Joshua to succeed Moses?
What did he do for the Hebrew people?

The Judges

Who were the Judges?
How did Deborah help the people?
What trick did Gideon play against the enemy?
Who were the Philistines?
Who was Samuel?
Why did the people want Samuel to choose them a king?

The Early Kings

What farmer was made a king?
Who was his son?
Who was the second king?

What did he do for Israel?
Who was the third king?
What famous building did he build?

THE GREAT REVOLT

How did a young king lose part of his kingdom?
What were the names of the two Hebrew kingdoms?

THE PROPHETS

Who were the prophets?
How did a shepherd-prophet win the people to listen to him?
What did he say they should not do?
What prophet was often in the court?
Why did he once put on clothes like a captive in war?
Why did Ezekiel make a map of Jerusalem?
How did the prophets show they were brave men?
Can people be brave in the same way now?

ASSYRIA AND THE HEBREWS

What was Assyria?
How did Assyria make life hard for the Hebrews?
Where were some of the people of Judah taken?
Have strong nations a right to oppress weaker nations?

AFTER THE EXILE

What is an exile?
Did the exiles forget God in Babylon?
What great nation conquered Babylon?
Why did their king, Cyrus, allow the Hebrews to go back home?
Why could they not all go back?
Why was life hard for those who went back?
Who was Judas Maccabeus?
What did the Hebrews hope for?
What was the Messiah?
What did the Hebrews teach their children about God?
Have we to-day any reason to love God?

The Persons of the Ancient Stories of the Hebrews

I. THE EARLY DAYS

ABRAHAM, who came into Canaan from Haran. Abraham's sons were:

ISAAC and ISHMAEL. Isaac's sons were:

JACOB and ESAU. Jacob had twelve sons:

REUBEN, SIMEON, LEVI, JUDAH, ISSACHAR, ZEBULUN, DAN, NAPHTALI, GAD, ASHER, JOSEPH, BENJAMIN. Joseph was sold as a slave into Egypt, and became the next to the king. Joseph's sons were:

EPHRAIM and MANASSEH.

MOSES was the great leader who brought the Hebrews out of Egypt. Moses had a brother and a sister:

AARON and MIRIAM.

JOSHUA was the successor of Moses, who led the Hebrews into Canaan.

II. THE JUDGES

There was a group of leaders called Judges. They lived in the days before the Hebrews had kings, and fought off the peoples who wanted to take their land. These peoples were the Canaanites, who had held the land before; the Moabites, Midianites, and Ammonites from the east; and the Philistines, from the land near the Great Sea in the southwest. The names of the six greatest Judges were:

EHUD, who dared to go alone and kill an invading Moabite king.

DEBORAH, who urged a war for freedom from the Canaanites.

GIDEON, who routed a great army of Midianites with three hundred brave men.

JEPHTHAH, who drove back a great invasion of Ammonites.

SAMSON, who was a strong man and fought the Philistines single-handed.

SAMUEL, who gathered an army against the Philistines.

III. THE GREAT KINGS

Samuel chose the first king for the people.

SAUL was the first king. Saul's son was JONATHAN, who died in the same battle with his father, Saul.

DAVID was the second king.

David's son

SOLOMON was the third king. He was famous for his wealth and his great buildings. He built a temple which stood for four hundred years. But he taxed the people heavily, and when he died the kingdom divided.

IV. THE TWO KINGDOMS

THE NORTHERN KINGDOM
ISRAEL

The kingdom of Israel had many kings of different families.

Some of the most famous were:

JEROBOAM, who founded the kingdom.

OMRI, who fought with a great empire, Assyria. His son was

THE SOUTHERN KINGDOM
JUDAH

The kingdom of Judah was always ruled by kings of the house of David.

Some of the more famous kings were:

REHOBOAM, son of Solomon, whose foolish and arbitrary conduct caused the division of the kingdom.

AHAB, who reigned in the days of a great prophet, Elijah.

JEHU, who tried to reform a falling nation.

JEROBOAM II, who had a long and prosperous reign.

HOSHEA, at the end of whose reign the kingdom was destroyed by Assyria.

ASA, a good king with a long reign.

UZZIAH, who ruled at the same time as Jeroboam II.

HEZEKIAH, a good king, who foolishly fought with Assyria.

MANASSEH, a bad king, who did great harm to Judah.

JOSIAH, who tried to reform the worship of God.

ZEDEKIAH, whose reign ended in the conquest of Judah by Babylon.

The people of the Northern Kingdom never came back from captivity to reestablish the nation as did the people of Judah.

THE CAPTIVITY

For fifty years Judah had no rulers.

AFTER THE CAPTIVITY

Cyrus, King of Persia, conquered Babylon and let the Hebrews who wished return to Palestine.

Two men are famous in this period:

EZRA, a priest who was a reformer.

NEHEMIAH, a governor, who rebuilt the walls of Jerusalem.

Memory Verses for the Weeks of the Year

I. GOD

1. God is love. —I John 4:8.

2. God is our refuge and strength, a very present help in trouble. —Psalms 46:1.

3. Know ye that the Lord, he is God:
   It is he that hath made us, and not we ourselves. —Psalms 100:3.

4. God is able to make all grace abound toward you. — II Corinthians 9:8.

5. God is a Spirit; and they that worship him must worship him in spirit and in truth. —John 4:24.

II. GOD'S WORLD

1. In the beginning God created the heaven and the earth. —Genesis 1:1.

2. The heavens declare the glory of God. —Psalms 19:1.

3. He causeth the grass to grow for the cattle,
   And herb for the service of man. —Psalms 104:14.

4. He appointed the moon for seasons;
   The sun knoweth his going down. —Psalms 104:19.

5. He gave us rain from heaven, and fruitful seasons. —Acts 14:17.

III. CHRIST

1. He that hath seen me hath seen the Father. —John 14:9.

2. In him was life, and the life was the light of men. —John 1:4.

3. God so loved the world that he gave his only begotten Son.

—John 3:16.

4. We have peace with God through our Lord Jesus Christ.

—Romans 5:1.

5. I live; yet not I, but Christ liveth in me.

—Galatians 2:20.

IV. Thanksgiving

1. O give thanks unto the Lord, for he is good.

—Psalms 107:1.

2. Bless the Lord, O my soul, and forget not all his benefits.

—Psalms 103:2.

3. Be thankful unto him and bless his name.

—Psalms 100:4.

4. In everything give thanks.

—I Thessalonians 5:18.

V. Prayer

1. O thou that hearest prayer, unto thee shall all flesh come.

—Psalms 65:2.

2. Watch and pray, that ye enter not into temptation.

—Matthew 26:41.

3. Teach me thy way, O Lord, and lead me in a plain path.

—Psalms 27:11.

4. Our help is in the name of the Lord, who made heaven and earth.

—Psalms 124:8.

VI. Obedience

1. Obey my voice, and I will be your God, and ye shall be my people.

—Jeremiah 7:23.

2. This is the love of God, that we keep his commandments.

—I John 5:3.

3. Teach me, O Lord, the way of thy statutes, and I shall keep it unto the end.

—Psalms 119:33.

4. Be ye doers of the word, and not hearers only.

—James 1:22.

VII. Love

1. A new commandment I give unto you, that ye love one another. —John 13:34.

2. All the law is fulfilled in one word, even in this: Thou shalt love thy neighbor as thyself. —Galatians 5:14.

3. A friend loveth at all times. —Proverbs 17:17.

4. I say unto you, Love your enemies. —Matthew 5:44.

VIII. Kindly Thoughts and Words

1. Be kindly affectioned one to another. —Romans 12:10

2. A soft answer turneth away wrath. —Proverbs 15:1.

3. Let us follow after the things which make for peace. —Romans 14:19.

4. Let not mercy and truth forsake thee. —Proverbs 3:3.

5. Be ye kind one to another, tenderhearted, forgiving one another. —Ephesians 4:32.

IX. Generosity

1. It is more blessed to give than to receive. —Acts 20:35.

2. Freely ye have received, freely give. —Matthew 10:8.

3. Give and it shall be given unto you. —Luke 6:38.

4. God loveth a cheerful giver. —II Corinthians 9:7.

X. Truth-telling

1. Thou shalt not bear false witness against thy neighbor. —Exodus 20:16.

2. Lying lips are abomination to the Lord. —Proverbs 12:22.

3. Putting away lying, speak every man truth with his neighbor. —Ephesians 4:25.

4. Keep thy tongue from evil, and thy lips ·from speaking guile.

—Psalms 34:13.

XI. INDUSTRY AND LAZINESS

1. We commanded you, that if any would not work, neither should he eat.

—II Thessalonians 3:10.

2. The labor of the righteous tendeth to life.

—Proverbs 10:16.

3. Whatsoever thy hand findeth to do, do it with thy might.

—Ecclesiastes 9:10.

4. In all labor there is profit.

—Proverbs 14:23.

XII. HONOR FOR PARENTS

1. Honor thy father and thy mother, as the Lord thy God hath commanded thee.

—Deuteronomy 5:16.

2. A wise son maketh a glad father,
But a foolish son is the heaviness of his mother.

—Proverbs 10:1.

3. Children, obey your parents in all things.

—Colossians 3:20.

4. Keep thy father's commandment,
And forsake not the law of thy mother.

—Proverbs 6:20.

UR OF THE CHALDEES

This shows the foundations of ancient houses in the old city of Ur.

Bible Dramas
and Pageants

COURTESY BRITISH BROADCASTING CORPORATION, LONDON

"And Jesus increased in wisdom and stature,
and in favour with God and man." LUKE 2:52

"And the child (John) grew, and waxed strong in spirit."   LUKE 1:80
"And the child (Jesus) grew, and waxed strong in spirit."   LUKE 2:40

Bible Dramas and Pageants

ACTING-OUT BIBLE STORIES

DO YOU ever ask, "What can I do?" on a long summer day? Do you ever wonder what to do during a dreary, rainy afternoon? Do you get tired playing the same old games over and over? Why not try acting out Bible stories? This is something anyone can do any time and any place.

First, get some of your friends together—in fact, you can act out many Bible stories with only two people. Decide what story you will act out. There are many Bible stories that will be fun to do—some exciting, some challenging, and some heart-warming. Read the story over several times. You might take turns reading it aloud. Or have one person read the story, then tell it to the others.

Next, decide who will act out the different parts. You might take turns choosing which parts you want. Don't have one person always get the big parts. Sometimes it's fun to let the quiet person play a noisy part, like Goliath; or a talkative person play a quiet part, like the poor widow who gave two mites.

Now collect your costumes and props. For costumes, use old bathrobes, sheets, pieces of cloth, sandals, sashes— anything you can find. Props are things you hold in your hand or use in the story, such as David's harp or Peter's fishing net, or the baby Moses' basket. For baby Moses

you'll need a doll, or you can use a rolled-up towel. Will
you need any chairs, or tables, or benches? Put them in
place.

Each person should think very carefully about the part
he is to play. Was Miriam afraid when she ran to the
princess and asked if the baby needed a nurse? How did
David feel when he was all alone in the hills with his
sheep? What did the water feel like under Peter's feet
when he walked on it toward Jesus?

Now you're all ready to begin! Don't try to say the
words exactly as they are in the Bible story. Instead, try
to say the words in your own way. Add in extra words
if you wish. Say and act out as much of the story as you
possibly can. If you need to, have a narrator explain the
parts of the story that the characters can't act out or say.
If you like, you may act out your Bible story for your
family or friends. If you do, be sure to practice it several
times first. But it's just as much fun to put on your play
for yourselves. After you've done one story, try another,
and another, and another.

When you choose your story, try to get one with a lot
of action and conversation. Don't worry about having
girls play women's parts and boys play men's parts.
Switch around. Let everyone try every part. There is
one part, however, that most people do not feel they
should act out. And that's the part of Jesus. If you
choose a story with Jesus in, it would be best to have one
person sit on the side, away from the rest of the group,
and read Jesus' words from the Bible story.

When you act out a Bible story, pretend to be Joseph,
or Abraham, or Ruth. Try to do and to say and even to
think what that person would do and say and think.
After you've acted something in the life of Joseph, or
Abraham, or Ruth, you'll feel that you really know that

"And it came to pass in those days that He went out into the mountain to pray. And He continued all night in prayer to God." LUKE 6:12

"And He took them in His arms and blessed them."   MARK 10:16

person. This is a good way to make many new Bible friends.

A different way of acting out Bible stories is playing Bible charades. Divide everyone into two groups. Then each group secretly decides on a story. Act out the story in front of the other group, without using any costumes, props, or furniture (maybe just a chair). Do it in panto-mime—that is, don't say any words. See how soon the other group can guess what Bible story you are acting out. If you do a good job of acting it out, they will guess right away. But if you don't do a good job, they might never guess what Bible story you are acting!

PEOPLE IN THE BIBLE WHO ACTED STORIES

Many of the prophets acted out their sermons instead of just preaching them. Jeremiah went to a potter and got an earthenware bottle. Then he called the leaders of the people together in the valley of Hinnom. He held the bottle in his hands while he preached a short sermon about the sins of the people of the city. Then he threw the bottle down on the ground and broke it into pieces.

After he had broken it, he said, "Thus saith the Lord of Hosts, 'Even so will I break the people and the city as one breaketh a potter's vessel, which cannot be made whole again.'" See 5:287-291. When the leaders went home and thought about Jeremiah's sermon, they would see that bottle broken in pieces and remember what Jeremiah had said.

The prophet Ezekiel made a little model of Jerusalem in clay. Then he added a camp with the forts and mounds and battering rams of a besieging army. Then he took an iron pan and placed it between himself and the city. See 5:352. He was acting out the manner in which the city would be besieged.

Jesus did not act out His stories. But He told many stories about everyday things which the people could picture in their minds. The people felt they knew the boy who left home rich and returned a beggar, but whose father loved him just the same. They knew about rich men who planned to pull down their barns and build bigger barns, but who died suddenly in the night. People felt they could see the shepherd as he went out in the darkness to find his little lost sheep.

LIST OF BIBLE STORIES TO ACT OUT

The following list includes many Bible stories with action and conversation—both of these are requirements for stories which are to be acted out. These stories could also be used for story-telling. Start out with a short, simple story. Later you might like to try the longer, more difficult stories.

In this list short incidents are sometimes suggested. If longer stories are suggested, parts of them may be used, if desired, for acting out or telling.

1. The Story of the First Ship
   (a) The Warning of the Flood; see 3:33.
   (b) Getting the Ark Ready to Sail; see 3:34.
   (c) The Voyage in the Great Storm; see 3:35.
   (d) The Landing at Ararat: Sending Out the Raven and the Dove; the First Rainbow; see 3:37–39.

2. Building the Tower Which Was to Reach the Sky; see 3:43.

3. The Life of Abraham
   (a) The Pioneer Goes to a Strange Country; see 3:51.
   (b) Choosing the Land; see 3:54, 56.
   (c) The Rescue of Lot from the Hostile Kings; see 3:59.
   (d) The Messengers at the Tent; see 3:64–69.
   (e) Hagar and Ishmael; see 3:73, 75.
   (f) The Sacrifice of Isaac; see 3:77–79.
   (g) The Flight of Lot—Sodom and Gomorrah; see 3:70–72.

"He departed thence by ship into a desert place apart: and when the people had heard thereof, they followed him on foot out of the cities."   MATTHEW 14:13

"Jesus said, Suffer little children, and forbid them not, to come
unto me: for of such is the kingdom of heaven." Matthew 19:14

4. Isaac and Rebekah
   (a) Sending Out the Old Servant; see 3:84.
   (b) The Journey; see 3:87–93.
   (c) The Return; see 3:93–96.
   (d) Isaac and the Philistines; see 3:96-99. This seems a simple incident, but it might be made very effective. Isaac is camped with his family. He decides he must dig a well for his flocks. He discusses the matter with Rebekah and his herdsmen: "Yes, this is a good place." He begins to dig. The Philistines come up in a quarrelsome mood. They threaten and order him off. He protests. He has a right to dig a well here. "No," they say. "We will fight you." He refuses to fight. He will go somewhere else. They call him a coward, but he goes. This scene is repeated twice. Then the Philistines go away. Isaac digs his well in peace, and thanks God for His bounty and protection.

5. Jacob and Esau
   (a) The Selling of the Birthright; see 3:101.
   (b) The Deception of Rebekah and Jacob; see 3:103–105.
   (c) The Blessing; see 3:105–107.
   (d) Leaving Home—a Night in the Wilderness; see 3:107–110.
   (e) Laban's Home: Meeting with Rachel; see 3:111–112.
   (f) Back to the Old Home; see 3:118–128.

6. Joseph and His Brethren
   This story almost entire is especially adapted to both simple and elaborate presentation; see 3:129–196.

7. The Life of Moses
   (a) Finding the Baby in the Nile; see 3:203.
   (b) The Encounter with the Egyptian and the Flight to the Wilderness; see 3:205.
   (c) The People Making Bricks in Bondage; see 3:215.
   (d) The Contest with Pharaoh; see 3:219–222.
   (e) The Plagues; see 3:222–240.
   (f) The Passover; see 3:236–240.
   (g) The Exodus; see 3:243–250. The story of Moses and

Pharaoh may be made very simple. Pharaoh sits upon a draped chair for a throne. Moses and Aaron appear before him and make the demand, "Let the people go." Then they threaten the successive plagues, and Pharaoh refuses to yield. After each plague, he seems to grant the demand, and each time repents and refuses. At last, Moses says that they will come back no more. Then comes the scene of the Passover. Moses makes his final entrance, and says the people are marching to freedom. Music from piano or recorder, a stirring march! The sound of marching feet is heard. The crossing of the Red Sea may be represented: the dismay when the pursuit of Pharaoh is announced, the triumph on the other shore, the songs of Moses and Miriam, the Egyptians dead on the seashore.

8. In the Wilderness

This period abounds in opportunities for dramatic representation and story-telling.

(a) The Halts in the Desert: Marah; Elim; see 3:256.

(b) The Giving of Quails and Manna; see 3:257.

(c) The Fight with Amalek (the Arms of Moses Held Up); see 3:265.

(d) The Scenes at Sinai; see 3:271–294.

(e) The Sending Out of the Spies and Their Return; see 3:298–301.

(f) The Water from the Rock; see 3:307.

(g) The Brazen Serpent; see 3:309.

(h) Building the Tabernacle; see 3:285–294.

(i) The March into Edom; see 3:311.

(j) Moses' Farewell; see 3:326–344.

(k) The Digging of the Well, and the Song of the Well; see 3:312.

The whole wilderness story may be made into one dramatization or divided into separate episodes.

9. The Age of the Judges. This period is also very dramatic.

(a) Crossing the Jordan: the Command of Joshua, the

"And Jesus went about all Galilee, teaching in their synagogues, and preaching the gospel of the kingdom, and healing all manner of sickness and all manner of disease among the people." Matthew 4:23

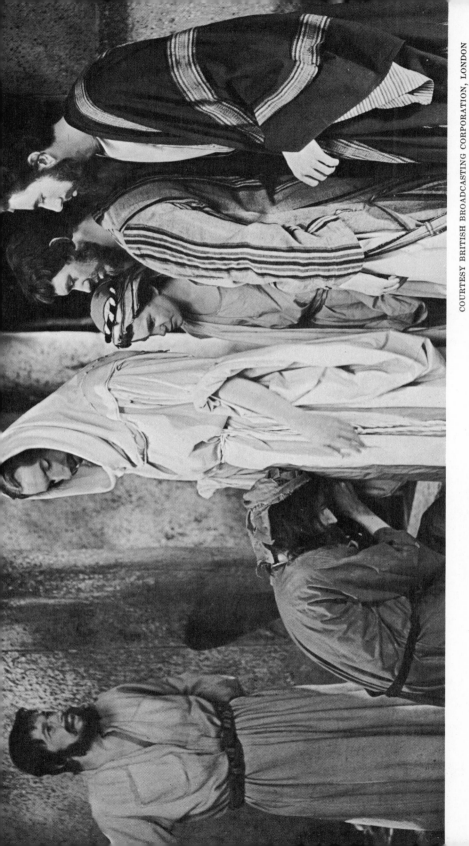

"Now when the sun was setting, all they that had any sick with divers diseases brought them unto Him; and He laid His hands on every one of them, and healed them." Luke 4:40

Meeting with the Captain of the LORD's Host, Making the Memorial; see 3:406–411.

(b) Rahab and the Spies; see 3:400–404.

(c) The Capture of Jericho; see 3:411–415.

(d) The Trick of the Gibeonites; see 3:423.

(e) Ehud; see 3:455.

(f) Deborah and Barak; see 3:458.

(g) Jael; see 3:461.

(h) Gideon. This story is full of possibilities:

    (1) The Young Farmer Working in the Pit to Save a Little Grain from the Midianites; see 3:467.

    (2) The Call; see 3:468–472.

    (3) The Gathering of the Men and the Test of Their Fitness; see 3:472–474.

    (4) The Night Adventure in the Camp of the Midianites, the Defeat of Midian; see 3:474–477.

Mr. Caldwell Cook, who used this material for his boys at the Perse School, Cambridge, England, suggests that as even a limited number of pitchers would be expensive, a satisfying clatter can be made with old cans outside!

(i) The Story of Abimelech; see 3:481–488.

(j) Samson, the Man Who Was Strong in Body but Weak in Will. Some of the episodes at least can be given, and it is a fine story to tell; see 3:501–516.

(k) Samuel.

    (1) The Little Boy in the Temple; see 3:531.

    (2) The Death of Eli; see 3:533–535.

    (3) The Warning to the People Who Want a King; see 3:544.

10. Saul

(a) The Boy Who Looked for His Father's Asses and Found a Kingdom; see 3:545–549.

(b) The Episode of Jonathan's Victory, His Father's Sentence of Death, and the Saving of Jonathan by the People; see 4:20–28.

(c) Saul's Disobedience and Samuel's Rebuke; see 4:29–33.

(d) Saul at Endor; see 4:34–38.

(e) The Last Battle of the Old King; see 4:38.

11. David
    (a) The Shepherd Boy Who Killed a Giant; see 4:43–51.
    (b) The Shepherd Boy in the Court of Saul.
        (1) David Soothing the King; see 4:33.
        (2) The King Angry and Jealous; see 4:57–67.
        (3) The Friendship of David and Jonathan; see 4:55–67.
    (c) David in the Wilderness, leading an Outlaw's Life; see
        4:67–97.
        (1) In the Cave of Adullam, the Water from the Well at
            Bethlehem. This episode was later, but it may be
            introduced here; see 4:116.
        (2) David and Nabal; see 4:80–86.
        (3) Sparing Saul's Life.
            (a) In the Cave; see 4:78–80.
            (b) In the Camp; see 4:86.
    (d) David the King; 4:98–184.
        (1) Receiving the News of Saul's Death; see 4:98–101.
        (2) Anointed King at Hebron; see 4:101, 102.
        (3) Doing a Kindness to Saul's Family; see 4:135.
        (4) Receiving News of the Rebellion and Death of
            Absalom; see 4:143–163.

12. Solomon
    (a) The Rival King; see 4:188–190.
    (b) The Building and the Dedication of the Temple; see
        4:200–221.
    (c) The Wealth of Solomon: Messengers, Workmen, Sailors
        from the Fleet, All Coming to Report; see 4:227–232.
    (d) The Visit of the Queen of Sheba; see 4:228.

13. The Divided Kingdom: the Revolt; see 4:250–254.

14. The Kingdom of the South
    (a) Jehoshaphat: His Reforms and Troubles; see 3:263–274.
    (b) Athaliah, the Wicked Queen; see 4:280.
        (1) The Good Aunt Who Concealed the Little Prince;
            see 4:281.
        (2) The Plot to Put Him on the Throne; see 4:281.
        (3) The Crowning of the Boy-king; see 4:282.
    (c) Uzziah: His Good Works, His Conflict with the Priests;
        see 4:294–297.

"On the next day much people that were come to the feast, when they heard that Jesus was coming to Jerusalem, took branches of palm trees, and went forth to meet Him, and cried, Hosanna: Blessed is the King of Israel that cometh in the name of the Lord." JOHN 12:12, 13

"Jesus saith unto her, Mary. She turned herself, and
saith unto Him, Rabboni; which is to say, Master." John 20:16

(d) Hezekiah. The reign of Hezekiah, with Isaiah as one of the leading characters may be made very impressive; see 4:305–326.

(1) The Cleansing of the Temple; see 4:307.

(2) Rabshakeh's Mission; see 4:319.

(3) The Sickness of the King; see 4:316.

(e) Josiah, the Little Boy Who Was a Good King; see 4:333.

(f) The Last Days of the Kingdom; see 4:346–351.

15. The Kingdom of the North. The most dramatic events of this kingdom center about Elijah and Elisha.

(a) Elijah's Appearance at the Court of Ahab, and His Retirement in Zarephath; see 4:392–394

(b) The Contest on Mount Carmel; see 4:395–401.

(c) Elijah and Jezebel: His Flight to the Wilderness; see 4:401.

(d) Naboth's Vineyard; see 4:410–416.

(e) The Appointing of Elisha and the Passing of the Old Prophet; see 4:404, 420.

(f) Elisha and the Poisoned Pot; see 4:435.

(g) Elisha and the Man Who Lost His Ax; see 4:442.

(h) Elisha and the Rich Woman of Shunem; see 4:432–435, 449.

(i) The Little Captive Maid and the Great Captain; see 4:437–442.

(j) Elisha and the Syrian Host: see 4:444, 445.

(k) The Siege of Samaria; see 4:446–449.

(l) The Anointing of Jehu; see 4:452–454.

(m) The Last Days of Elisha; see 4:454, 455.

(n) The Fate of Ahab and Jezebel; see 4:456–462.

(o) The Last Days of the Northern Kingdom; see 4:476.

16. The Daniel Stories

(a) The Hebrew Boys at the Foreign Court; see 5:470–482.

(b) The Fiery Furnace; see 5:482.

(c) The Young Man Who Was Not Afraid to Worship God; see 5:494.

(d) Daniel at Belshazzar's Feast: see 5:490.

17. Nehemiah, the Builder
    (a) Mourning in Exile; see 5:551.
    (b) Nehemiah, the Cupbearer; see 5:551.
    (c) The Return to the City; see 5:553.
    (d) The Building of the Walls; see 5:555–569.

18. The stories of Esther and Ruth are a little more difficult; see 4:545–566; 3:527–542.

19. The Prophets.   The prophetical material does not, as a rule, lend itself to dramatic representation, because there are fewer stories.   Something might be made, however, of Isaiah, Amos (the meeting with the priest is very dramatic), and Jeremiah.   All the prophets might appear one after the other and give a characteristic speech; see vol. 5.

20. Tales of the Maccabees.   These great stories are full of dramatic incidents; see 4:487–524.

21. The New Testament

The story of the nativity is a favorite for dramatization.   A suggestion has already been made with respect to the parables.   This is a field which is particularly adapted to the telling of stories.

The adventures of Paul furnish much material both for dramatization and story-telling: only a few incidents are given.
    (a) The Conversion of Paul; see 8:23.
    (b) Paul Writing the Letter to the Romans at Corinth and Sending It by Phebe; see 8:159.
    (c) The Conspiracy at Jerusalem; see 8:95–123.
    (d) The Journey to Rome—the Shipwreck; see 8:123–136.
    (e) Paul at Rome; see 8:137.

The American Passion Play

BLOOMINGTON, ILLINOIS

THE American Passion Play was first presented in 1923 and has been presented every year since then. Over a million people have seen it.

There are no professional actors in the Play. The two hundred and fifty men, women and children who appear have had no dramatic training, but have put their souls into their work and undertake to live and act the parts they portray.

The American Passion Play is distinctly a community effort. All members of the cast serve without pay or compensation of any kind. Their labor and sacrifice in the production of this great religious drama are unstinting in their efforts to present the story of the life of Christ to those who come to see it.

Every scene in the American Passion Play has been constructed with a view to accuracy, so far as research and study are able to determine, and has been built especially for the setting that is to be portrayed.

A Passion Play is the portrayal primarily of the events in the last week of Jesus' life. Earlier events in His life can be included, but the concentration is on the Triumphal Entry, the Last Supper, the Prayer in the Garden, the Arrest, the Crucifixion and the Resurrection of Christ.

Passion Plays have their roots in the Middle Ages, when Mystery Plays and Miracle Plays, as they were called, showed Biblical events to people who probably did not own Bibles and could not read.

407

THE AMERICAN PASSION PLAY
BLOOMINGTON, ILLINOIS

THE SERMON ON THE MOUNT (*Opposite page*)

"And seeing the multitudes, He went up into a mountain: and when he was set, His disciples came unto Him: And He opened His mouth, and taught them." MATTHEW 5:1, 2

Jesus was followed by eager throngs of people who listened to the great truths which He gave them. The chief means of communication was by word of mouth. Therefore, people would go long distances in order to hear some new doctrine.

JESUS AND THE WOMAN AT THE WELL (*See following page*)

"Jesus answered and said unto her, Whosoever drinketh of this water shall thirst again: But whosoever drinketh of the water that I shall give him shall never thirst; but the water that I shall give him shall be in him a well of water springing up into everlasting life."
JOHN 4:13, 14

Jesus was never too busy or too tired to talk with individuals, as well as with great crowds. Jesus stopped by a village well to rest, and engaged the Samaritan woman in conversation by asking for a drink of water. He then told her about the eternal water of life.

THE SCOURGING (*See following page*)

"Then Pilate therefore took Jesus, and scourged Him." JOHN 19:1

Jesus was loved and revered by many. But there were others who hated Jesus and were jealous of Him. So they arrested Him on false charges. He was tried before Pilate, the Roman governor, who could find no fault in Him. But fearing the people, Pilate ordered Jesus to be punished by scourging. This was a cruel beating, with the customary number of blows, forty less one.

THE AMERICAN PASSION PLAY
BLOOMINGTON, ILLINOIS

PILATE WASHES HIS HANDS (*Opposite page*)

"When Pilate saw that he could prevail nothing, but that rather a tumult was made, he took water, and washed his hands before the multitude, saying, I am innocent of the blood of this just person: see ye to it."   MATTHEW 27:24

Pilate was unwilling to condemn Jesus, as he knew Jesus had committed no crime. He was also unwilling to release Jesus, because he wanted to gain the favor of those who sought to harm Him. He wanted all of them to know he took no responsibility for whatever might happen to Jesus.

THE CRUCIFIXION (*See following page*)

"And it was the third hour, and they crucified Him." MARK 15:25

Jesus was crucified between two thieves. Crucifixion is said to be the most cruel type of punishment ever devised by man. It was reserved for the most despised criminals. First, the victim was nailed to the cross. Then the cross was carried to a place where a hole had been dug in the ground where it was pulled to an upright position and dropped into the hole. There the victim was left until dead.

THE ASCENSION (*See following page*)

"And He led them out as far as to Bethany, and He lifted up His hands, and blessed them."   LUKE 24:50

He had given them His last instructions. As the disciples watched, Jesus raised His hands, blessed them and slowly ascended upward. He soon disappeared from sight and the disciples knew that He had ascended into heaven.

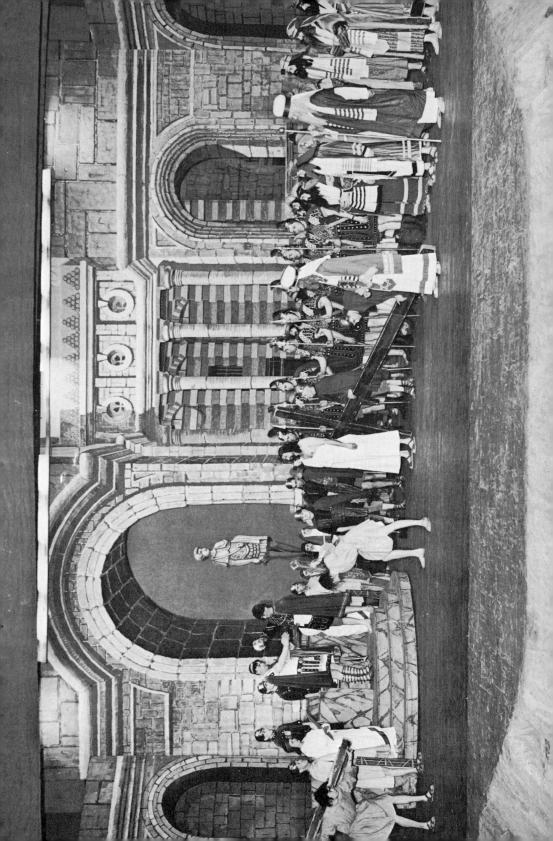